'Hatred is a delicious feeling – it comes so easily and makes me feel good about myself … superior to someone else.'

The Perfect Gentleman

this is at least a trilogy

The Perfect Gentleman
(you really should read this first)
(originally published as *Unimagined*)

The Imperfect Gentleman

The Gentle Man
(coming soonish)

(author intends to write more books if you read these three)

The Imperfect Gentleman

on an Unimagined Journey

Imran Ahmad

Sequel to *The Perfect Gentleman*

www.unimagined.co.uk

Published by New Generation Publishing in 2020

First Edition

Published worldwide by New Generation Publishing, an imprint of Legend Times Group, 2020

ISBN: 978-1-78955-872-2

Translation and other rights available – contact author via website:
www.unimagined.co.uk

www.newgeneration-publishing.com

Acclaim for
The Perfect Gentleman / Unimagined

Selected in 'Best Books of the Year' lists of:
Guardian
Independent
Sydney Morning Herald
Belfast Telegraph

'Yes, you can laugh while having your consciousness raised; this Pakistani immigrant's memoir of aspiring to be the ideal Englishman proves it.'
O, The Oprah Magazine (No 1 in '10 Titles to Pick Up Now')

'Imran Ahmad's light touch and sense of humanity displayed so skilfully in *The Perfect Gentleman* ensures that his words have a deeper meaning and a wider application … If you read nothing else this year, discover this book.'
New York Journal of Books

'A feminist and a peacemaker … impatient for the sequel.'
***Maclean's* magazine, Canada**

'Hurrah for a memoir that isn't miserable! Hurray for Imran Ahmad's terrific sense of humour … an entertaining, moving and thoroughly thought-provoking tale of our times.'
Daily Mail

'Wonderfully evocative and strangely touching.'
The Sunday Times

' … a compelling quest for belonging …'
The Guardian

'… successful in striking that balance, by presenting a thought-provoking debate even as it makes you laugh out loud.'
The Hindu

'What a very strange book. There's more to it than meets the eye … this Trojan horse of a book.'
The Book Magazine

For Sabrina and Aleena – my greatest teachers.

With love and gratitude.

Contents

ACKNOWLEDGEMENTS

Thank you to those of you who have been pestering me for years to write this sequel. I hope that it was worth the wait. In actual fact, had I written this immediately after the first book, it would be rather drab – because I had not yet had so many of the extraordinary experiences related now.

I am grateful to *everyone* who is part of this journey – even the 'negative' characters.

We are all teachers and classroom assistants for one another – my worst enemy in this life may actually be my closest friend in Eternity.

CUSTOMARY PROFOUND QUOTES

'… the distinction between past, present and future is only a stubbornly persistent illusion.'

Albert Einstein

'Time is an illusion. Lunchtime doubly so.'

Douglas Adams

'I died as a mineral and arose a plant,
I died as a plant and rose again an animal,
I died as an animal and arose a man.
Why then should I fear to become less by dying?
I shall die once again as a man
To rise an angel perfect from head to foot!
Again when I suffer dissolution as an angel,
I shall become what passes the conception of man!
Let me then become non-existent, for non-existence
Sings to me in organ tones, "To him shall we return!" '

Jalāl ad-Dīn Muhammad Rūmī (1207 – 1273)

Translation by Edward Henry Whinfield (1898)

… *he seems to be describing some kind of developmental journey* …

AUTHOR'S NOTE

This book is written as a direct sequel to *The Perfect Gentleman*. You really should read that book first, otherwise this one won't make complete sense. *I'm just sayin'*.

This book may surprise you for various reasons.

One reason is that it is not as consistently funny as the first book – this is inevitable (as per the wisdom quoted opposite).

Another reason is that it does not follow a uniform genre. A life cannot *authentically* be viewed through the lens of only a single genre. (Surely no one's life is *always* a romantic comedy, or *solely* a misery memoir?) Life is a rich tapestry of diverse experiences in different dimensions – or at least a thick tangle of threads. (Like your VHS tapes all got entwined: romantic comedy, drama, soap opera, spy thriller, corporate intrigue, documentary, National Geographic, religion, supernatural mystery.)

Perhaps it might be possible to untangle individual tapes …

Everything narrated in this book is completely true – just a few names have been changed. I could have selected content that might help the reader to like me more – but that would not be authentic. I had *absolute certainty* ... and I was wrong about everything. (Please remember this paragraph whenever you read anything in this narrative which outrages you – and you will do.)

The vignette memories I have labelled 'Age 3' are all authentic. I know that I must have been under four years old for these, because we moved to the Putney house before I reached the age of four in September 1966, and these memories are set in Fulham, where we lived before Putney. So by simple logic I have worked out the timeframe of these memories.

How I have managed to retain them is another story.

'When I was a child, I spoke like a child, I thought like a child, I reasoned like a child; when I became a man, I put an end to childish ways.'

1 Corinthians 13:11

The Imperfect Gentleman

Student

1999 Age: 37 Minneapolis

Even our American television news, which is generally very inward-looking and superficial, is covering the fact that NATO is bombing Belgrade and surrounding regions, to put an end to the Serbians' genocidal intervention in Kosovo. This is just wonderful. The thought of bombs dropping on Serbians fills me with utter joy. Ever since the evil Serbians' genocide against Bosnia's Muslims and the horrible siege of Sarajevo – which left hundreds of thousands of people suffering and starving for nearly four years – I have utterly hated those evil Serbians and view them all with absolute contempt. Serbians seem to have some deep-seated irrational hatred of Muslims … and we can hate them right back.

The Americans accidently hit the Chinese embassy in Belgrade with five guided missiles, which is rather unfortunate. Apparently, the CIA got the coordinates wrong for a military target in the same street. This is what they call 'collateral damage' and it happens sometimes.

The Serbians are so insanely deluded, they even gather on bridges and at other strategic locations, forming human chains by linking hands and singing defiantly – hoping this will deter NATO from bombing those places. *Of course it shouldn't!* NATO should bomb the bridges just when they are crowded with these arrogant, despicable Serbians.

In the end, this beautiful bombing campaign lasts for 77 glorious days. But it would have been so much more effective and much less trouble to decimate that cesspit Belgrade with one righteous nuclear missile. *Isn't that what nukes are for?*

In my honest opinion: the only good Serbian is a dead Serbian.

Australia

1973 Age: 11

In Mr Todd's class at Hampton Hill Junior School, I sit in the same cluster of desks as Grant Langford. He is mad about Australia. He has never been there, but everyone knows it is his favourite country. He knows everything about it. When we make continents in our clay workshop group after school on Tuesdays, I get assigned South America – a place about which I know nothing. Grant, of course, manages to bag Australia, because Mr Todd knows that he would be devastated not to get it.

I don't know much about Australia either, except for the obvious. There were dark brown people living there called Aborigines, Britain sent convicts there, and now it's a white country. Everything else I know comes from watching *Skippy the Bush Kangaroo.*

One day, in a classroom quiz, Mr Todd asks the question: 'What animals caused havoc in Australia and resulted in fences being built across the entire country?'

I know this! I just read a whole chapter about it in one of those general knowledge books my parents bought me. It was rabbits. They multiplied so fast across the country that they became like a major natural disaster. My face lights up with enthusiasm and my hand shoots up eagerly.

But everyone is looking at Grant. Anything to do with Australia is his domain. He puts his hand up too, but without my energy. He seems hesitant, unsure … but he has to take the question, because it's about Australia.

Of course, Mr Todd picks Grant, and his answer is, 'Kangaroos.'

There is a palpable shock in the classroom when Mr Todd says, 'No.'

Grant responds with some desperate comments about kangaroos jumping on crops, but Mr Todd points to me with his finger of authority. 'Imran …?'

'Rabbits!' I blurt out, eagerly and with absolute confidence.

There is surprise, almost commotion, and something else in the classroom, when Mr Todd confirms that I am right. I am triumphant. Grant looks visibly shocked, humiliated even. Sitting near to me, he can't look me in the eye.

The something else … it's irritation. Everyone already knows that I'm the cleverest boy in the class (there are a couple of very clever girls). Most of the boys sat the entrance exam for Hampton Grammar School, and I am the *only one* who will go there. When we each had to give a talk to the class, mine was on 'Atoms and Molecules', which apparently went completely over some people's heads (this made me feel quite smug).

Now I've humiliated Grant, a popular boy, and some of them despise me for it. This is why I don't have any friends. I don't have anyone to play with during break time – I wander around the playground, possibly reading a book and longing for lessons to resume. I'm a complete outcast in junior school, for being too clever and knowing it.

1987 Age: 24

I use the payphone in the corridor of the Chemistry Department. I'm quite nervous, as I always am when I speak to Janice. I insert a ten pence piece and punch in her number. She seems happy enough to hear from me, and I go directly to the dreaded question.

'What happened about that job in Australia?'

Seems like a long pause.

'I'm going,' she gushes gleefully.

I congratulate her with false enthusiasm, and we talk excitedly about what a great opportunity this is for her – a two-year secondment with Rowntree Macintosh, her chocolate bar company, to Melbourne. Inwardly, I'm feeling frustrated and upset. Just when I've secured a great job with Unilever – good enough to quit my PhD for – and I have a fighting chance to secure Janice's affection (and her hand in marriage) by being on the same socio-economic level as her (instead of being a poor student), she slips once again out of reach. I've known her for nearly six years, and my stubborn conviction that we are destined to be together has hardly ever wavered. So, now I'm going to be tested for another two years.

She does ask me if I'd like to buy her immaculate and fastidiously maintained Honda Accord for an elevated price (which no stranger would ever contemplate), and I readily agree.

1996 Age: 34

On Saturday afternoon, I am sitting in the front row of First Class on a Northwest Airlines DC-10, heading from Minneapolis to LA, on my way to Australia.

The aircraft thrusts down the runway and takes off. Immediately, a storage unit door in the galley in front of me opens by itself and an ice bucket comes out and rolls down the aisle into Economy Class, followed smartly by a tray, then a carton of orange juice, and then a carton of milk.*

As a management consultant, this is the most impressive customer process re-engineering that I have ever seen. Not only has Northwest reduced the delivery time of the beverage service to the Economy Class customers to practically nothing, they have also zeroed the headcount required to perform the process.

This is my first trip to Australia ever. I can't believe that I'm finally standing on Australian soil. This country seems to have long been in the back of my mind – I know why.

At the Sydney office of Honeywell on Monday morning, I call Janice in Melbourne. We haven't spoken in years. She is doing well: she has a fine husband; two children and one more coming; a beautiful house with a huge backyard; a four-wheel drive vehicle; a large yacht. (*I don't think that we will be getting married, after all.*) She invites me to come to visit them. I think about it, but realise that if I fly to Melbourne, I won't have any free time at all in Sydney. I decide to give it a miss.

These days in Sydney are indeed wonderful. It's the height of summer; I'm staying in the elegant Sheraton hotel in a beautiful downtown location; the work days are pleasant;

* This really happened. I told you already – *everything* in this book is true (even 'spend about two hours').

the evenings and weekends are mine. Most importantly, I'm free of the misery which is my estranged marriage, the spiteful, manipulative control and the enforced chaos. My hotel room is always tidy; my clothes and personal effects always neatly stored; my day is always carefully planned and executed.

I am addicted to walking. I return from the office, shower, change and walk. I pass the evenings and weekends in dedicated walking. (Since I have fixed meal allowances, I prefer not to spend my time and money in expensive restaurants, but to keep the cash and eat McDonald's.) I walk all over what they call the Central Business District of Sydney, weaving in amongst the lives of people who work here, but clearly not really one of them – a tourist gone astray perhaps, in my shorts and training shoes. The Sydney Harbour Bridge is my favourite. I cross it by taxi twice a day, between the Sheraton and the Honeywell office, but to walk across it is a real treat – the view is spectacular, with its blend of colours and visual textures. On my one side there's the rumble of traffic, which seems to reverberate through the whole structure, and on the other side is that amazing blurring of divine and human architecture – God and Man have worked together to create something exquisite. The brilliant blue sky, the blazing sunshine and the shimmering green-blue water blend so breathtakingly with the architecture of the Opera House and harbour. I can practically feel myself losing weight as I pound back and forth across that bridge, drunk on the view, the freedom and the endorphins.

There's a flea market near the bridge, and I wander about in it sometimes, not really wanting to buy another material possession (which would merely lie around my huge, untidy American house, unappreciated), but yearning to engage in human contact. There's a blonde girl I notice who runs a stall selling odds and ends: art or junk – *what's the difference?* I wonder if this is just a hobby for her, whether she has a real career, or does she have to make her living this way? I would love to chat with her, to be her friend, maybe her lover. But I never speak with her, never take that first step.

Throughout my walking, my mind is chattering incessantly – streams of thoughts and connections and recollections. I'm always talking to myself, in my mind – angrily contemplating the world's problems and imagining how they could be fixed by force. But all of this frantic activity, this dedication to getting out there and walking all over downtown Sydney, is just trying to mask one unpalatable reality – I am desperately lonely. One of Sabrina's favourite shots to take at me is: 'You don't have any friends!' *Is this true?* Just because I'm not interested in the shallow, ignorant people that my estranged wife and her family associate with, does it mean that I'm not worthy to have friends? I'm not interested in friendships based on alcohol, or on football teams, or on common ethnicity, or regressive cultural heritage, or everyone getting involved and excited to unthinkingly arrange a passionless marriage. I'm only interested in friendships based on our full intellectual and human potential, freed from all old constraints, freed to be all that we can be. (Friendships based on *Star Trek*.)

There's one thing that is always on my mind, because I haven't had it for so long. *The unbearable longing that burns deep within.*

In my hotel room in Sydney, I flick through the Yellow Pages, getting a forbidden thrill just reading the entries under Escort Agencies. There are many of them. *Could any of them be the police, just waiting to entrap decent people like me?* I play through the scenarios in my mind, imagining what might happen and the implications. I am so desperate to hold a woman in my arms, to kiss her, every square inch of her. Not really believing that I'm doing this, I dial one of the numbers, to ask how much it would be. I am conscious that this number will appear on my hotel bill, but it's just an ordinary Sydney number – George, my boss in Minneapolis, would never have any reason to think it was anything disreputable.

There is a long message played on the line, explaining the services available. Apparently, this agency offers women in four categories. 'Level One' women are attractive. 'Level Two' women are beautiful. 'Level Three' women are absolutely gorgeous. 'Level Four' women are stunning top models.

My first question is obvious – how much is it going to be? And which level could I afford? And what would I get for my money? My fingers trembling, I hit the key which will connect me to a real person. An Australian voice answers, her manner surprisingly friendly and relaxed.

'I'd like to get an understanding of the rates you charge, please.'

Her explanation is business-like, but patient. Apparently, it's not possible to give me specifics – it all depends on the woman and the duration – but it starts at a couple of hundred Australian dollars, and could be as much as one thousand Australian dollars, for a Level Four girl for all night. Trying hard not to seem nervous, I thank her and tell her I'll call back after I've thought about it.

Well, of course I'd want all night. And it would have to be a Level Four girl, otherwise I would be wondering how much better I could have done. One thousand Australian dollars would be about seven hundred US. I could get that from an ATM using a credit card. But it's a lot of money and we are really short of cash *(aren't we always?)*. The new house in Minnesota still needs air-conditioning and sprinklers – these are all essentials which we couldn't pay for upfront. I just don't see how I can afford it.

Reluctantly, I put this to the back of my mind, and continue to long unbearably. Perhaps I'll meet someone in the lobby – we'll become friends and lovers (for free).

On my next trip to Australia, I arrive at the Sheraton on the Park in Sydney at about 7:00 a.m. on Monday morning, after another short fourteen-hour flight from LA. When I booked this trip, the hotel said that I could have the same excellent room which I had last time.

Well, when I check in, it seems that being a *Sheraton Club International Gold Card* member means nothing to them. They say that I can't have my 'usual' room, but a different one of identical specifications, because they are 100% full.

When I get to this room, it turns out to be identical to my preferred room, but of opposite symmetry, which leaves me confused and disoriented. Every time I want to go to the bathroom, I walk into the closet.

Later, I learn why they are 100% full. I read in the local paper that an American entertainer known as 'Jacko' is coming to Sydney and has booked four complete floors of the Sheraton on the Park. I vaguely remember him from when I was a boy (although I avoided any interest in pop music on principle). There was a cartoon series called '*Jackson 5ive*' when I was nine years old.

A couple of days later, I call a taxi from the office at about six and head back downtown. It is a beautiful, sunny afternoon in Sydney. We drive over the harbour bridge and past the magnificent opera house, which I had always wanted to see, and now I am taking for granted.

As we approach the Sheraton, the traffic grinds to a halt. We can see a vast crowd outside the hotel, and a mass of yellow and green balloons. I decide to walk the rest of the way. As he is writing my receipt, the taxi driver asks me who is coming to the Sheraton. 'I think it's Michael Jackson,' I say. (I have now learned this fact from people at the office – his arrival in Australia has been greatly publicised, after a tepid reception in New Zealand, apparently.)

I walk along and across the road to the hotel. The crowd is about eight-people deep: screaming and pushing and generally being hysterical.

I assume that there must be a break in the crowd where the police are controlling the entry and exit of genuine hotel guests. I hold my key card in my hand as a symbol of my *right* to enter the hotel. But, looking at the police officers immediately in front of the door, who are struggling to keep the crowd from invading, I realise that this is not going to be straightforward. I try to push through the crowd, but it is futile.

Looking around, I see other business people with briefcases and computer bags who are also milling about, wondering what to do.

The bar of the Sheraton has an exit to the street. I walk about thirty yards down the road, to where the crowd has thinned to nothing, and up to the glass door of the bar. There is a thuggish man in a leather jacket standing in front of it, possibly one of Jackson's security entourage.

I hold up my key card and my *Sheraton Club International Gold Card.* He barely glances at them and doesn't appear to be at all impressed.

'Sorry, this door is closed,' he says abruptly (in a British accent!), before I say a word.

'How am I supposed to get to my room?' I demand.

'You'll have to wait until Michael Jackson arrives,' is his non-negotiable (and smug) response.

I nearly go ballistic with rage. WHY should ***I*** have to wait for Michael Jackson? Now I am *positive* that he does not work for the hotel; he shows no courtesy or respect at all. He must be a local security thug hired by Jackson's organisation and he has been placed in a position of authority and power over me. I am a paying guest of this hotel (and a *Sheraton Club Gold* member!) and he is denying me entry. I feel the outrage swell inside me. It's his male ego confronting my male ego, and he has the upper hand, which gives him pleasure and makes me very angry. There is no point in trying to reason with this individual or discuss the matter with him any further.

I evaluate my opponent. He has about one hundred pounds of solid muscle on me, and several inches of height. I, on the other hand, conservatively estimate that I have about fifty IQ points on him.

I consider swinging at him with my attaché case. Laden with my laptop computer inside, the case is heavy and makes a plausible weapon. A moment of déjà vu comes over me (something about a bully at school).

This action might knock the wind out of him slightly, but not enough to conclude the conflict, and probably wouldn't do my computer any good either. Also, if I take this physical approach, he will respond physically, and I am not likely to fare well. I decide to leverage my IQ advantage.

I know that the Sheraton has a back entrance; I used it myself on the last trip, but it means walking all the way around the block. I set off, looking out for an alternative route. A few yards down is an office building, with a large foyer. I enter, go straight across the lobby and find an exit to the street at the other side of the block. Looking ahead towards the hotel, I see that there is no crowd at the back, although there may be another hired thug at that entrance. As I walk along this backstreet, a completely discreet door, in a featureless wall, suddenly opens and some hotel workers come out, with the look of people going off-duty.

The door has no handle on the outside. Before it closes, I grab the door and rush inside.

I am in the underground service area of the hotel, a dark netherworld not to be seen by guests: grey concrete corridors, no natural light, signs that say *Laundry*, *Goods In*, *Human Resources.* I wander through and pass a few people who do not challenge me. Eventually I find a lift that takes me up into the lobby of the hotel.

There is a crowd inside as well, but they are controlled so that a large open space is being kept clear immediately inside the front doors. The hotel has a spiral staircase leading up to the mezzanine floor, which overlooks the lobby. That floor and the staircase are crowded with camera people. Looking up, I see that the several other floors which overlook the lobby are lined with hotel staff all looking down.

I walk around the back of the crowd and into the bar, which is curiously peaceful and has a few normal people in it. I proceed down to the end of the bar, and to the very glass door that is guarded by the British thug on the outside. I am now standing right behind him, only the glass separating us.

I want him to *know* that I have succeeded and that he has not been able to stop me; that I have *won.* I consider whether to tap on the glass and make that rude sign with a finger (the Americans call it 'giving the finger'), but I fumble with my British fingers and I'm not sure which one it is supposed to be, or which way around. I decide to be spiritually superior, by walking away. (Besides, he might open the door and pull me out.)

Back in the lobby, the crowd goes wild as Jackson walks in. I permit myself to stand on my toes and stretch up only once to see above the crowd, from the back. I glimpse a black hat and a white face (or mask?).

I retire to my room. Having showered and changed, I nonchalantly return to the lobby with absolutely no interest in seeing Michael Jackson; I am not going to lose my dignity at any cost. The crowd has nearly completely dispersed. A few sad individuals are loitering around, instead of going home to revise for their school exams.

I relax in the bar and observe a Michael Jackson look-alike in a leather jacket and tight trousers, wearing black glasses despite the subdued lighting. He is strutting around trying to look completely cool. I observe two Japanese women wearing Michael Jackson leather jackets, trying to look nonchalant while they have a drink – although it is obvious to all that they are loitering around on the off-chance that Michael might come down to the bar for a drink.

I decide that if I meet him in the gym the next morning, I will completely ignore him.

Later in the week, I get back from the Sydney office one evening to witness a lot of people buzzing around the hotel – but nowhere near as many as that first day when I couldn't even get into the hotel. I learn from one of the hotel staff that Michael Jackson is about to leave for his first concert.

I leave my attaché case in my room, comb my hair and go back down to observe what is going on, not because I am a Jacko fan, but merely to use my privilege as a paying hotel guest to the full – and because there are many beautiful women loitering around, who look as if they need some focus in life, which I may be able selflessly to provide.

I am wearing a smart fawn suit from Next in London, a pale blue shirt from Hong Kong (one of those ones which I had made for me), an elegant Marks and Spencer tie which blends the shirt and suit colours perfectly, and brown suede lace-up shoes. I really look like I should be in a catalogue.

I go down to the mezzanine floor and take up a position at the railing, overlooking the lobby. It is an indication of how much quieter the hotel is today – the day that Jackson arrived, I would not have been able to get anywhere near the balcony.

I lean against the railing and watch the goings-on. There is an odd assortment of characters: Japanese tourists, children, beautiful women, hippies, business people. Some are loitering like me, obviously waiting for the big event, others are going about their business.

A beautiful woman, in an elegant but revealing dress, comes and leans against the railing next to me.

'I suppose you guys have had a busy day,' she says.

Looking at her, I do not recognise her as having any involvement with my project at work, and I cannot discern how she would know anything about the relative eventfulness of my day.

'And who might we guys be?' I ask coolly.

'Security,' she replies confidently.

Now, I usually don't mind if someone attributes any mysterious, exotic persona to me – but to be mistaken for a Jackson entourage thug like the one that I had dealt with earlier is too much.

'I'm a paying guest of the hotel,' I say indignantly. 'I'm only curious to see what all the fuss is about.'

She seems disappointed and after a few seconds wanders off.

What an idiot I just was! My Ego, outraged at being associated with the Jackson entourage, just prevented me from having exactly the kind of erotic encounter I have been *longing* to have. I should have implied that I *am* Security, she might have found it irresistible. *Idiot.*

A middle-aged English woman comes and stands next to me and we both assure each other that we are not Jackson fans – we just want to see what all the fuss is about.

Suddenly there is silence. Then a group of men appears on the other side of the mezzanine floor, and they begin a measured descent down the spiral staircase.

'I didn't know he had a moustache,' I say to the woman next to me. I'm being deliberately flippant and those within earshot laugh.

'That's his bodyguard,' she enlightens me.

There are four bodyguards, all tall African-American men, with short hair and wearing sharp designer suits and collarless shirts.

The scruffy man with them is, I think, Michael Jackson. He is anorexically thin, and wearing tight black clothes and a black hat. His skin is surprisingly brown, not pale white as I have seen in pictures. An African-American boy about ten years of age walks along beside him. Jackson waves casually to the people in the lobby and his group exits the hotel.

After he leaves, there seems to be that excited buzz that occurs after we've had our examination papers collected; everyone wanting to share and discuss their experience and thoughts with everyone else.

I go back to my room and have an apple for dinner, saving my corporate meal allowance.

Apparently, on his return later that night, Jackson gets married in a private ceremony in the hotel. *I am there!* (Somewhere in the same hotel, several stories below the wedding, probably sound asleep.)

During my on-going process of being considered by Ernst & Young, a different Big Six firm, KPMG, also comes into the picture, through a different headhunter. (I already worked for KPMG back in London – they made me redundant a few years ago!) American KPMG wants me to run its (as yet not-established) Oracle practice in Minneapolis. Ernst & Young has its global Oracle headquarters in Minneapolis – so although I wouldn't be running it, I would be a senior person in it.

In the end, they both offer me a position (for virtually the same money). They are in touch with me by telephone and fax, even while I'm in Australia. It's great to be wanted again.

One evening I go to the Sheraton's health club, on the top floor, and work out on the various machines. This physical exertion relieves some of the stress of having to make this very real and difficult decision. I finish, grab a cup of water and step out onto the balcony. The magnificent Sydney skyline presents itself to me.

Directly in front of me is a tall, modern office building, and emblazoned across the top of this building is a huge illuminated set of letters and a logo: ***Ernst & Young***.

It's a tough decision, but this brightly lit sign clinches it; I choose Ernst & Young.

The day I'm leaving Sydney on this trip, I don't go into the office, even though it's a weekday. I'll spend the day packing and head out in the afternoon.

I take the opportunity to go for an early morning walk, over the Harbour Bridge, of course. It's stunning as always – and at this time in the morning, the air is so fresh. As it's a working day, I'm walking against the streams of commuters heading towards the city. I think about how wonderful it would be to have an apartment on that side of the Harbour Bridge, and every day to walk over it towards the business side. What a joyful commute that would be.

I could have had something similar in London. A small apartment I could afford, somewhere near the City; a walk to work and back (over a more modest bridge); an evening meal I prepared myself in my tidy kitchen; a bowl of lemons on the worktop; Joni Mitchell playing in the background; freedom to come and go as I pleased, to stay out late, to date women and have intense, meaningful relationships.

I reach the other side, pause at the top of the stairs, looking at the neighbourhood, thinking how ordinary it seems, and then reluctantly head back over the bridge for the last time. I'm walking with my head turned more or less permanently to the left, enjoying the view with bittersweet feelings. A woman in a dark business suit overtakes me, striding to work, much faster than me. She is reading a gossip magazine as she walks, her face buried in it, oblivious to the view. I am stunned. *How could anyone, ever, take this for granted?*

2008 Age: 45

I am invited to a reception on Saturday evening – for the international writers who are speaking at the Sydney Writers' Festival – at Government House, hosted by the Governor of New South Wales, Her Excellency Professor Marie Bashir.

As we walk in, we are greeted by the Governor herself, who kindly spends a moment welcoming each of us individually. I present the Governor with an inscribed and signed copy of my book, which she seems to greatly appreciate. She thanks me generously for the gift.

I appear to be the only writer who gives a copy of his/her book to the Governor, but I don't think this is the main reason I make an unforgettable impression on Her Excellency. That is to come later …

I am standing with the Governor and her Chief of Staff, Brian Davies Esq LVO, as Her Excellency kindly recounts a fascinating story about the First Fleet. The Governor is on my right and the Chief of Staff is opposite me – we are huddled quite close together. I sip nonchalantly from my glass of orange juice.

A tray of canapés comes by …

To show how at ease and relaxed I am standing in the company of the Governor, I reach for a canapé. I notice it is topped with a creamy white blob of sauce.

This is a substantial two-bite canapé, so I take the primary bite. The magic of this dignified private moment with the Governor seems to suddenly evaporate as I feel the blob of white creamy sauce miss my mouth and slide down the side of my chin … and fall into oblivion.

The Governor stops talking.

The Governor, the Chief of Staff and I all look down to the floor. The large creamy white blob has landed on top of my right shoe. I have the orange juice in my left hand, the other half of the canapé in my right hand, and it seems a long way down to my right shoe. There is silence. Time stands still.

I have a vague awareness of Her Excellency's voice: 'Brian …'

Suddenly, the Chief of Staff is addressing me: 'Don't worry Imran, we'll take care of this' and simultaneously he is crouching in front of me, wiping the creamy blob off my shoe with a paper napkin.

I apologise profusely to the Chief of Staff, but he dismisses it as nothing to worry about.

Words cannot express the embarrassment I feel. *Idiot, idiot, idiot!* Never, *ever*, eat a complex canapé in front of distinguished company.

Her Excellency finishes her story, but somehow I feel that the dignity has gone from my private audience. She moves on.

When something really embarrassing happens, I believe that the best way to overcome the pain of the humiliation is to recount the incident as a funny anecdote, as many times as possible. The pain is then anaesthetised by humour.

A little later, I am chatting with an officer of the Australian Airforce. He is a Squadron Leader, his blue uniform emblazoned with medals – a very distinguished gentleman indeed. So, I decide that I will begin the self-healing process, by telling him the anecdote.

'Something really embarrassing happened to me this evening,' I say, by way of introduction.

His reply is swift. 'You mean with the Governor and the canapé? I already heard about that.'

2009 Age: 46

This whole trip is a magical experience, from end-to-end. The fact that I have no job and no money left since being laid off from GE is constantly at the back of my mind – but the fear is tempered by the possibility of that project manager job at Regus I already had an interview for, with the final meeting deferred until my return to London.

I arrive in Sydney and check back into the Sebel Pier One hotel – feeling a wave of warm memories from my experience at the Sydney Writers' Festival over a year ago. But the people now sitting in the lobby … they're not fellow writers, they're complete strangers.

I have a speaking event at Gleebooks, the famous independent bookshop, and I am introduced by the British Consul-General, Richard Morris. There are so many familiar faces in the audience, so many different threads of my life. There's Duncan, my colleague from General Electric in London; my cousin Khalid, from my Dad's side in Karachi; Nancy, who loved my book so much, she organised so much publicity for me last time; Becce, the breathtakingly beautiful woman I met on the last trip, intelligent, spiritual, gracious – and not the least bit interested in me; Benjamin, a film maker and fellow writer I met at the Perth Writers' Festival and with whom I share an Australian publisher. There are many strangers, but no sign of Janice, who has moved to Sydney from Melbourne recently – I have not met her in person since the day I bought her Honda Accord (I did send her an email about this event).

I have a radio interview with a bearded Australian man at the ABC studio in Sydney one evening. I have to ask him his name in order to inscribe his copy of my book. He calls me a 'delightful fella' on air, and subsequently many people mention to me that they heard me on Phillip

Adams' show, which was broadcast several times, all over Australia. Apparently, he's very famous.

The Byron Bay Writers' Festival goes even better for me. I had said 'yes' to every event when Jeni Caffin – the Festival Director I met in Bali last year when we were both at the Ubud Festival – was doing the planning. Consequently, I have many events: the schools' day; the Writers' Cabaret; various panel discussions. I seem always to be able to make people laugh. On the second day of the Festival, I'm wandering around the grounds in a state of pure joy, when an attractive woman comes up to me and says, 'Excuse me. I just wanted to tell you that I think you're going to be the big hit of the Festival.' *How can pure joy get any better? It just did.*

After my final panel event, the other three writers – we are all seated in a line at an extended table – have long signing queues, but I have no one. *What happened?* The answer is unexpected … *Unimagined* has completely sold out.

The icing on the cake is the article in the *Sydney Morning Herald*: 'The best-selling book was *Unimagined*, a memoir by the entertaining Imran Ahmad, one of three international guests.'

'Oh Imran, this is just fantastic, I'm so pleased for you, you've conquered Oz!' writes Lynne Hatwell to me in an e-mail. She writes the famous literary blog called *dovegreyreader scribbles*, in which she chose my book as her 'best non-fiction read of the year'.

It's nice to think that. But what I can't stop thinking about is this: does Janice read the literary section of the *Sydney Morning Herald*?

2010 Age: 47

Having been unemployed for months after being let go from that dreadful company Regus, and now living on the state benefit called 'Job Seeker's Allowance', I can no longer afford to pay the Council Tax for our house (equivalent to Property Tax in the US). I apply for the Welfare stream known as Council Tax Benefit, which is quite a humiliating process. I have to submit endless documentation and copies of bank statements which show what a horrendous state my finances are in.

The Benefit is granted, and the letter is signed by the Housing Benefits Manager – Grant Langford.

This is most unexpected. I really thought that he would have moved to Australia.

Tangle

Life is not a straight and uniform cable – it is a mesh of many threads of different colours and textures, all tangled together.

And, apparently, Time is not linear. It is simply the means by which we try to make sense of everything.

If there's any particular distinctive thread that bores you in *Tangle*, you can skim through and skip over those segments – giving you a personalised reading experience. (You don't have to watch *all* of your VHS tapes.)

As a writer, I appreciate you reading my book and I have no desire to torture you. (I am not one of *those* writers who believes that s/he has the right to make you suffer.)

Whatever segments and threads you might choose to skip, everything does come together in the end. You can even read the vignettes of *Tangle* in any order you like.

We all create and interpret Reality in our own unique way.

Club
2019 Age: 57 Kuala Lumpur

I am so absorbed in my very enjoyable work that lunchtime slips by and I don't notice. (This often happens when I'm in my office.) Only around mid-afternoon do I realise that it would be more productive to stop to eat something. My office is on the 34th floor of Tower 2 of the Petronas Towers, which I first saw in the film *Entrapment* over twenty years ago. (I don't recall how Catherine Zeta-Jones got to the outside of the building, because at this height I have never found a window that can be opened.) The Skybridge which joins the twin towers is about ten storeys above my office, and on that level is the Malaysian Petroleum Club, of which I am automatically a member by virtue of my seniority. (It makes me think of the Oil Barons Club in *Dallas* – without the drunken fighting, of course.) The MPC is an excellent place for lunch or afternoon tea, and occasionally Jasmina joins me there. I message her and she is able to make it today.

The place is empty and we are able to sit at my favourite table immediately next to the panoramic windows, looking out over Jalan Ampang and the route that I walk to work from my dream apartment nearby. I order my usual *Kampung Fried Rice*, and Jasmina just has iced lemon tea. She wants to tell me a story, and she is content to relate it while I eat and listen.

'You know I like to volunteer, Imran. Sometimes is my time that I volunteer, sometimes my skills, my knowledge or my money. I also volunteer my positive energy, hugs and smiles to those who lack them in their lives.

'You remember that it's thanks to volunteering that I came to Malaysia five years ago. It's thanks to volunteering that I met so many of my dear friends and colleagues. It's thanks to volunteering that few months ago I went on visit to Asrama Cahaya.

'When I signed up, I thought I was going to visit orphanage and play with kids for few hours, but when we came to the building that is sharing its space with Bukit Nanas Convent School, I was told that we are visiting 'senior orphans'. I never heard of that term before, but my wondering mind kept quiet because we were just greeted by the lady who was our host.

'And then we entered a room with more than thirty grandmas – blind, deaf, disabled, in wheelchairs, bedridden, mentally challenged, old and very old, smiling, indifferent and sad, present or lost in their minds and memories.

'It took me a while to understand that these ladies were either orphans that were brought to orphanages in Penang, Ipoh, Taiping or KL when they were small kids and due to their disabilities they never had an opportunity to leave the orphanage, or they have been abandoned by their families and because of their disabilities had no other place to go. It was hard for me to absorb these information and even harder to understand what kind of life they had lived within so many institutional walls.

'During the first hour all I was able to see was their sickness, sadness and disabilities. I tried my best to engage in various activities with them – singing, throwing balls, celebrating August birthdays. Each activity was supposed to stimulate one of their senses and inspire them to be proactive.

'And then they were supposed to make something from a clay in order to improve motion of their fingers and hands. I looked around for the grandma that would need my help and I saw back of one tiny woman sitting in wheelchair that was twice her size. I approached her from behind, kneel down and only then looked at grandma face. She was skin and bones, blind, with glued eyelids, she had no tooth, her head was constantly moving as well as her hands. I took deep breath and put a bit of clay in her palm. Her small hands were too weak to press the clay and she moved it away. I tried to put my hands over hers and by simultaneously moving them make small ball of clay but she refused that too. I put clay aside and just started to touch her hand, slowly and gently. First her palm, then finger tips, then her whole hand, wrists – slowly and gently. After while her hands and her head were not shaking anymore and she looked very peaceful. I continued until she placed my hands in her lap and started patting me, slowly and gently. Like a caring and loving grandma who is soothing her grandchild. I almost started to cry because it was a long time since I felt that genuine and unconditional kind of tenderness.

'Few minutes later our hands were playing together and for good five-ten minutes we were gently exploring our palms and even arms. Then I raised her hands and placed them to my face and grandma started laughing. Her face lit up, her mouth made the most beautiful curve and both of us were overwhelmed with joy. I closed my eyes and put hands on her face. Our fingers saw more than our eyes. It was one of those rare moments of complete happiness when there is nothing more to ask from life.

'As I was on my way home I was still under strong impression of everything that I felt and experienced during those few hours with grandmas. I went there to give my time, my positive energy, my smiles and hugs … but I was coming home feeling like I was the biggest beneficiary of that visit. It is *me* who got the most.'

I have been eating as quietly as possible, not clattering the cutlery, delicately sipping the Coke Light. I am determined to make it clear to Jasmina that she has my full attention.

Whatever hollow words I speak are merely to reinforce that I am listening.

'Wow. That's amazing …'

'But Imran, it did not end there. I have been going every week. Something more amazing happened.

'Yesterday I went to spend some time massaging my grandmas and they prepared me a surprise. When I arrived they pretended that they had to do something in one of empty rooms. I saw how deaf were helping those in wheelchairs, some in wheelchairs were helping blind, and I was left alone with just few bedridden grandmas.

'Suddenly one of those who disappeared called me to come and when I entered that room they all started to sing happily: "Happy Birthday, dear Jasmina." Those who do not talk were clapping and smiling. I was almost in tears when they continued to sing: "God bless you, child." I kissed all of them and they hugged and kissed me. Room was full of pure joy.'

I am speechless. Nothing I can think of saying can possibly be an adequate response to Jasmina's narration. I am somewhat used to this – lunch or afternoon tea or dinner with Jasmina is always profound, there's always something remarkable and moving to discuss … but this one beats them all.

'Wow. That's amazing …'

Joy
2009 Age: 46 London

One quiet Saturday afternoon in leafy Surrey, I am walking back to our house from the nearby shops, lost in thought as usual. I become vaguely aware of three teenage boys on the other side of the street, walking towards me, but pay no attention to them.

Apropos of nothing, my wandering mind reflects appreciatively on how much Britain has changed just in the span of my lifetime: *I haven't been called 'Paki' in so long. I actually don't remember the last time I was called 'Paki'. It's been years since I was called 'Paki'!*

As they draw level with me across the road, one of the boys calls out to me: 'Paki!'

My heart explodes with joy. I am so overcome with happy emotion, I want to hug all of them. (This probably would not be appropriate.)

That fellow soul just confirmed again what I have been learning recently. There *is* a Universal Consciousness and we are all connected by it. I was never so happy to be called 'Paki' in my entire life!

Paradise
1990 Age: 28 London

Apropos of nothing, Sabrina asks me: 'When you go to Paradise, do you have to be with the same person you're married to in this Life, forever?'

I think about it for a moment, then mumble hesitantly: 'I think so.'

We both contemplate this in sombre silence.

Bathrobe
1995 Age: 33 Hong Kong

To pass the time this evening, I go out for a walk. Whenever I step outside the cool, quiet tranquillity of the Sheraton, I am slapped in the face by the heat, humidity and noise of Hong Kong – but I'm getting used to it now. It's dark already (not that it seems any less busy) and I head off down Nathan Road.

Just half-a-mile away is the beautiful and elegant Kowloon Mosque, which I discovered only recently. I proceed through the metal gates, up the steps, and slip off my shoes outside the large wooden doors, which are flung open and welcoming.

Inside it is subdued and peaceful, with very few people around, and it's a pleasure to walk barefoot on the carpeted floor. I prefer mosques when they are in-between the congregational prayer times which bring crowds of men and a somewhat uptight atmosphere as the prayers are performed in a rigid collective ritual. Instead, now it's very calm, and the pleasing acoustics produced by the domed roof help to enhance the soothing ambiance. I pick an isolated spot beside a marble pillar and perform the sunset prayer (late) and the night prayer together, because I'm taking the travelling exemption – being thousands of miles from home. Islamic prayer – properly performed, not hurried, not regimented – is incredibly calming and spiritually elevating. You have to immerse yourself in the recitation and the movements, so that you can completely disconnect from the anxiety and the frenzy of life. I think it's similar to how Buddhists focus on Breath during meditation – something to anchor on so that you can let go of your transient surroundings and state. But in Islam we use the whole body (like in yoga) – which I think makes it easier to detach yourself from externalities.

Afterwards, I sit cross-legged with my back against the column, breathe gently and reflect on my unimagined life. I failed to get into medical school; studied Chemistry in Scotland; quit my PhD to join Unilever; was hassled into a marriage that was arranged but not forced, and turned out to be a total mismatch; became a management consultant; spent six months in Africa; was blessed with the loveliest daughter possible, whom I love more than anything; became an expert in Oracle systems; was offered a job and relocation to Minneapolis; now travel to exotic locations around the world to work on Oracle projects. I never dreamed of any of this when I was young, and now I'm never sure where my life will lead next …

Well, there is one thing I am absolutely sure about … Islam. That's why I'm sitting in this mosque, completely at peace. It's been a long journey … from the enforced, unquestioning, unreasoning, sombre misery of imposed ritual and superstition in my childhood … struggling with the relentless efforts of hardline evangelical Christians to convert me with their *absolute certainty* … through observing the hypocrisy of ignorant, culturally regressive, medieval Islamists … to the joyful understanding and faith that come from factual study and rational analysis. And Islam is the answer. Of this I am certain. So, I sit here in this oasis of dignity, savouring the stillness, until it's time to go.

Back at the hotel, I have another shower and put on shorts and a fresh T-shirt, deodorant and aftershave – then put my feet up on the sofa and wait.

The phone rings sooner than I expected.

It's Penelope, of course, and she sounds overjoyed to speak with me. The joy may not be solely because of me, as she explains excitedly that she has been upgraded to a lovely suite.

I go up there right away. She has left the door ajar and I stride in and lock it firmly behind me, also hitting the 'Do Not Disturb' button which activates a red illumination outside. I glance around and get the impression of a spacious suite, with separate bedroom and living room. Penny always dresses well – today she has flown thousands of miles from the US in designer jeans, a slim white shirt and an elegant blue jacket. I embrace her and can feel that she is clammy from the long journey. Her mouth is that usual blend of lingering cigarettes and freshly swirled mouthwash which I find curiously exciting.

Of course, she will shower first. I release her and she hangs up her jacket, then heads into the bathroom. I slip my clothes off, place them on the armchair on my side of the bed, and slip under the covers, relaxing with my hands behind my head on the pillows. With the room being so cool, inside the bed feels absolutely perfectly cosy. There's just the calm hum of the air conditioner in the bedroom … until I hear the steady gush of the shower coming from the bathroom. I can almost feel the hot pressurised water washing away the sweat of Penny's journey. I wait with delightful anticipation.

But this is a bittersweet moment of reflection. I feel both excitement at the imminent pleasure, but also sadness in the knowledge that this is only transitory. Penelope and I have an understanding that this is a 'long-distance relationship' in the sense that it only takes place when we are both a long distance away from home. It provides occasional relief for both of us, but we know it can only be for as long as we are on projects which bring us to the same destinations.

I have guilt also, but it's easy enough for me to justify this. I'm locked in a miserable non-physical marriage with a woman who abuses me, but won't let us get divorced. Every time I try to discuss this possibility in a civilised way, she drags our precious three-year-old daughter into the argument, and I cannot bear the pain which it causes Aleena, so I back off. The stress of my home life is unbearable, and I get my relief from business travel – as far away as possible and two or three weeks at a time.

I am an exceptionally passionate man who does not have a steady sex life. From my marriage I came to believe that sex is something that men want and women grudgingly allow. But from Penny I learned that this is not true – women have the desire also! She doesn't seem to carry the same level of guilt as me, although she is a Christian from the Deep South. She is divorced and pragmatic about the fact that we both need this and it's good for both of us. We have quality time together too, dinners and conversations – although I steer away from any discussion about religion. (Penny did mention Rapture once, as in something like: 'The Rapture may come before this project ends.' I think she noticed my aversion reaction and never mentioned it again.)

The sound of the shower stops and my body tenses with excitement.

Finally, the door opens and Penny appears exactly as I want her to be – wearing a white Sheraton bathrobe, with her blonde hair and ivory skin still damp. She is incredibly desirable. I never imagined that I would be attracted to a woman more than ten years older than me.

She slips into the bed still wearing the robe and I unknot the cord, slipping my hands around her taut body. This is what I dreamed of and longed for since I was twelve years old – *real passion.*

Her first climax comes in less than one minute. Even I'm surprised, and say so. 'You've relaxed me!' is her explanation. So appreciative. *I really appreciate being appreciated.*

Her second climax takes a couple of minutes, and the third and final one we spend about two hours working on, steadily and sensually – using every part of the suite, including the shower and the sofa in the living room. (When I was a boy, I flicked through an Astrology book in a gift shop. For Virgo, under Sex it said: 'You prefer the chase to the kill.' I assumed this meant me running around the bedroom chasing the woman, who laughs and squeals in *faux* protest, as I had seen many times in *Carry On* films and other vulgar British comedy. But now I know what it means.)

When she's had her third climax, I allow myself my own release, and then we collapse in blissful exhaustion – drifting away in the cool air and the steady hum of the air conditioner …

… I have a horrible, disturbing dream. Aleena has been kidnapped and is being held somewhere in a derelict and deserted grey building, which has dozens of windows. It is night-time, and I am standing across the street in front of this building, desperately looking at all of the black windows, and from somewhere in the darkness I hear Aleena's frightened voice cry out: 'Daddy, where are you?' …

… The telephone rings. Penny answers it, of course, as I remain completely silent. It's our colleague Greg and he's asking if she's seen Imran. She tells him that she hasn't seen Imran, but she is sure that he's been informed about the group teleconference this morning with our boss back in the US.

Cayenne
2002 Age: 40 London

I read a car magazine article that reports that the Porsche Cayenne has the highest depreciation and running costs of all the cars surveyed. The emission and fuel consumption figures also indicate that it is actually an environmental catastrophe on wheels.

I occasionally, very occasionally, see a Cayenne on the road in London and I am always filled with contempt and hatred for the owner. *What arrogance and irresponsibility!* How can a Porsche have five doors? How can a Porsche look like that? And why do these smug assholes feel the need to drive an SUV in London, when the roads are perfectly fine? We are not in a desert or in a jungle. They don't care about the pollution and the unnecessarily high petrol usage. They drive a Porsche Cayenne purely for the purpose of flaunting their wealth, no matter what the environmental impact. *Idiots!*

Whenever I see a Porsche Cayenne, I always imagine spraying back and forth all over it with a machine gun. *That would be fun!*

I hate anyone who drives a Porsche Cayenne.

5 - 1
2005 Age: 42 London

The test will be difficult, I know, but I also know it will require clear and methodical thinking, and I've always been good at that. In school, I emulated Spock, who was always 'logical'. Most people aren't able to be so dispassionate and rational – they make assumptions. But, as it says on my CV, I am 'able to understand and analyse any complex issue and then explain it in the appropriate level of detail'.

They are a completely mixed bunch of people, of all shapes and colours, waiting in the lobby of the Thistle Hyde Park Hotel. For some reason I notice: a silver-haired white man in a dark blue pinstripe suit, perhaps looking for a career change before retirement; a slim young woman of Far Eastern ethnicity; an overweight black woman in her forties. It takes all sorts to be British secret agents these days.

There is total silence as we proceed into the function room when directed. It's laid out like a school examination hall, but since we all are strangers to each other, there is no talking at all. I help myself to a bottle of sparkling water and take a seat in the front row, which I've always believed is the least distracting. The recruitment agency woman in charge explains the test procedure, the timing and so on, and then asks if there are any questions. A question does cross my mischievous mind, but I don't have the courage to ask it: *'After joining MI5, is it possible to transfer to MI6?'* I almost laugh out loud; it would be so funny to ask in this atmosphere of deadly seriousness. (I know they can't answer the question – they are an external contractor employed by MI5 to administer the test.)

What is it about me? I've never taken anything completely seriously. But isn't that why I still look and feel so young? My hair and teeth – they are all there and all original!

The test is indeed very difficult. It is somewhat similar to an advanced verbal reasoning test – I've always been very good at these (in the one for Price Waterhouse management consulting, my score put me in the top 1%). You must be very careful to understand and identify the difference between a deduction, an inference and an assumption. This is very important in order to evaluate the quality of intelligence data you are receiving from agents and informants. It is only possible to arrive at sound answers by categorising and tabulating the data, so that you can make quantitative comparative evaluations – and thus make balanced decisions about the use of limited resources. I know that I enjoy the whole sexy James Bond genre, but this is actually why they call it 'intelligence'.

I am able to complete the test within the available time, but I am mentally exhausted. Unlike an exam in school, when we get up to leave no one says a word to anyone else – there is an uncanny silence. People avoid eye contact even. We flow out of the exam room, out of the hotel, and disperse into the fresh air of early May and the unknowing general community – carrying our secret with inner pride and excitement (*well, I do*). I return to the GE office and don't have to tell anyone what my 'appointment' this morning was about.

The plain white envelope comes within a few days and conveys the good news that I passed the test (I was actually quite confident that I had done so). The letter advises that they will be in touch soon and reminds me to treat my application with absolute confidentiality. *I have done!* I haven't told anyone: not Sabrina, *not even Milton!*

Milk Bottle
1966 Age: 3 London

Nearly four years old, I am allowed to wander the streets around our Fulham bedsit by myself. It's a hot, slow day as I trudge about, bored, listless. There's no one around.

One of our neighbours has a car, which is quite an extraordinary achievement (*imagine having a car!*), and I come upon it parked nearby. Seeking some self-importance, I take an empty glass milk bottle from a nearby doorstep, then place it against one of the wheels of the car – the idea being that, when the car is driven, the bottle will shatter, and the broken glass will puncture the tyre.

But this is the calamity that I, as the hero, must prevent. With a deep sense of urgency, I ring their doorbell and then frantically tell one of their family members, a teenage boy, that he must come with me as I have something most important to show him. He follows me out to the car and observes, as breathlessly I show him what some criminal has done. Almost indifferently, he thanks me and takes the bottle and places it outside their doorstep for the milkman to collect as usual.

Disaster has been averted, thanks to me the hero, but the expected acclaim and admiration appear to be disappointingly missing.

Travelin' Man
1996 Age: 33 Mexico City

Everyone I know has been signing up to this new 'Internet' – either through CompuServe or America Online. My preference is CompuServe (which is how I met 'Lady Samantha' from New York – that didn't work out too well; you should always meet someone in person before you conclude that they must be the love of your life). I still use the chatrooms to look for a woman, albeit more cautiously now, but there's something else going on as well. The passionate debate between Islam and Christianity, which for years has been using my heart and mind as a battleground, has a new venue – the Religion Forum of CompuServe. I'm mostly spending my days on a project in Mexico City; Penelope is in Europe somewhere, so evenings in my hotel room are quite barren. This Forum is where I spend my time.

The problem with the Internet is that there is no quality control or truth validation. There is such a motley bunch of characters in this Forum – they all have their own agendas, and many of them seem unencumbered by truth, facts or rationality (and some are only semi-literate). There are obnoxious so-called Christians viciously bashing Islam – as well as gentle, thoughtful, articulate Christians seeking to engage in mutually respectful dialogue (with a view to conversion, I'm assuming). There are Atheists, who are always coldly rational, of course. There are superstitious primitives who believe in reincarnation, astrology, karma and other such mumbo jumbo. What annoys me most are the so-called Muslims who actually believe all sorts of nonsense and some of the cultural values which are always attributed to Islam – and then they try to defend these and end up making Islam look primitive, barbaric and incoherent.

And then there is one regular Muslim poster who is always: well-informed, absolutely rational, totally logical, brilliantly coherent.

He goes by the name of *Travelin' Man.*

Shoe Shop
1973 Age: 11 London

We are in a shoe shop. My mother is buying new shoes for my brothers, while I wander around aimlessly. All shoe shops look the same to me.

There is a song playing over the speaker system, the sound coming down from the ceiling all over the shop. It's not a song I know, but I stand still, listening intently, my head tilted, and looking up at the ceiling. They keep singing the same phrase over and over again: *'All you need is Love … All you need is Love.'* There is a variation, *'Love is all you need'* and also just *'Love, Love, Love …'*

My mother appears from nowhere, sees me listening intently, listens herself for a moment, and then declares loudly in a disparaging voice, to break the spell on me: 'What a silly song!'

Yes, that's right. I withdraw into myself again. It *is* a silly song, just repeating the same words over and over again, about 'Love' – that vulgar thing the white people are obsessed with in all their songs, their films, their television, their whole culture. That's not for us. We don't do 'Love'.

Eternal
1975 Age: 12 London

At the Islamic Sunday school, our Egyptian teacher asks the class: 'How old is the Qur'an?'

I do some quick arithmetic in my head (roughly 2000 minus roughly 600) and call out: 'Fourteen hundred years!'

'Wrong!' he replies.

He then explains that the Qur'an is actually Eternal – not only into the future, but from the past. It has existed Eternally.

I don't say anything … but this doesn't make sense.

I thought that God created everything, that God Himself wrote the Qur'an and that *only* God is Eternal. So if only God is Eternal, then He must have existed before the Qur'an and therefore the Qur'an cannot have existed *since* Eternity. So what the teacher is saying doesn't really make sense.

But this also raises another issue, which I process endlessly inside my head. If we agree that the Qur'an is *almost* Eternal and existed before Creation, then that means that everything mentioned in it is pre-ordained. The Qur'an is full of guidance, explanation and reassurance which is very specific to the life of the Prophet and the situations in which he and his early followers found themselves. This means that those events were known to God in advance. If they were known in advance, does that mean they were all planned and meant to be?

I keep being told that God controls and determines *everything.* So, what do *we* do? If God determines everything, then it means that I have no control or influence over anything. It's more important to pray to God and please God and let God decide an outcome – rather than try to achieve it myself. I feel totally disempowered, apprehensive and afraid.

At the Grammar school, I feel disconnected from all my classmates – none of whom spend any time worrying about these critical dilemmas. They just seem carefree, frivolous and happy. They have no idea about the darkness in my mind.

Concerned
1997 Age: 34 Minneapolis

My first assignment with Ernst & Young is to Imation, based in Oakdale, a satellite city of Minneapolis-Saint Paul. This company is implementing Oracle software all around the world, and E&Y is leading it for them.

I drive every day, in my new leased silver Toyota Camry, through the snow and ice the thirty-five miles to Oakdale Mall – which looks like any small American shopping mall, with about one hundred cars in the car park. But inside, the mall is curiously empty. There are few outlets open, and very few potential customers to be seen. Where are all the people who parked those cars outside?

In *The Man from U.N.C.L.E.*, the agents entered an ordinary looking New York tailor shop, and then went through a hidden door in the back of a changing cubicle to enter their secret underground headquarters. There is a similar arrangement at Oakdale Mall. In a long bare wall, there is a plain and discrete door marked *Private*, alongside which is an electronic card reader to give access. Behind the door is a vast windowless network of huge project rooms, with scores of (mostly Indian) programmers working at keyboards, and many E&Y and Imation staff having endless meetings. The company has rented a lot of cheap disused retail space in this empty shopping mall, to house the big project team.

This is very exciting for me and I am assigned a role looking after a specific aspect of this huge programme.

One of our most experienced Oracle consultants is Greg Brendan, who knows the software very well, apparently. He looks like he's a couple of years out of college, like many of the E&Y consultants. One day I'm discussing something with Greg, and on his computer I show him an aspect of the basic functionality which will really help to solve the problem which he is working on. He practically falls out of his chair with surprise; he was unaware that the software could do this.

I reflect how worrying it is that we have kids out of college who have learned about the software through trial and error, and these are our best 'experts'. Meanwhile, an army of Indian programmers are writing modifications under their direction. This is most perturbing.

More customisations mean more work for my consulting firm, which subcontracts programmers to write them, and will cost the client a lot more in both the short and long terms. I'm very uncomfortable with this. As professional advisors, we should be steering clients towards modifying their business processes, rather than messing around with the software – but the additional revenue can amount to a lot of money for the consulting firm.

As I become familiar with the project, something else also troubles me deeply. Imation is requesting many changes to the standard software, and E&Y is going ahead with these. The system is due to 'go live' in September, and we are already in March. With all this new software being written, all the testing and training which will need to be done, all the phases of a properly run IT project … I cannot see any way that we can be ready with a reliable working system by September. It doesn't make sense. But the senior people in charge *must* know what they are doing; *I must be mistaken.*

Ridley Juergens is the Senior Manager in charge of this vast, profitable programme for E&Y; he will soon be made a Partner for bringing so much income to the Firm. Every two weeks, he summons the entire E&Y team (and no one else) to a restaurant where he books a big private room. As

I look around, it is always sobering for me to see how young the team is; I am an old man by comparison.

This week Ridley has an interesting request, as we wait for our starters. We will go around the very long table, and each one of us is to convey in just *one word* how we feel about the likelihood of this big project being delivered successfully by September.

The exercise starts and all the young people are saying words like 'excited', 'confident', 'upbeat', 'energised', 'positive', 'certain', 'optimistic'.

My term comes and I say 'concerned', in a suitably concerned voice.

Ridley looks slightly taken aback (I am the only other Senior Manager in the group), but the focus moves on to the next person. By the time that we have been around the whole table, every single comment has conveyed absolute confidence that we will deliver on time, except for mine.

Oops. I said what I genuinely believe, but should I have said something else, something more politically expedient?

Ridley brings my role on his programme to an end fairly soon after this – I am to be redeployed on another project, far away.

Awkward
1988 Age: 25 London

The wedding goes as planned, although the bride is one hour and twenty minutes late (no explanation is ever provided). I sit on the stage of the Porchester Hall in Bayswater, waiting in front of a vast crowd – only a handful of whom are my friends (even Milton isn't here, he gave himself food poisoning from a dubious prawn sandwich) – until she arrives, bedecked according to tradition. I hate what South Asian weddings do to an otherwise beautiful woman: she is garbed in vivid, garish clothing; shackled with vulgar jewellery; her body is graffitied with hideous designs in henna. The ceremony treats her as a brightly decorated piece of property being transferred from one man to another. I hate this cultural slavery and ignorance.

We arrive at my parents' house around 11 p.m., and many photos are taken of us sitting on the sofa. I have an arm around Sabrina, grinning like the Cheshire Cat, and she smiles but looks awkward.

We are driven around the corner to my own house and, by the time everyone leaves, it's about 1 a.m. (Everyone except my uncle and his wife from Vancouver in the spare bedroom, and my brothers downstairs in the living room.) (My uncle actually did marry the woman in the black-and-white photo, and they appear to be very happy together.)

Finally, this is the good bit. I'm an expert at this theoretically – I've read *The Joy of Sex* three times. She is sitting on the bed, looking uncomfortable, when I return from the shower in my new blue pyjamas (which I now know should be thrown aside casually on to the floor).

It doesn't go quite as I expected.

'Bond was too tired and too stressed to achieve the necessary state of mind. He and the beautiful woman just went to sleep.'

Which book was that in?

When I go to the bathroom in the morning, I hear from the spare bedroom my uncle's wife moaning gently as they make love. *In the morning!* (Well, I'm glad someone's getting some action.)

Football Kit
1974 Age: 11 London

Now that I've been accepted into Hampton Grammar School, the school sends my parents lots of information in the mail about what to expect and what we need to do to prepare. I study all of it – my parents don't really bother. There is even a little yellow book entitled 'School Rules' which I read reverently several times ('Smoking or bringing cigarettes to school is strictly forbidden'). The book mentions the concept of a Saturday Detention as a possible punishment for misdemeanours. It's very scary.

The information on uniform is quite explicit, as well as on the attire for PE and sports (white shorts, white T-shirt, white socks, white sneakers for PE; black shorts, rugby or football shirt, socks, boots for sports). I nag my parents about this until finally they take me out one Saturday afternoon to get the uniform. But on the sports attire, they seem unconvinced or non-committal. They say we'll get it after we return from our vacation in Canada during the long summer break. They imply that they can't afford everything all at once.

The term at Hampton Grammar School will begin on Thursday September 9th, and we return from Canada on the afternoon of Saturday September 4th. We are all exhausted and sleep well into Sunday. We still need to get my sports kit, but of course the shops are all closed on Sunday. My parents return to work on Monday and now my anxiety is embedded. Since the shops close at 5:00 p.m. or so, there seems to be no opportunity for them to take me to buy what I need. My mother says it's okay, we'll go on Saturday. But that is Saturday *after* school starts.

It's Thursday morning at Hampton Grammar School, and my form teacher Mr Holman is writing out our weekly timetable on the blackboard. Four lessons of English, three lessons of French, four lessons of Mathematics, three lessons of Latin, double-Chemistry, double-Physics and so on … I am hoping desperately that PE and Games will be on Monday, Tuesday or Wednesday – so that it won't matter that we will buy my gear on Saturday. But it is not to be. The main session of Games and one of the sessions of PE will be on Friday afternoon.

With a feeling of panic, I go up to speak with Mr Holman and explain that I have not yet got my sports kit and we are going on Saturday to buy it. He seems quite sympathetic and relaxed about it, and asks me to bring a note from my parents.

My mother writes the note in the evening, explaining that we came back late from our vacation and were not able to buy the sports clothes before term began.

On Friday afternoon, my class all arrive at the rather drab, musty and spartan changing rooms at 2:00 p.m., and they all begin transforming into their brand new, pristine white PE kit. All except me. I stand around awkwardly and they regard me with curiosity, perhaps disdain. When the rather severe and humourless Mr Foster appears, I immediately present the note, addressing him as 'Sir' in the most respectful and pathetic tone I can muster. He reads the note quickly and then tells me in a rather gruff voice to stand to one side and just observe everything.

The PE lesson looks terrifying. Mr Foster explains all the equipment, the bars on the walls, the mats and the wooden structures. His tone is scary – we are not in school anymore, we're in the Army. The gym has terrible acoustics and the whole place seems like a torture chamber. I feel so awkward standing around, hoping no one will pay any attention to me and that Mr Foster will forget about me.

After the PE lesson is over, it's time for our entire year group to join my class for double-Games. Now, instead of just 26 boys noticing that I don't have the necessary clothes and shoes, there are 107 boys doing so – crowding all of the changing rooms. We all move out on to the school field, and I walk self-consciously alongside Mr Foster, as he and other teachers yell loudly to direct the organisation and playing of the football games. We will play football and rugby on alternate Friday afternoons, apparently.

As I stand awkwardly on the field in my black blazer and trousers, my black formal shoes getting dirty in the muddy grass, I feel totally humiliated. It's only the second day at Hampton Grammar School and already I've made myself stand out from everyone else – not in a good way.

Macbeth
2011 Age: 48 Southeast Asia

Mark Hemstedt is a great guy – we reconnected recently, thanks to the Internet. Now that we both live in Southeast Asia (he in Singapore, I in Malaysia), we are actually neighbours and meet occasionally. He runs an institute teaching self-empowerment and has offices in both countries. I sometimes speak about my personal journey of failure and success in special seminars for the graduates.

On one occasion, it's a long weekend for me and I take a slow six-hour train ride from Kuala Lumpur down to Singapore, at total peace as I observe the endless palm oil plantations along the route. I stay at Mark's apartment, and this evening we go to an extraordinary 'Shakespeare in the Park' performance of *Macbeth*. The following evening, we visit a fairground near Clarke Quay and share a terrifying ride in which we fall from the sky in a giant swinging pendulum.

One of the best parts of reconnecting with Mark is that his actual home is an extraordinary villa in Phuket, Thailand, complete with its own pool and housekeeper, and he lets me use it by arrangement. It's in a private estate, and there's an excellent spa just across the road, with an endless variety of massages and treatments.

One time I take Aleena and one of her friends from medical school for a few days at Mark's villa.

Another time I take Nina's daughter and her Australian boyfriend for a long weekend – although Nina is furious when she hears about this, as she wants all ties with me severed. Nonetheless, we have a most relaxing time.

Park
1980 Age: 17 London

Andrea is all I can think about. Ever since I met her at our two schools' combined sixth form plays, I have been totally in love with her. I dream of dating her, of marrying her, of making love with her. The only problems are that there's no scheduled opportunities to meet her (only random encounters between her school and mine); the dating part would be impossible to get past my parents; the marriage part would be contrary to all the parameters which are clearly defined, as she's not Muslim and not Pakistani. The making love part I visualise so much, it makes my brain tired.

I walk around with a constant heaviness in my chest; a longing for what I cannot have and which I desire more than anything. I totally lose interest in Biology, Chemistry and Physics, which I am studying for the A-level exams next year. This doesn't matter too much, as God controls everything and He will get me through those exams – as it surely is my Destiny to go to medical school and become a doctor.

But wasn't it also my Destiny to meet Andrea? That was also ordained by God, so it must have some purpose, some ultimate meaningful conclusion.

I long to see her, so I go for random walks which take me past her cul-de-sac. I never walk into the cul-de-sac, of course, as that would not appear random. But there is a park behind her house, and one evening I decide to go for a random walk there. It's nearly summer, so the light lingers long. As I casually walk around the park, I try to figure out which of the adjacent houses must be hers – but without making it obvious that I'm looking. Just a casual glance in that direction. But as I reach my closest approach, I can see in one of the windows a figure with brunette hair, and clearly the figure is watching me. *It's Andrea!*

Of course, I don't acknowledge her or look directly at her. I just continue to casually walk around the park on this random excursion. I hurry away, without trying to look in a hurry.

For some reason, I tell Mike Allen about this the next day at school, emphasising that I was just on a casual random walk and Andrea happened to see me from her window.

His response is quite severe. 'Don't do it again. Don't go to that park again. She'll think you're creepy.'

Systems
1987 Age: 25 UK

The weeks in October leading up to my house purchase are spent in Banbury, a delightful market town in Oxfordshire, where we are auditing Mattessons-Wall's.

Banbury is actually the head office of Mattessons, which the Board of Unilever decided to merge with Wall's recently, to reduce overhead costs. Both are meat companies, but Mattessons was considered more *upmarket* (pâtés) and Wall's more *mass market* (sausages). The merger was pushed through under intense pressure in a short timeframe and was a complete disaster. The incompatible computer systems are completely messed up and no one knows which invoices have been printed, sent, paid, not paid and so on. This means that the Finance department is in crisis.

What really troubles me is that the person in charge of the merger project is likely to lose his job over this, and yet that is exactly the kind of prestigious, responsible, highly-paid job to which I aspire. It's very scary. As a lowly internal auditor, I am much less likely to come to the attention of the Board.

We auditors hang out in a conference room, our portable computers and printers spread out over the big table, cables strewn everywhere, files and papers in various piles. We each come and go during the day, to our individual audit meetings, reconvening for lunch and to leave at the end of the day (which can *never* be before 6:00 p.m. and more typically 7:00 p.m.). Then there's always dinner, usually in an Indian or Chinese restaurant – not too expensive, so that we don't exceed our meal allowances. It's okay to leave around 5:00 p.m. on Fridays, to travel back home or to a pub near Unilever House for someone's leaving event. Monday morning comes back around very quickly.

Somewhere in amongst all this we are supposed to be studying for our accountancy exams, which I find very difficult. Fortunately, we will be given three weeks' study leave before each set of exams, to be able to focus on these without the burden of our auditing work.

My parents are determined to use these three weeks of study leave to get me engaged as soon as possible after I move into my new house. Any period of time I spend as a bachelor with my own place is considered very high risk. I might fall in (mutual) love with a white woman (which is exactly what I want to do).

Galen
1975 Age: 12 London

There is a television series *Planet of the Apes* on Sunday evenings, and my family generally watch it together. Two American astronauts in a deep space probe have gone through a time warp and returned to Earth in the year 3085 (June 14th to be precise) – to find that intelligent talking apes are now the dominant species and humans are relatively backward and subservient.

Although we all enjoy it, one evening while we are watching *Planet of the Apes* my mother rather dampens the mood by suddenly articulating an issue I have kept suppressed.

She scoffs contemptuously: 'The *Goreh* [white people] don't believe in Adam and Eve. They think people came from monkeys. The whole western world believes this!'

My father smiles awkwardly and nods in agreement, although clearly not so bothered about it.

I don't say anything. I am deeply troubled by this. I know that in Hampton Grammar School we will study Evolution one day. I have entered classrooms where the Evolution stuff is still written on the blackboard, from a previous lesson. And I know that *everyone* in school believes in Evolution except me – or rather that I am *not supposed* to believe in it. I don't want to be different from everyone else and this is very unsettling. I cannot believe in Evolution because it's un-Islamic and we believe in Adam and Eve.

[A few years later, I learn from strictly Christian boys in the school that they don't believe in Evolution either.]

Honeymoon
1988 Age: 26 Florida

The honeymoon is a nightmare, almost from the beginning.

The slightly severe INS officer in Orlando examines our passports and notes the poor quality of my US visa. She holds it under a UV light to show me, then compares it to Sabrina's good quality one, which is newly obtained. I can see her point, but I already used that visa a few years ago, on a day trip driving from Vancouver to Seattle and back, with my uncle and his wife. (The INS officer then had laughed, when my reply to his question about the purpose of my visit had been 'to go on a picnic'. There was a torrential rainstorm in progress. We went shopping in K-Mart instead and I bought a pair of very smart, brown corduroy trousers.)

However, making a point of being kind to us because we are on our honeymoon, she stamps the passports in a methodical way and lets us in to the land of my dreams.

Immediately afterwards, as we are walking through Customs, Sabrina makes what she thinks is a joke. 'Well, Imran, you *really* should stop smuggling cocaine.'

'Don't say stupid things like that!' I snap at her, conscious that if any Customs officer has heard her, he must also hear my sharp rebuke and understand that the woman's comment has been in jest. But you never, *ever*, joke with US Customs about drug smuggling. *Everybody knows that!*

Sabrina immediately goes into a bad mood because of how I just spoke to her and she won't communicate for the rest of the evening. We get the rental car; check in to the International Inn on International Drive; go to bed (as in 'to sleep').

Sabrina and I argue all the time. I want to go on the rides in Disney World; she wants to go to all the bloody shops. She insists we must buy a present for every single member of my family and her family. My credit cards start to creak under the weight. Hers are already maxed out, even though she lived at home and had no mortgage to pay. I think she's reckless and frivolous, and preoccupied with silly little material things. She thinks I'm a miserable control freak.

Our personalities do not sit comfortably together. I never realised that women can have a broad range of different personalities (the arranged marriage process is not based on personality, it is based on superficial appearances and various status measures). I thought that marriage would be like having a permanent girlfriend.

When we talk, which is rare, it's awkward and I don't like what I'm hearing. She didn't really want to get married – she had no choice, her parents hassled her into it. Her father's apparent vast fortune is mostly locked in a legal dispute with his first wife and the children from that marriage. They are all grown up and have seized his assets in Pakistan, apparently. They even had him thrown in jail for a while, by bribing police officers, judges and government ministers. That's Pakistan for you. I've always known it was utterly corrupt, ever since I was told what happened in the Karachi 'Bonnie Baby' contest of 1964.

There is another problem too. Our marriage isn't yet consummated. For whatever reason, it just doesn't seem to happen. The fact that we are arguing all the time doesn't help at all – but to make it worse, Sabrina says I must agree now that when we return to London, I will see a consultant in this field. Otherwise she will kick up a stink about it with her family and everyone in the Pakistani community in London will get to know about it. This additional encouragement is extremely helpful.

Conscious of how recklessly we are spending money on family presents, I economise any way that I can. I buy the biggest value takeaway meals from Kentucky Fried Chicken ('extra crispy') at night, and then eat and drink the ample remains for breakfast. Sabrina lies in bed, looking at me with her wide beautiful eyes, as I sit in the blazing sunshine at the round table by the huge window of our ninth-floor room – writing postcards to Audit department and Janice and others about what a great time I'm having.

One afternoon there is a very heavy downpour and most people decide to leave the Magic Kingdom for the day. On the packed ferry boat, people notice us arguing in our poorly suppressed tones. There's a German couple nearby; I see her listening intently to us and then she says to him: '*Sie sind Englisch.*'

This marriage was a terrible mistake. I *knew* that before I went into it. The right thing to do is to get it annulled. But nearly everyone from Unilever Internal Audit was at the reception (everyone except Timson, I deliberately didn't invite him). To have it annulled would be unspeakably embarrassing – I would never be able to live it down at work.

One day we get into another argument in the hotel gift shop (about what we don't need to buy) and Sabrina storms off. I head off in another direction and go for a long walk, dipping in and out of the shops in order to benefit from the air conditioning.

When I return to the hotel room, she is there, lying on the bed. We don't exchange a word. I lie down next to her, and our rage turns to passion. We both end up laughing with relief when it finally happens. We go out to dinner this evening, and it's as if a weight has been lifted. I don't have to see a doctor back in London, and maybe this marriage will work out alright after all.

Welcome
1981 Age: 19 Scotland

It's my first week on campus at Stirling University and there's a knock on my door one evening. This is quite exciting – it could be a beautiful woman.

I open the door to reveal two foreign young men: brown skin, pathetically scraggly beards, slightly Chinese-looking-but-not-quite. They could pass for Klingons, without much make-up work.[*] I have no idea *where* they're from.

They seem taken aback on seeing me and immediately apologise.

'Sorry to bother you. We are from the Malaysian Muslim Students' Association. We saw your name on the room list and we thought you must be Malaysian.'

I assure them that I'm not Malaysian and we politely disengage. *Malaysia*? I know it's vaguely near China, but apart from that I know nothing about the place.

The presence of Muslims on campus is a bit troubling, as I don't want to feel compelled to be overtly Muslim and I do want to appear normal – in order to attract the right kind of woman. This would be a beautiful white girl who is not too bothered about religion. I've been wanting this for about seven years.

The next evening there is a knock on my door. Maybe this time?

I open the door to reveal a young man and a young woman: casually dressed, white, English accents.

'Hi there! We're from the Christian Union.'

Inexplicably and inadvertently, I reply enthusiastically: 'Oh, hi!'

---

[*] In those days the Klingons in *Star Trek* looked like dark brown Chinese people.

They think my enthusiastic response must be sarcastic, but actually it was just because I'm at ease with white people who speak English clearly and don't use bad language. Just like the Christians back at Hampton School with whom I had a lot in common – we were well-behaved, didn't use foul language, believed in God and Satan, and weren't quite ready to unquestioningly accept Evolution. We could also have fascinating and engaging discussions.

They tell me about their weekly meetings on campus and assure me that I'm very welcome. We cheerfully disengage.

Like Hell I would go to an actual Christian Union meeting! I'm very happy to engage with them in neutral territory (I guess now that I'm a student far away from my parents, I'll be spending a lot of time in bars), but I would never place myself into a large group of them – that would be like walking into a lion's den. They'll start doing miracles and stuff and I'll be terrified.

And so it begins …

Flame
1967 Age: 4 London

In our new house in Putney we have a hot water maker in the bathroom. It is called a 'boiler' and it runs on gas – you can see the blue flame inside through a little glass window.

One day it is not working, and an English gas man comes to fix it. My father is standing with him in the bathroom, and I am also here watching.

The gas man needs to light the gas again and takes out a match to do this. He strikes it on the side of the matchbox. The match looks like a birthday candle – as soon as it is lit, I huff and puff it out. My father tells me not to do that and the gas man smiles a little.

The gas man lights another match and immediately I huff and puff it out. My father reprimands me. But I know that I'm a child and children are allowed naughtiness fun.

The third time my father loses his temper, yells at me and gives me a slap on the shoulder.

I burst out crying and lunge out on to the landing … at the top of the stairs, I lose my balance … I fall headfirst down the stairs … head over heels over head over heels … I can't do anything, I have no control … each time my head hits the stairs it really hurts … I'm crying and crying as I'm being hit on the head … finally, I hit the ground with one last blow to my sore head … I get up and stagger about …

I'm crying and crying … and no one feels sorry for me.

100
2001 Age: 38 Manhattan

I'm going to attend project planning meetings with GE Commercial Finance in Stamford, Connecticut – my first business trip to America since moving permanently back to London. I fly American Airlines into JFK one Sunday morning in January and check in at the Radisson in Manhattan in the early afternoon. I'll stay here on Sunday, before heading for Stamford first thing on Monday morning. This is a pure indulgence on my part, of course – I could have gone directly to Stamford.

Being able to do this, I feel that I'm at the high point of my career – a job I love; a job I *think* I'm good at (I'm never quite sure); a company I'm proud to be in (*'I'm with General Electric'*); the freedom to do things like this, under the umbrella of 'work'; and to get away from Sabrina (although I miss Aleena, who is now eight years old). A million years from Unilever Audit and being the worst auditor ever, or the constantly conflicting parameters of management consulting (maximising billable hours *vs* doing what is actually best for the client).

General Electric is a very demanding and professional company. The people are very sharp, high-energy, focused and results-driven. There is no room for bullshit. I always have a deep insecurity about whether I'm really up to scratch. Consulting was a much less competent environment than this one and was always about making the most out of your bullshit. But also, in GE there is no mandatory drunkenness, no 'strippergrams', no lewd jokes, no humiliation of women, no overt racism. It seems almost too good to be true: a professional environment that is not in conflict with my personal values. Is this because of GE values, American culture, or the fact that it's been thirteen years since my earliest experience of corporate life in the UK? Perhaps a combination of all three?

It's cold and the wind is biting, but it's quite bright. Wearing my stylish cream trenchcoat from Paris and black gloves from Wilson's Leather, I go on a long, reflective walk. New York means so much to me, has been so important at different times of my life. I've always stayed in the heart of Manhattan. It's a place where I've always been alone and free, where Sabrina wasn't in the picture, and so I could have a glimpse of how exciting life might have been – if I had seized it properly and not let myself be enslaved by culture, and obligation, and wanting to make my parents happy, and my own limiting sense of non-entitlement.

Although it's Sunday afternoon, the streets are still busy – plenty of tourists and shoppers. Here's the confident Ernst & Young building on Broadway, where I conducted so many recruitment interviews for the Firm. That logo always makes me feel proud – I was a Senior Manager and people treated me with respect. Here's the stately building near Park Avenue, housing Sumitomo Bank – where the Partner of the engagement gave a glowing review of me to Brad, but the client wouldn't pay for my Manhattan expenses (they wanted a local resource), and so I had to go. That reflected badly on me, even though it wasn't my fault. I could have spent months on that project and built a life in Manhattan (perhaps with a New York girlfriend).

Moving on, I am compelled to wander along to the corner of Fifty-Seventh and Third. Here's the dignified, low-key building housing Samantha's Parisian-style apartment; next to it, the basement Japanese restaurant where we had a sushi dinner – passionately conversing now that we knew we weren't going to be lovers. She's gone now, married long ago.

The reminiscences I have about New York yet again isolate and accentuate the core emotion of my life – loneliness. I'm always alone.

There's something about the wind when you're deep in thought on a walk – it senses your reflections and provides an evocative background.

I take a limo to Stamford on Monday morning, to Commercial Finance's office on High Ridge Road. Corporate America welcomes me back with steaming black coffee, muffins and donuts. As soon as we have a break, I trudge in the snow down to 260 Long Ridge Road, flash my GE London ID to the delightful, nearly-retired woman who sits at Reception, and go in to see Steve. He seems happy to see me, polite and enthusiastic as always. It's very hard for me to gauge whether he regrets hiring me, whether he thinks I'm not up to the job.

This week passes in the planning meetings with Commercial Finance, followed by the inevitable evening dinners. Next week, I'm remaining in Stamford for six sigma Quality training at GE Capital's training facility. A couple of the CF guys ask me what I'm doing at the weekend, and I tell them I'm spending it in Manhattan – I'm planning to walk all over. 'Don't go north of 100,' they advise me.

Mindful of the expense implications of spending the weekend in Manhattan, instead of the reasonably priced Sheraton in Stamford, I forego a limo – taking instead the commuter train to Grand Central Station, and then I walk over to the Marriot Marquis hotel in Times Square. I hope that no one will pay attention to my expense claims and the unnecessary switch of accommodation over Friday to Sunday nights. This hotel has 49 floors and, by some miracle, I am given a room on the 44th. The glass elevators ascend up the sides of a central atrium which runs all the way up to the hotel roof – giving the impression of the vast central shaft of the Death Star in *Star Wars*. My elevator takes off like a rocket, and through the glass I watch the hotel lobby disappear into the distance below.

The room looks like a regular hotel room – with one important difference. The huge glass windows look out on the magnificence, the sheer joyful, arrogant *joie de materialisme* of New York City and capitalism and branding and luxury logos and huge high-tech widescreen *we-can-do-anything* technology. I look down upon it from the 44th floor, which makes me part of it, and I don't worry about what's happening in the darkness and the shadows beneath the dazzling screens, and in the alleyways between the warm, glowing buildings. I let my breath be taken away in this spectacular high … and yet I know that something is not right on a deeper, spiritual level.

A weekend spent with no agenda, no hassles, and no emotional blackmail – with the only objective being to find somewhere to eat breakfast, lunch and dinner on expenses – is the height of self-indulgence. On Saturday morning, breakfast in the Europa Diner is heavy in eggs and pancakes and coffee refills – it's pure America. Back on the 44th floor, I log into AOL and try to find a New York soul mate willing to meet with me immediately for a deeply spiritual experience, but with no success. Sadly, I reflect how pathetic it is to be sitting in my hotel room on the Internet, when I'm in Manhattan on a beautifully sunny (if bitterly cold) day.

As I'm still digesting breakfast in the afternoon, I decide to forego lunch in favour of an ambitious walk. In my training shoes and trenchcoat and black leather gloves, I head out of the Marriott to Fifth Avenue and 42nd Street, and then northwards. In my mind I have an idea where I'm going, even though it's *forbidden.* I am determined to go 'north of 100'.

I have thought this through very carefully. I am not carrying my passport – that is securely locked in my hotel room safe, with most of my credit cards. I have only my Corporate credit card, which is in my trouser pocket, along with my GE ID, and a small amount of cash is in an otherwise empty wallet in my trenchcoat. My AT&T calling card number is, of course, memorised. So, I could surrender the wallet without a significant or inconvenient loss. My cell phone is in another trenchcoat pocket, readily to hand in an emergency.

I have chosen Fifth Avenue because it runs north alongside Central Park, instead of being interrupted by it. I want to experience the city streets, not the park. I proceed at a brisk pace and the street numbers steadily climb. It's good this way – I can see the park on my left and the streets on my right. The Guggenheim Museum at 89th Street is an extraordinary, almost alien building, and I take a few minutes to have a look inside the lobby. By the time I cross 100th, darkness is falling. Once Central Park has ended, the streets become more ordinary, the flow of pedestrians ceases. At 120th Street, Fifth Avenue runs into something called Marcus Garvey Park (I remember that name from *The Autobiography of Malcolm X*). This coincides with an urgent desire to use the restroom – my late breakfast having included James-Bond-like quantities of orange juice and coffee. I find some kind of community recreation centre, which has just closed, but the black caretaker – who is sweeping the floor and reminds me of Morgan Freeman – listens patiently to my plea in the strange accent, and very kindly lets me run to the restroom.

So far, it's all very unremarkable, unthreatening. Clearly real people live here, leading real lives – not just muggers and drug dealers and gang members (which had been the implication in the advice not to go 'north of 100').

By the time I've reached 130th, I'm in a neighbourhood bustling with families and grocery stores and ordinary cars parked in the street and there is nothing threatening or unusual about any of this – although I do note that *everyone* is black. No one, however, seems to pay any attention to me. In its ambience and atmosphere, it feels a lot like Southall in west London, where virtually everyone is South Asian.

I take a moment to make my dutiful call home from a phone booth, trying not to sound as if I'm having too much of a good time – because that always annoys Sabrina and she starts laying on the emotional blackmail about me travelling all the time and completely neglecting my family. Duty done, I head back south, with dinner in mind.

Once I'm away from the shopping area, the streets are deserted, although clearly the houses are inhabited, each one exuding that warm human glow of 'home'. Just south of Marcus Garvey Park, I notice the African Grill, which has a completely entrancing look (there's something *Live and Let Die* about it). Inside, it is relatively small and cosy, the décor is tastefully and authentically African, and the people are all black – staring at me, not with hostility, but with an idly curious *'you're unusual'* look. It must be the trenchcoat with the training shoes.

Dinner is a grilled fish which still looks like a fish, unlike in most American places. They don't serve alcohol or take credit cards – I realise with a start that this place is probably Muslim. It's annoying to have to pay cash, as it means I must safeguard the receipt and make a cash claim (which is more work for me than using my Corporate card).

My trek home is just over seventy blocks. I don't seem to encounter anyone until, slowly, Harlem turns into central

Manhattan again. My legs are aching, but it's a pleasing, self-satisfied ache. Back home at the Marriot Marquis, my shower pressure doesn't seem to be any the worse for being on the 44th floor. I feel like I've been on an adventure. Between the calorie-laden American breakfast, the healthy grilled fish, and the 180 blocks of walking, I wonder if I gained or lost weight?

Hotel
1975 Age: 12 Frankfurt

Immediately after the one-week midterm break at the end of May, it will be exam week and we will have our first-year exams in all subjects – my first exams in Hampton Grammar School. My parents decide that I will skip the week before the midterm break and we will all go on a two-week family trip via Pakistan to Saudi Arabia – to visit the holy cities of Mecca and Medina. (This would not be the pilgrimage known as the *Haj*, which takes place only once a year on specific dates, but a lesser pilgrimage known as *Umra*, which can be performed at any time of year.) The fact that I will be missing the final week of school before the exams could be an issue, but my mother writes a note for me to pass to the Headmaster and permission is granted.

Because my father works for Pakistan International Airlines (PIA), our journey is via the hub of Karachi and we stay at my grandparents' house before and after visiting Saudi Arabia. We always travel on very cheap standby tickets which are granted to airline staff and their immediate families. But 'standby' means exactly that – we can only board if empty seats are available. Once we are back in Karachi, a problem arises: the Karachi to London flights are running full and there is no chance that all five of us can get seats. A working solution is found: we will fly from Karachi to Frankfurt on Saturday; spend Saturday night in a very cheap hotel used by airline staff; then pick up the Frankfurt-to-London flight on Sunday, which apparently is showing plenty of seats available. My exams begin with French on Monday morning, Mathematics on Monday afternoon.

The flight to Frankfurt is fine, but it seems odd and uncomfortable to be getting off the plane so close to home. (This flight will continue to London, but is sold out apparently.) It is exciting to see Germany, which I have never been to before, but our visit consists of a trip on the subway into town, some fried carry-out from a fast food place, and checking in at the hotel. It's not really a 'proper' hotel like, say, a Sheraton (which I cannot imagine staying in) – it seems to be converted from a grand old terraced house and is staffed by one somewhat indifferent elderly German man. I am troubled by the exams to be on Monday, but sleep easily enough, as I'm exhausted.

We all awake very early, being on Pakistan time, and go for a brief walk around the neighbourhood on this sunny morning. As we head out across the street, the hotel owner sees us from his own bedroom window and calls out something, but we can't make out what he's shouting. When we return to the hotel for our continental breakfast, served by the same gentleman, he seems a bit gruff.

After breakfast, we gather our stuff and head back to the airport on the subway.

My brothers and I settle down with our mother in a seating area in Departures, while our father goes off to make the arrangements with his Frankfurt Airport colleagues. Our intended aircraft is currently on its way to Frankfurt. It is now Sunday afternoon and all I can think about is that the exams start tomorrow morning at 9 o' clock. In London.

Our father returns with shocking news. Some other flight was cancelled and many of those passengers have been transferred to *this* flight which we are waiting for. It no longer has plenty of empty seats. The next PIA flight from Frankfurt to London is on Wednesday! With a sense of urgency, he leaves us again, to see what can be done.

This is a dire situation. Our parents are due at work tomorrow, my brothers and I are supposed to be at school, and I have exams. If we don't fly until Wednesday, I will miss more than half of the subjects. Everyone will think I'm an idiot. It really wasn't a great idea to skip school before exams in order to visit Arabia, instead of studying for them. But to miss the exams altogether? *That will be catastrophic!*

Our mother makes no secret of her concern at our situation. She laments: 'What are we going to do? We don't have any money. We can't pay for a hotel! Where will we stay? What are we going to do?' My brothers and I, to whom this uplifting monologue is directed, have no answers.

Her distress totally exacerbates mine. I have a deep sinking feeling in my stomach. *What if I miss so many of the exams?* We sit in glum-faced, anxious silence.

After about an hour, our father returns with good news. Because he is expected at work tomorrow, and due to this situation with the cancelled flight being unforeseen (and because everyone always like my dad), the Frankfurt station manager has given approval for us to be upgraded to First Class![*]

This is an enormous relief and it is a joy to watch the enormous PIA DC-10 taxi up to the gate (only a couple of hours late).

It seems obvious to me that the 'real' First Class passengers can tell that we don't belong, but nonetheless I am relieved to be heading back to London and the food is good.

---

[*] In those days, there was no intermediate 'Business Class'.

Back at home, I go straight up to my bedroom and start flicking through my French textbook. From my desk at the window, I can see a teenage boy and girl sitting on a short wall across the street, embracing and kissing (also French). I ache with desire.

Air
1988 Age: 25 London

My three-month secondment to UK National Accounting has significant drawbacks, despite being a prestigious assignment. I have to travel to Unilever House every day, commuting into London like a regular office worker, instead of an executive business traveller enjoying comfortable hotels all through the week. Not only do I *not get* the precious travel allowances which I desperately need to give me some disposable income (after paying my huge mortgage), but I also have *to pay* to travel into London every day.

On top of this is the misery of getting up every morning in the dark, and walking twenty minutes to the station. I stride briskly in my suit and cheap C&A trenchcoat (bought in a sale during college days), carrying my attaché case, and I arrive at Hampton station, hot and slightly breathless. (The days when I could jog effortlessly up the hill to the Wallace Monument near my university campus seem to be long gone.) I take my usual place on the platform and wait for the 7:35 a.m. to Waterloo. The train is always hot, but nobody else seems to mind. What is the point of heating the train so much, when everyone is dressed for the outdoors anyway? I approach this problem logically: I always take the starboard window seat at the very back of the front carriage, where I can open the window without the resulting draught troubling most other passengers. With my attaché case, trenchcoat and jacket placed on the overhead rack, I sink into the seat and lean against the window to place as much of my upper body as possible in the precious stream of cool air.

There is one attractive woman who always sits in my carriage. She is slim, dark haired and in her mid-thirties.

She reads the *Daily Mail*, so she probably wouldn't be interested in me. But she does reveal herself to be a nice person. One day, she comes to sit opposite me just as I'm taking my usual by-the-window-at-the-back-of-the-carriage-seat.

'Do you mind if I open the window?' I ask anxiously.

'Not at all,' she replies, most unexpectedly. She really is a nice person.

There are a couple of men who know each other – one has a beard and one is Dutch (I can just tell) – and I'm convinced that they talk about my window-opening habit. One morning it is pouring heavily with rain – it reminds me of my first day at Hampton Grammar School – and everyone is soaked as we wait for the train. My trenchcoat is completely drenched. Nonetheless, I still scurry anxiously to the back of the carriage to secure my window seat and open the window, at which point they both burst out laughing. It is obviously because they have noticed my habit of opening the window and that this supersedes everything – never mind the awful weather. I see the funny side, but I still feel slightly offended at being laughed at.

One morning, as the train pulls in, there is a catastrophe. There is a man already sitting in my seat. The starboard window seat at the very back of the front carriage – that's *my* seat. He is silver-haired, wearing a dark blue, heavy woollen coat over his blue pinstripe suit, and he's reading the *Financial Times*. My precious window is closed. The aisle seat next to him is empty.

Completely thrown by this upheaval in my ordered existence, I find myself unable to think through the challenge of choosing another seat, and I gravitate towards the empty seat next to my usual one. I put my attaché case, trenchcoat and jacket on the overhead rack, and then, before sitting down, ask him if he would mind if I open the window. Being next to the window, the cool air would affect him more directly than me. He says that he would prefer it closed, declines to swap places, but then agrees to let me open the window to determine if it would disturb him. This conversation of ours goes far beyond what is permitted in normal strangers-on-a-London-commuter-train etiquette.

Perhaps it will be alright after all. I concentrate on my book, *The Fourth Protocol* by Frederick Forsyth (a mutual understanding that countries in a state of cold war hostility agree not to set off nuclear weapons in each other's territory), and I hope for the best. But after a few seconds he says, 'No, it's not acceptable' and he slams the window shut. The precious stream of cool air is cut off and I feel I'm locked in an oven with all these stupid people in their absurd winter coats, all terrified lest they feel a shiver.

He adds insult to injury by saying, 'If you're so hot, you can always stick your head out of a window.'

I keep my eyes rigidly on the pages of *The Fourth Protocol*, but my mind is seething with anger and my inner dialogue is running wild. I want to make some biting response to him, something about his age – perhaps that's the reason he feels the cold. Why does he think that cool air is something to be frightened of? Why does he cocoon himself in a thick woollen coat over a suit, in an already over-heated train carriage? It's because he's afraid to live, because inside he's dead already …

The anger makes me even hotter. I'm not even reading the book.

I can't bear the thought of this appalling situation occurring again. I come up with a perfect solution. From the next morning, I start taking the 6:35 a.m. train. This is the same train I would take if I was travelling on an away audit on a

Monday morning, but now I'm taking it *every* day. I leave my house promptly at 6:15 a.m., in complete darkness. I see a bread van making its regular morning delivery to the corner shops. I pass a woman, at more or less the same spot every day, walking her dog. I reach the virtually deserted platform and take my preferred seat in the virtually deserted front carriage, every day. I open the windows on both sides, creating a delicious draught across the carriage, and there's no one there to object. I arrive at Waterloo and walk to Unilever House in a London that is just waking up. This is wonderful. *That's shown him!*

The downside is that I feel very tired and get anxious if I'm not in bed by 10:00 p.m. Between the accounting job, the commute, dinner at my parents' house, finance exams to prepare for, the ironing of five shirts every Sunday, life seems very empty.

The only relief is that there's *Dallas* to watch on the video recorder. I've always loved *Dallas* – what a place, what a life! I would love to go there.

Mrs McKenzie
1981 Age: 19 Scotland

My place is confirmed, and my parents will be dropping me off at Stirling University on the Saturday that rooms become available before the start of the semester. It's over 400 miles away (in Scotland!), and my father and I will take turns driving the Mercedes!

My parents will need to stay overnight, of course, so I call the University accommodation office to ask about a cheap place to stay (not an expensive hotel, obviously). They recommend Mrs McKenzie who runs a bed & breakfast on Causewayhead, a road very close to campus.

I call Mrs McKenzie and the friendly Scottish lady advises that it's five pounds for a double room. I say that my parents would like to stay on Saturday night, and she confirms the reservation taking only our last name – she doesn't ask for our address or phone number or my full name.

The day I arrive at Stirling University is one of the most exciting in my life so far. Seven years ago, when I walked into Hampton Grammar School, I was so scared – now this could not be more different! (As if to emphasise the contrast, it's a beautiful blue sky sunny day, whereas on my first morning at the grammar school there was a torrential downpour.)

We make it in time to unload my stuff into my room at AK Davidson Hall, before attending the Chancellor's Welcome Address at 2:00 p.m. in one of the largest lecture halls. By about 4:00 p.m., we're free and easy.

My parents suddenly decide that there's no point in paying to stay the night here in Scotland. They can easily make it to my mother's cousin near Manchester, before returning to London later on Sunday. They use the payphone outside the Library to confirm the arrangement with our relatives.

I say that I'll phone Mrs McKenzie to let her know they won't be coming, but my mother is adamant that I should not, because she will surely charge us for the cancellation. I really feel that we should tell her, but then I'm scared about being charged. So, I don't do anything.

Mrs McKenzie will only know that she reserved a double room for some people called Ahmad – but they never showed up and she never received any explanation.

Eclipse
1979 Age: 17 London

In my general studies optional class, 'The History and Philosophy of Science', which is led by the headmaster himself, we are discussing the historical tensions between the Church and Science, particularly in the field of Astronomy. Galileo was an exceptionally courageous and principled man to assert that the Earth is *not* the centre of the Universe with all the heavenly bodies revolving around it – but that in actual fact the Earth and the other planets revolve around the Sun. Galileo made observations and then formulated a simple model of the solar system which explained all the observations, and this model was much less complicated than the cumbersome one which was required to support the Church's position that everything revolved around the Earth. This theory brought him into direct conflict with the ruthless Inquisition, which tolerated no disagreement with the Church's precepts, and he was forced to recant in order to survive. No one can blame him for doing that.

In talking about the body of evidence Galileo was working with, we discuss eclipses and the headmaster mentions that the next total solar eclipse that will be visible from Britain will take place nearly twenty years from now, on the eleventh of August in 1999 – and it is well known that the best place to observe it will be from Devon or Cornwall, apparently.

'You had better book your hotel rooms now,' he quips, only half-jokingly.

From deep within leaps out a programmed thought reflecting my embedded belief and sense of inadequacy: *'I can't afford a hotel room. Only wealthy people can stay in hotels.'*

Paratha
1966 Age: 3 London

There is no sign of our parents today, a Sunday. When we woke up, they were not here. Some other Pakistani people from our street are looking after my baby brother Rehan and me, in our bedsit. I don't know what is happening and no one tells me.

Later in the day, our parents return. Our mother has a big white bandage wrapped around her hand. By listening carefully to all the chatter, I come to understand what happened. Our mother decided to make *paratha** for our father as a weekend breakfast treat. She had an accident with the hot oil and burned her hand. Our father took her to the hospital to have it fixed.

Our father berates our mother, as if it's her fault: '***Who*** asked you to make *paratha*?'

She looks hurt and says nothing.

---

* *Paratha* is a round flatbread, like *roti* (*'chapati'* to white folk), but it is soaked in butter and fried, making it more delicious (and more lethal in the long-term).

Idolatry
1974 Age: 12 London

I hate Sundays. The apprehension begins on Saturday night. Not only have I left six or seven or eight subjects of homework untouched and locked in my attaché case since Games on Friday afternoon, but we have to get up early to go to the Islamic school in Hounslow. It's an ordinary, local junior school, but it's borrowed or rented by some Muslim organisation on Sunday mornings between 10:00 a.m. and 1:00 p.m. My parents feel compelled to give us some form of Islamic education, so we must go.

It's arranged in classes, according to attainment, and my brothers and I are all in the entry level class. To move up to the next class, I have to demonstrate that I can read Qur'anic Arabic aloud, accurately and articulately. But this is never going to happen, because I am just not interested enough to put any effort into it. I can't. I'm already so exhausted learning Latin and French and everything else at the grammar school, that I just don't have the brain capacity left to do it. Also, I know that I'm never going to be fluent enough in Arabic to interpret the Qur'an directly, so I might as well read it in English. Amongst some Pakistanis, I know that they only care that their children should read through the Qur'an in Arabic, memorising some or all of it like parrots – without understanding a word. The understanding and interpretation, the thinking and debating – these activities are not on the agenda. All that seems to matter is reading and memorising the sacred text – so sacred that it must be preserved for all generations, never mind what it means.

It's the discussions I'm interested in, not the Arabic. We hear about the Prophet's life, again and again. He lived in Mecca in the seventh century, and his fellow Arabs had forsaken the way of Abraham, to worship countless idol gods of wood and stone. But obviously, there is *only* one God, and Muhammad's mission was to remind people of this.

This is the message which is programmed in, again and again. There is only one God, He is omniscient, omnipresent, and absolutely omnipotent, and the one thing that *really annoys* Him is people who worship many gods, instead of just Him. That really makes Him angry.

So, who does God not like?

Muslims worship only Him and constantly reaffirm His Oneness – that's what He wants to hear, that's what will keep us from the flames of Hell (along with doing good deeds and avoiding bad ones).

Jews worship only one God, so we have a lot in common with them. They don't acknowledge Jesus, so that's one issue. Another is that, apparently, they don't like Muslims, so we don't like them – and there's the whole Israel problem.

Christians are a difficult case. They say they worship one God, but they've split Him into three, making Jesus into the Son of God. This really annoys God, because He is eternally One. Some Christians pray to Mary, which must be even more annoying. But Christians have their famous good deeds, compassion and kindness going for them – and ultimately that might get them through.

Hindus believe in many gods. They make idols and worship them. This is the worst of sins – an insult to God and guaranteed to make Him very, very angry. So, I deduce that God really must not like Hindus. In fact, they are in the deepest trouble of all.

This is confirmed in both the Qur'an and the Bible. God in the Old Testament was always getting angry with any people who worshipped any other god, especially an idol god, and He used His infinite powers to punish and destroy them. So Hindus must be the people who upset God the most, they are in the most danger from His omnipotence, and it is best not to be too close to them because you don't know when the lightning will strike.

It's all confirmed in the cheaply printed Islamic textbook we all have, which in some parts is organised as questions and answers.

Q: Which is the worst of sins?

A: Idolatry.

Q: What is idolatry?

A: Worshipping false gods and idols.

Q: Who make God angry the most?

A: Idolaters.

So, it's obvious who God doesn't like the most – it must be the Hindus. And there's a whole country of them, called India.

Simmering
1989 Age: 26 London

It's Saturday morning, I'm tired and miserable after another painful, depressing week in Unilever Audit, and we are to go to Shepherd's Bush to buy some cakes from a very special bakery, apparently.

Saturday is supposed to be that joyful day, a holiday, when you delight in your free time – safely buffered from work by another entire day – and it still resonates with the anticipation of *Doctor Who* in the evening, of dinner and a movie. But Saturday isn't special for me anymore – its only redeeming feature is that it isn't Sunday.

The Alfa Romeo is tired and old. Its pale orange colour is paler still, broken up only by the increasingly obvious spots of rust. The Alfa no longer generates the excitement it did when I was a student, when having a car was a privilege and life was unwritten. Now it speaks of someone with no money, someone low down the socio-economic order, someone who can't even afford a half-decent car. Someone so *not* James Bond, so *not* Simon Templar.

We set off, with that simmering tension between us, of two egos trying to assert dominance, of neither wanting to be here – in this place, in this car, in this marriage, on this Saturday. As usual, conversation is limited, as too much conversation just provides more opportunities for disagreement. The traffic is painful everywhere, but in Shepherd's Bush it is absolutely awful. There is no humanity here, only a miserable jostling to get ahead, as if it's a matter of survival. Now she wants me to make a U-turn across three lanes of snarling traffic, and then pull onto a double yellow line. I protest in alarm and outrage – but this only serves to anger her even more. *Any normal man could do this.* The tension in the car is unbearable; life is unbearable; *is it supposed to be like this?*

Miraculously, I push my way across the three resentful lanes without collision, and pull onto the double yellow lines, which seem to be disrespected by many others anyway in this awful, frantic place. My abrupt instruction for her to 'Hurry up!' is met with further anger – a slow, defiant walk to the infernal *what's-so-special?* bakery.

The wait is an eternity for me. I've always followed the rules. I've always represented the forces of order, of social responsibility. I was a Prefect, dammit. Now, making me wait on a double yellow line in a horrendous traffic jam is like mental torture. This is *not* who I am – *I don't do these things!*

Finally, she emerges, head turned up, a frown on her face, an absurd, extravagant stack of cake boxes in her arms – more reckless spending of money we don't have – the same slow, defiant walk. The princess must carry her own shopping, and how it must grate her to be seen walking to this old car, orange and rust, missing a spoiler. This is so *not* who she is.

We have another shouting match, it doesn't matter what the details are, it's always the same – two completely incompatible people pushed into the same space, unwilling to compromise, driven to react from within, without choices, powerless, all energy negative, digging deeper and deeper into debt and despair and resentment. This is not how my life was supposed to be, not how I pictured it. *(Bond relaxed and considered how he was going to spend his free weekend – there were so many possibilities.)*

At her parents' house, where some of the cakes are to be delivered, we lie on the ancient, broken twin beds in her old room, two young healthy people, so many possibilities, exhausted.

Wives
1987 Age: 24 Liverpool

One evening during this audit of John West Salmon in Liverpool, Daniel King and I go to dinner in a Chinese restaurant. The place is empty. We specifically request to sit by the window. The 50-something Chinese woman takes our order, and then asks us to pay in advance. We are surprised and a little bit offended, but pay up anyway.

I figure it out. 'They probably have a problem of people running out without paying. And *we did* ask to sit *here*, which is right by the door.'

Daniel King agrees that this must be the reason. We are both humbly aware that we are privileged to be employed in fast track positions in a prestigious global company like Unilever; we stay in a luxurious (looking) hotel; we receive allowances which enable us to eat in restaurants every day – but here in Liverpool we are in the midst of self-evident unemployment, poverty, crime, despair and desperation. The Chinese family running this business are just trying to make a living. Some of their 'customers' obviously try to enjoy a free meal when they can get away with it.

I do enjoy my conversations with Daniel King – who is an articulate, intelligent, good humoured, nice guy – but this evening he does not give me an easy ride. It's always been obvious that I am Muslim, and tonight he has a question about something: *Why does Islam allow a man to have four wives?*

As the *de facto* Ambassador for Islam in the Liverpool business district, I immediately deliver my standard explanation (which I long ago perfected in my mind).

It is not that Islam *encourages* many wives – it is that Islam *permits* up to four, for a variety of reasons. Islam is a set of universal principles, not an imposed uniform culture – therefore a broad spectrum of cultures can exist under the umbrella of Islam. Although Daniel and I are culturally monogamous, not all cultures are thus inclined. In fact, in some cultures a woman would be mortified at the thought of being a man's *only* wife (I saw an African woman on a daytime television show explaining this once).

Also, in times of war, there is often a resulting surplus of women unable to find husbands. Polygamy enables such women to have the protection of a man and the dignity of married status. In Britain, after the Second World War, there were many households which consisted solely of two women, because neither could find a man.*

Even in modern times and in our western society, there are many reasons why a man might need a second wife. Perhaps his first wife cannot bear children, but she really wants him to have a family, because it's important to him. She might actively seek a second wife for him.

Perhaps the first wife ends up in a coma and no one knows if she'll ever come out of it.

Perhaps the level of their sexual needs is different, especially when she's pregnant, and they are both better off if he has another wife.

Perhaps his first wife was in a plane crash and was cast away on a tropical island with Chuck Connors for several years, presumed dead, and her husband is left in legal limbo. Is it fair that he must be celibate all this time?

Adultery and prostitution are rampant in the western world, and yet taking legal and moral responsibility for a second wife is viewed as primitive. *What utter hypocrisy!* Adultery is the worst kind of betrayal. Prostitution is barbaric exploitation of a vulnerable human being for one's own selfish pleasures. *Hypocrisy!*

---

* Sociologists later surmised that this wasn't necessarily the reason in all cases.

(My explanations stick to 'second wife', not 'third' or 'fourth'.)

Daniel King is not convinced that the Islamic position is fair and compassionate, rather than patriarchal and somewhat misogynistic. (And neither am I.) But fortunately the food comes, and I steer us to focusing on that.

Maril

2012 Age: 49 Kansas City

I'm about two-thirds of the way through my speaking tour of the entire mainland United States and it's been going well – apart from the heavy ache in my chest which shows no sign of fading. It's a cliché – but it's true and real and like nothing I have ever felt before. The weight is always there, especially when I wake up in the morning. Curiously, it makes me feel more human and *alive* than I have ever felt. It's as if I never really lived before, never truly experienced Life without a safety harness.

It's a beautiful, blue sky Saturday afternoon when I arrive in Kansas City a few hours before my speaking event – having driven two hundred miles from Omaha. I park the rental car at the venue and then meet up with Maril Crabtree, as arranged. I haven't seen Maril for three years and I give her a very sincere hug. I have a lot to tell her (maybe she can help me with the pain). We are walking unhurriedly towards a restaurant, when Maril points to something on the pavement.

'Well, what have we here?!'

It's a perfect, pure white feather, and it's enormous – about eight or nine inches long. It is lying on the sidewalk, right across our path.

Maril continues: 'I haven't seen a feather all day, and now here's one right when we meet.'

My response is even more excited: 'I've been on the road for weeks and I haven't seen a feather *anywhere*. And now here's a giant one right in front of me, just when I meet you. What does this mean?'

Maril is quite relaxed and confident in her response: 'It means you are *exactly* where you are supposed to be and all is well. The Universe has your back.'

Smiffy
1988 Age: 25 Warrington

Everyone in Unilever Audit goes off on three weeks' study leave, except me. I get only one week, as I am re-taking a Stage 1 paper. As there are no audits in progress during study leave, I sit around the department doing odd jobs for managers. I study diligently when I get home in the evening, and more so during my week of study leave. I finally get it. You divide a Trial Balance into Balance Sheet and Profit & Loss items, and then organise these to generate the financial statements. It makes sense. If only I'd applied myself last November, instead of assembling bookcases and getting engaged and dis-engaged. I re-sit the *Financial Accounting* paper, this time in nearby Kingston. It goes okay.

I'm feeling slightly left out when we reconvene in Audit Department, as everyone else is discussing the Stage 2 exams. We get the Audit plan for the forthcoming quarter. Finally, after months of no travel, I'm on an away assignment again – with the accompanying allowances. I will have some money, at last.

It's Crosfield Chemicals in Warrington; we travel by train from Kings Cross at 7:30 a.m. (I have to take the 6:05 a.m. from Hampton, to achieve this); and we'll be staying in the Liverpool Moathouse hotel – a modern hotel with a gym, sauna and swimming pool. This is all very satisfying.

But there's a slight problem. Putting aside the long-distance train travel, the hotel, the dinners and so on – once I am seated at a desk, and I've already had a coffee, and I have a list of business areas to audit staring up at me, there is a troubling realisation: I don't really enjoy auditing – not at all. This is most unfortunate.

The problem is compounded by the fact that Smiffy is the Group Manager of this audit, which means he turns up once in a while and shows everyone he's the boss. We have settled into a routine of meeting at 8:00 a.m. in the lobby of the Moathouse hotel, to drive to Warrington in the rental cars, which takes about forty minutes. Smiffy comes to visit and his first management decision is that the meeting time should be 7:45 a.m. every morning. I guess that's why they pay him the big bucks.

Smiffy has just returned from a six-week audit trip to Africa. He has a thick stack of 216 photos of his visit, to show to everyone. One afternoon, in the meeting room we auditors have been assigned, he proceeds to show these photos to the team, but talking through them individually in mind-numbing detail. The entire team is huddled around him – except me. I sit resolutely at my desk and go through the motions of working. I actually wouldn't mind seeing the photos, but having to sit through Smiffy's commentary is a violation of human rights – it is cruel and unusual punishment.

At the restaurant in the evening, I offer to pay the bill with my credit card (so that I can collect the cash from everyone *now* and pay Barclaycard several weeks in the future). When my card is returned with the credit card slip, Smiffy immediately reaches for the tray and fills out the voucher for me (including the tip amount) and then passes it to me for signature. I almost tear up the voucher in anger, my inner voice raging: *Why don't you sign it as well?!*

On Friday afternoon, he is leading eight of us home to London. When the train pulls up at the station platform, we find ourselves standing alongside a smoking carriage. I point this out immediately, but Smiffy ignores me and leads the team on board, to some empty seats. Looking around me at the smoking going on, I refuse to sit down.

I say, 'I'll see if there's anything in no-smoking' and I head off down the aisle. Without any difficulty, I find a block of eight empty seats at the end of a no-smoking carriage, and I sit down in them, spreading my suitcase, attaché case and jacket over them. I don't want to leave these seats, lest they get taken by someone else.

After a while, Richard Kingsbury comes along to find out what has become of me, I point out the empty seats, and he goes to inform the team – who all come along a few minutes later.

Now we have to endure a long journey to London with Smiffy leading the conversation and providing the entertainment with his appalling jokes. When Smiffy goes to the lavatory, there's relief in the air. Richard makes a joke about him and even Clive, the Assistant Group Manager, laughs.

You don't have to be an intuitive psychic woman to spot my sullenness, my cool hostility to Smiffy. Unfortunately, despite his self-centricity, Smiffy has the minimum level of sensory function required to notice this attitude. One day, he calls me into a meeting with Clive and himself, in a private room. He asks me if I'm having any problems, and then, somewhat bluntly: 'Is there someone on the audit you don't like?'

You mean, apart from you, Smiffy?

'No, not at all. I'm just preoccupied thinking about my wedding and everything I have to do and the exam preparation I have to do now, because September will be all tied up with the wedding and the honeymoon.'

'Okay, well you can always ask Clive or me if you need any help with anything on this audit.'

Infinite
1975 Age: 12 London

One morning at Assembly, the Headmaster reads from a book about Astronomy and the nature of the Universe. There is one theory that the Universe is in an infinite cycle of: Big Bang, rapid expansion, slowing down, reversal, contraction, Big Bang … for all Eternity (whatever Eternity is).

He reads about the implications of this, which are staggering. I listen with rapt attention.

In an endless series of enormous Universes – each existing for billions of years and consisting of countless galaxies – there would be many instances of Life evolving and, in some cases, intelligent civilisations developing. Each civilisation would have its own history, cultures, conflicts, stories – for thousands and millions of years.

But, with the contraction of each Universe, all would be ended. However rich and wondrous a civilisation was, however many souls and stories it had … there would be no way for it to survive the contraction of its Universe or leave any evidence of its existence. No cave painting, no scrap of fabric, no parchment … nothing.

Imagine the history, the people, the art, the music, the literature, the loves … of countless races through endless time … and nothing, not an atom left in evidence … not an echo in the void. Imagine that.

A shiver runs through me and I feel sombre, numb, subdued at the thought of civilisations flourishing and then being lost forever.

But this theory of the Universe can't be true – it's against everything I'm taught in the Islamic Sunday school.

Sign
1988 Age: 25 London

My parents have not been very effective at introducing me to viable marriage candidates. All they can find is a limited series of young women of Pakistani heritage whom I don't find attractive and who never have any 'spark' of energy or independence. There's no way that these candidates will have the same drive as the women I meet in Unilever who, like me, passed the stringent selection process to find effective high potential leaders. Thanks to Hollywood and the BBC, I have a very clear understanding of what an attractive woman looks like, acts like, speaks like – and my parents are never going to be able to find one.

Surely God will do this for me? I learned from my Islamic education that God pre-determines and controls everything, so something as significant as who I will marry will surely be ordained by God and He knows exactly the specification I want. But how will I know who it is? I suppose she'll be Muslim for sure, but will there be a Sign?

Fortunately, God makes the Sign clear as day.

One day at the office, I learn that someone from Unilever Malaysia will be joining us on secondment for a year. Her name is Rohana Rozhan. *Oh my God!* That's so obvious! My brothers' first names are Rehan and Rizwan. *Rohana* sounds like a variation of the Muslim name *Rehan*. *Rozhan* sounds like a variation of the name *Rizwan*. She's named after my two brothers!

I don't know much about Malaysia, but this woman is obviously Muslim — so my parents *should* be okay with that (although she's not Pakistani). And, being in Unilever on the global management track, she'll be really smart and competent. I can't wait to meet her. I *know* this is the candidate from God.

Helpline
1978 Age: 16 London

The O-level exams are approaching. I hate committing myself totally to studying for them in my bedroom, so instead I sit comfortably in the living room on the sofa, under the tall onyx lamp from Pakistan, reading my endless school notebooks which come in different colours, each colour denoting a different subject.

I can clearly hear the television which is in the family room at the back of our open plan house, next to the kitchen where our mother is preparing dinner – although both the television and my mother are not in my line of sight. There are local current affairs programmes which come on at 6:00 p.m. – both the BBC and ITV (Independent Television) have their own versions of these. Currently, I can hear *Thames News* running an item on teenagers' sexual problems and difficulties – unwanted pregnancies, venereal diseases, relationship problems and so on. I hear them explaining that teenagers often feel lost because they have nowhere to turn to for information, advice and support. But now there's a new adviceline service providing non-judgemental and sympathetic help to teenagers who can call in anytime with questions and issues.

'To get help and advice anytime and in total confidence, you can call this number …' Suddenly the television volume drops to silence.

I am surprised by this sudden loss of audio – but it takes me only a moment to figure out what happened. My mother had become concerned by the news item, and by the fact that I could hear it, and had somewhat in a panic hurriedly rushed out of the kitchen and turned down the sound just in time, before I could hear the telephone number of the adviceline.

Self-conscious and embarrassed, I continue to study my notebooks as if I'm completely oblivious to this.

Talaq
1988 Age: 25 London

On Friday evenings it's customary for us to return from whatever away mission we are on and to assemble in a pub near Unilever House for drinks (including Diet Coke in one case).

This summer evening it's very pleasant (although I do just want to get home and get out of my suit) and we are congregated overlooking the River Thames outside *The Blackfriar.*

Stuart Pickles is in the year above me and he studied Law at Cambridge. He has a question about Islamic divorce: do I agree that a man can issue a divorce just by declaring *'Talaq, Talaq, Talaq'* ('I divorce thee' three times)?

I immediately launch into my polished defence. *Of course not!* This is actually a three-month process. The three *Talaqs* are delivered at one-month intervals, the third making the divorce final. During this time, the man and the woman must live apart and cannot have physical relations – to do so cancels the process. This extended separation allows a cooling off period for consideration of whether this is really the right thing to do, time to miss each other, and also enables attempts at reconciliation by other parties. The entire process is civilised and humane.

I don't see any reason why a couple's future should be determined by a bigoted old man in a silly wig and black gown, rather than by the couple themselves. Islam is a beautiful eternal system which transcends all the vagaries and accumulated ignorance of Man.

It may be true some men give three Talaqs in an 'instant divorce' instead of over three months, but this is completely wrong – it's not in the spirit of the intended process.

Stuart is not at all convinced that this system is fair and reasonable, and that it is not skewed in favour of the man. He then asks about the Qur'an treating the testimony of *two women* as equal to that of *one man* …

… but fortunately, we are interrupted by someone else and this chain of conversation never resumes.

I'm tired of this. I seem to be constantly defending Islam by always having to explain that everything in the Qur'an needs to be understood in its proper cultural and situational context. And *then* it makes complete sense, is always fair and wise and reasonable. (But if the Qur'an is eternally binding, why couldn't the Creator have written it so that its inherent wisdom and justice does not need constant unravelment?)

Delicious, Broken
1988 Age: 26 London

The wedding album is delivered, along with a VHS videotape. After the experience of the honeymoon, I don't feel any positive emotions as I flick through the endless pages of bright, colourful photos of the events. Everything feels vulgar, garish and over-the-top – so many people I don't know and don't care about. I feel as if I was hijacked and put into that situation – which isn't really the true me. But my parents are happy, her parents are happy, and this marriage makes complete sense – she is beautiful, her father is rich, and (despite the miserable honeymoon) I love her (I think). I'm really lucky. God took care of me, as He always does.

One of the photos is particularly interesting. We are both sitting on the stage, after the formalities have been concluded. I am wearing my expensive Italian dark blue suit with the fine pinstripes, which I bought on Jermyn Street specifically for the wedding. My hair is absolutely immaculately combed. In front of me has been placed a large plate of all the most delicious Pakistani food imaginable: biryani rice, lamb, chicken, kebabs, naan bread. The food has my full attention and there is an expression of both intense focus and appreciation on my face as systematically I consume it, smiling with deep contentment.

Sabrina is a few feet to my left, but turned away, virtually with her back to me. Her head is bowed somewhat under the bright scarf that goes with her outfit, and on her face is an expression of utter despair – she looks despondent and completely broken. Her mother's youngest sister has her arm around Sabrina, supportive and consoling – she looks sombre and pensive.

Racquet
1974-75 Age: 11-12 London

I'm so excited that I will be going to Hampton Grammar School in September. I walk past the grammar school every day on my way to my junior school – *it looks amazing!* There are sports fields to the side and back, and at the front there are tennis courts.

One day, I'm talking animatedly to my mother about the imminent prospect of my new school.

'I can't wait to play tennis. I can be in the Hampton Grammar School tennis team!' I exclaim excitedly.

There is no glimmer of positive encouragement from my mother, or any discernible reaction at all. The prospect of me playing tennis or being in any sports team is clearly of no consequence to her. (These things aren't important – only Science is important, because you need to study Science to become a doctor.)

Nonetheless, as the time approaches, I am persistent in my request for a tennis racquet (or 'tennis bat' as we call it, in rather South Asian fashion, avoiding advanced vocabulary like 'racquet'). I will need this by the start of the summer term. My mother is adamant that this is something which should be purchased from Pakistan, because it will be cheaper and of very good quality – Pakistan having a reputation for the manufacture of sports equipment, apparently. My father is making a trip to Pakistan and he is duly instructed to buy me a 'tennis bat'.

The summer term begins after the Easter vacation and I can't wait to play tennis! (This is a much more upbeat beginning than the Autumn term some eight months earlier, when I was so embarrassed to not have the right clothes and to have to watch the first Games session from the sidelines in my school uniform.) I am proud and excited to take my new tennis racquet to school, with its handle poking out from my sports bag.

It's first-year Games on Friday afternoon as usual, and I'm delighted to change into our regulation white kit and join everyone outside at 2:40 p.m., casually waving my racquet as if I'm playing already.

It is David McDowell who notices first. He points out that my racquet is longer and narrower than *everyone* else's.

It is Simon Alloway who figures out why. 'That's a *badminton* racquet, not a tennis racquet.'

Totally deflated, in a trembling voice, all I can say is: 'Is there a difference?'

My dream of being in the Hampton Grammar School tennis team never materialises. I sign up for cricket instead of tennis (it doesn't require us to have any special equipment of our own) – but I can never meet everyone's expectations that because my name is Imran, I will play as well as Pakistan's very famous cricketer, Imran Khan.

Surrender

1996 Age: 33 Mexico City

'Welcome to CompuServe.'

Religion Forum
Author: Travelin' Man
Subject: Surrender

Islam is the most misunderstood and most misrepresented religion in the world.

It is misrepresented both by those who fear it and by some of those who profess to follow it.

Every behaviour we see in the news media attributed to Islam is totally contrary to the spirit and principles of Islam.

Killing innocent people, oppressing women, viewing people through a tribal lens, mistreating those of lower socio-economic rank -- these are all totally un-Islamic behaviours. Arabs (and people who revere and emulate them, like Pakistanis) are the worst offenders.

Even the translation of Islam as 'Submission' to the will of God is unduly harsh.

It's actually closer to 'Surrender' (to the will of God) as in 'go with the Flow'.

It's like this:

'Peace, Brother. You tried your hardest. You didn't get it. If it's not meant to be, your Destiny must lie elsewhere.'

Or this:

'Go easy on yourself, for the outcome of all affairs is determined by God's decree. If something is meant to go elsewhere, it will never come your way, but if it is yours by destiny, from you it cannot flee.'

Umar Ibn Al-Khattaab

It's this kind of 'Surrender'. Peace Brother. Don't fight it. Go with the Flow.

No!
1988 Age: 25 London

Rohana Rozhan from Unilever Malaysia will be joining us for a one-week training course for my year group. I'm so excited, but slightly apprehensive about meeting her for the first time. Obviously, I'm going to have to ask her out. We'll need to be married, or at least engaged, before her one-year secondment is completed. (Where will we live? London, of course – I'm not going to move to Malaysia, obviously.) I make sure I'm absolutely immaculate today (hair combed, shirt pristinely ironed, tie neatly knotted) as I travel to Unilever House and enter the meeting room early.

There's an unfamiliar woman already in here. My heart sinks as I realise it *must* be her. But she's not what I expected God to deliver. She's a bit Chinese-looking – well, Malaysia is near China, isn't it? To be honest, I've never found women of that region attractive. I learned from *Charlie's Angels* what I consider to be attractive (1. Jaclyn; 2. Farah; 3. Kate) and this isn't it. She *is* smartly dressed in a dark skirt suit, but she seems short and so skinny – her figure is almost childlike.

I say 'Hello', but my energy is clearly depleted.

Maybe it's because she's new (or possibly jet-lagged), but she seems a bit shy, introverted and meek – exactly how I expect stereotypical Asian women to be and exactly what I *don't* want. I don't say much to her.

This event triggers off a deep theological anxiety in me. For years I've argued that the Islam of the Arabs – in which women are subservient, passive, without empowerment – is *not* the true Islam. My specification for my perfect woman is totally culturally un-Islamic (one of *Charlie's Angels* or James Bond's wife, Contessa Teresa di Vincenzo). But, if this is the woman God has pre-ordained for me, then it means that Islam and God *are* as perceived by the Arabs. If *this* woman is what God wants for me, then I'm in deep trouble.

I generally don't chat or engage with her much. We are even assigned to the same away team, but I hardly speak to her. I feel like I'm on the run from God – a different God from the one I want to believe in. That's why the Christians say that Allah and God are not the same.

Timson
1988 Age: 25 UK

Just as I joined Audit department last July ahead of the annual graduate intake in September, we also have an early starter who has joined us on this audit. Like me, but so *not* like me. He is Mark Timson and everything about him evokes contempt in me. He smokes, he boasts about getting drunk out of his mind, he goes to illegal wild raves at weekends, he all but confesses to doing drugs ('Me and me mates have tried everything'), he describes women in terms of the size of their breasts. His fingernails are filthy. He brags that, while at university, he lived with a girl whose spending was so wild, MasterCard sent someone big and muscular around to confiscate his credit card – it was so far over the limit and behind in payments.* When we go out for the mandatory team dinners in the evening, he wears ragged jeans and T-shirts with holes in them, because these are trendy, apparently.

As a Muslim, I find this complete absence of dignity and self-discipline appalling. But I don't just have a moral repugnance at Timson. There is another issue. His presence in Unilever Audit undermines my sense of achievement and self-worth. I am proud that I got through such a rigorous and competitive selection process, to join the most prestigious department in Unilever – the *crème de la creme.* The fact that he also succeeded means that perhaps this was not such a great achievement. *Maybe I'm not doing so well, after all?*

---

* Ironically, he eventually ended up making heaps of money as a Credit Trader, before the Global Financial Crisis.

Fall
1966 Age: 3 London

Our bedsit is on the top floor of the three-storey house in Fulham. There's another brown family who live in the bedsit on the ground floor – I'm not sure where they are from. Their son is about my age and we play together sometimes.

Today Mansoor has been with me and we've been playing, while my mother has been busy in the shared kitchen which is upstairs. Now it's time for him to go and we are on the small landing at the top of the stairs. At this moment I remember something I saw on television recently – *it will be fun to try it!*

I'm standing behind Mansoor as he's about to descend the stairs. I put my hand into his back and quickly push him as hard as I can.

It's quite amazing to watch. He tumbles down the stairs head over heels over head over heels. It's like in slow motion. When Mansoor hits the bottom with a loud thud, he shrieks and then manages to get up. He skulks away back to his family's door, crying loudly.

My mother comes out of the kitchen and looks downstairs curiously.

'What happened?'

'Mansoor fall.'

Telex
1988 Age: 26 London

Our first morning back at work after the honeymoon, we'll take the train together from Hampton Station. I have to get up extra early to use the bathroom – I'm not used to sharing it.

I warm up the Alfa Romeo, while Sabrina puts on her coat and locks my front door (*our* front door, how strange). I manage to park near the station, though not as close as I would like. On the train, it's a bit later than the one I would usually take (even before I implemented my 'before dawn' strategy), it's busy, and we have to stand. I hold her hand, and look around, but I can't see the Dutchman or the bearded one. There's no one I recognise here, to see that the beautiful woman is with me.

In the days that follow, I discover that Sabrina is the Goddess of Chaos. My tidy and ordered house and life are ransacked. Clothes are discarded on the floor at the place of undressing; drawers and cupboards are perpetually left open; papers and letters are strewn everywhere; lids are absent from everything that should have a lid – toothpaste, jars, bottles, deodorant, tupperware. The kitchen looks like a disaster area. No shoe or sock can ever be found with its mate.

I could never have known about this incompatibility without living with this person first, or at the very least 'going out' with her, with no parents involved. That's the big flaw in 'our' noble and honourable system.

At least she doesn't want to drive the Alfa Romeo.

Hey, whatever happened to my wedding gift of a Honda Prelude? There's been no further mention of it.

We go to her parents' house every Saturday, usually staying for dinner. The food is always sumptuous and plentiful – that's one good thing. They have a servant they brought with them from Pakistan – a gentle old woman who was Sabrina's and her brother's nanny when they were children. She does some of the work around the house.

What does Mr Mayat actually do? Well, he's a successful businessman apparently, so he doesn't have to answer to anyone or worry about six-monthly performance appraisals. He sends and receives faxes, mainly.

Wearing his Pakistani white *kurta pyjama*, with perhaps a sweater or dressing gown over the top, he sits in his armchair with a wheeled mobile desk in front of him, and taps away on a distinguished, but antiquated, manual typewriter. These sheets are then passed through the fax machine and sent *who-knows-where*? He receives faxes too, and these are placed in ubiquitous piles around his corner of the family room.

I glance at them occasionally, trying not to appear prying. They speak of huge quantities of commodity items – petroleum oil of varying grades, vegetable oils, Johnny Walker whisky – and of these consignments being F.O.B. (I think that means 'Free On Board' – it's about who is paying for the shipping, the buyer or the seller). Prices are quoted in US dollars and expiry dates assigned to offers to buy or to sell.

So it seems that what Mr Mayat does is trade in goods, even while they are in the process of being shipped from one country to another. He offers to buy them from one party, offers to sell them to another party, and makes a profit in the middle. I *think* that is what is going on. What a great way to work – I wish I knew how to do this. Mr Mayat has all the necessary connections.

In the corner of the dining room is a defunct telex machine. That's how he used to operate, until the amazing new technology of the fax.

Verses
1989 Age: 26 UK

There's Islamic uproar over Salman Rushdie and his *The Satanic Verses* book. It's an enormously complex and weighty novel, having many dimensions. It begins with two characters falling out of the sky, after an explosion on a passenger plane. It explores many themes, but one of these is the phenomenon of Prophethood and divine revelation. For this, Rushdie uses characters unmistakably based upon the Prophet Muhammad and the Angel Gabriel.

Some Muslims are screaming about 'blasphemy'. In England, some are trying to get Rushdie prosecuted under the ancient anti-blasphemy law. The English legal response, quite correctly, is that this obsolete law applies only to blasphemy against Christianity. (The English authorities do not appear to have any inclination to have Rushdie burned at the stake.) Some Muslims want to have this law extended to cover Islam (and therefore, by extrapolation, all recognised religions, although they are not thinking this through).

I recognise the futility of this. One man's most deeply held belief is another man's blasphemy. Christians believe that Jesus is God – this is blasphemy to Muslims and Jews. Muslims believe that Jesus is not God, and Jews do not appear to believe in him at all – this is blasphemy to Christians. What about the question of One God, or many gods? Or no God? It is impossible to legislate about what people are allowed to believe and communicate. The Western world learned this a long time ago (*thank God*). The Islamic world appears not to have caught-up yet, although Islam absolutely guarantees religious freedom; the Qur'an says, '*Let there be no compulsion in religion.*'

The real issue here is that Rushdie *appears* to be mocking Islam, and especially the idea that Muhammad really did receive revelation from God, via the Angel Gabriel. Rushdie maintains that he is merely exploring this topic; that his characters are dealing with the real challenges and dilemmas caused by such a situation.

I'm very confused. As a Westerner, I believe in freedom of speech and of ideas. But, as a Muslim, it seems to me (based on the information that I am fed), that he has been deliberately offensive to Muslims, by knowing exactly which buttons to push.

There's nonsense on both sides. Ayatollah Khomeini, the spiritual leader of the Shia Muslims in Iran, issues a *fatwa* (a religious edict) that it is the duty of all believing Muslims to kill Rushdie (and this will bring a great reward in Paradise). This is embarrassing. Shias are not true Muslims in my opinion, there should be no clergy in Islam, and *fatwas* are man-made nonsense to exert control over people.

But I am also furious that the western *literati* support Rushdie; they are doing it out of spite against Islam; *ignorant, drunken bastards.* They want to give him all sorts of awards for his worthless book, instead of letting it slip quietly into obscurity. I feel betrayed by the publishers, Penguin Books, owners of the Puffin Club (of which I was once a loyal member). There is a long drawn out wrangle about the release of the paperback version.

Sometimes I imagine bursting in on an event where the *literati* are gathered with Salman Rushdie, and expressing my opinion with a machine gun. I play this out in my mind repeatedly. However, there's no need to do any such thing. These people will learn the error of their ways on the Day of Judgement, when they will be shocked and terrified to realise that Islam really is the Truth.

There are demonstrations and riots all over the world, even in England. The television keeps showing the same footage of a couple of Muslim men burning copies of *The Satanic Verses* in a street demonstration somewhere up North, where there are lots of Pakistanis. One of the men in the video is Hakim, the Chemistry postgraduate from Stirling University who gave the most miserable sermons at Friday prayers; there is no doubt about it. He looks really angry.

I am deeply troubled by this whole issue. I think it's a big misunderstanding, due to a huge gap in cultures and perceptions, but I also get drawn into it emotionally sometimes, becoming angry both with the Shia Iranians, for making this an issue, and with Rushdie, for what he has apparently written. Both are smearing Islam.

God shows clearly where He stands in this matter. I read in a quality newspaper a journalist's account of a closely guarded press conference between Salman Rushdie and specially invited members of the media. The journalist describes how security was very tight on the way in, because of the *fatwa*, but he also mentions something else very interesting and significant. As Rushdie began to speak, a table of champagne bottles and glasses mysteriously tipped over of its own accord, smashing its precious *haram* load on the floor. Everyone present was surprised by this, but surely it was a sign for those who Believe.

Lockerbie
1988 Age: 26 Manchester

It's the week before Christmas. I'm tapping away at my computer at nearly midnight, in a country hotel near Manchester. I've been auditing Mattessons-Walls again this year, and it's been going reasonably well. Nigel Bishton is the Assistant Group Manager, and he's a nice guy and quite intelligent. He has recently returned from a secondment in Bahrain, so he must understand Muslims (he was Finance Manager of a Unilever company selling them alcohol). Sarah Bunney and Brian Lever are my co-auditors (they're both from the year below me) and they are pleasant people – I feel comfortable with them. Sarah it turns out is a Quaker – like my old PhD supervisor, Dr Maskill. This means that she must be an inherently nice person – incapable of spite, deceit and intrigue. Brian is a softly spoken, gentle young man from Liverpool. These two are so *not* like the Audit crowd I am used to.

The reason I'm working so late is that I'm behind with my systems notes. I've enjoyed going out to dinners with Sarah and Brian, and have had interesting theological conversations with them, in the cosy bar with its crackling fireplace – this is unusual for me. It all depends on the company, I suppose.

The television is on in the background and whatever was on is interrupted by a news report. It's shocking, a catastrophe. A Pan Am airliner has crashed on to the village of Lockerbie in Scotland. *Lockerbie?* It rings a bell – I think that I pass it when I drive to Scotland. It's off the A74 – my route towards Stirling.

I shiver – I've always been sensitive to airline crashes. I've been flying all my life, my father works for an airline, many of my parents' friends and family do also. In fact, one of my mother's relatives works at check-in for Pan Am at Heathrow. (I learn later that she checked in this flight and remembered many of the people.) It always troubles me when something like this happens. To fall from the sky seems an awful way to die – because you have time to think about it, but there's nothing you can do. And what about children? It's just not fair on them.

And what is the role of God in such an event? My Islamic God is omnipotent. Therefore, He can just as easily prevent such a thing as make it happen – so it's His will, either way. There is no sense in which He is ever a powerless observer.

So He *could* have prevented this, but He *chose* not to – which makes Him complicit. This is uncomfortably difficult to analyse and rationalise and explain within my belief system. (That's why we shrug our shoulders and say something in Arabic equating to 'Oh well!') ('God moves in mysterious ways' – the Christians can't explain it either!)

Anyway, *please God*, let this be an accident. Because if it's terrorists, I know it won't be the IRA.

Photo
1975 Age: 12 Toronto

My brothers and I are in Canada again with our mother, for three weeks during the school summer vacation. Our mother has two brothers – both younger than her. The older of the two is married and has a lovely house in a suburb of Toronto. The younger brother stays there too – he's still single.

This vacation is very relaxing for us. Apart from the mandatory trip to Niagara Falls, my brothers and I mainly chill around the house, exploring the scores of TV channels (in England we only have BBC1, BBC2 and ITV) where you can find *Star Trek* and *The Six Million Dollar Man* every day.

One day I'm just lounging around in the living room, when the younger uncle bursts in from another room and appears to be crying. Suddenly, my mother appears behind him, in pursuit, cajoling him, clutching a black-and-white photo of a young woman. I recognise the woman as from a family we are vaguely related to in Pakistan. My mother is imploring her brother to be reasonable, to think about this seriously, she is pointing out how lovely the woman is, and the grown man is actually crying – he just wants to be left alone.

I feel a heavy foreboding in my stomach. I can see what's going on. One day it will be my turn. My mother will show me a photograph. (And the women in these photos – I never find them attractive.)

Inadequate
1989 Age: 26 London

Patrick van Hoegaerden calls to say he wants to give me some feedback on the audit we just completed at Van Den Bergh's oil works at Grays in Essex. I really hated the whole thing – getting up so early, driving so far in the rain and fog, auditing how they measure and calculate the volumes of oil. There had been a problem about anomalies in the volumes of oil being transported in the railway tankers, as if some was being stolen, but I never got to the bottom of it. I ran out of time towards the end, when I was auditing Fixed Assets, and left my conclusion open as to whether the processes in that function were 'adequate' and the controls were 'satisfactory' (which is the terminology we use). I expect that Patrick wants to discuss my views further.

I meet Patrick very early on Friday morning at Unilever House. Like everyone else in the department, he also enjoyed the food at my wedding reception – but now his manner is very serious, devoid of any warmth. It doesn't go as I expected.

He says that my performance on the audit was completely inadequate. Not finishing an assigned function is not acceptable. I should have completed Fixed Assets and reached a verifiable conclusion, whatever it took. 'Running out of time' is not an excuse. I shouldn't have been leaving as early as 7:00 p.m., if I thought I was running out of time.

He says that I am not fulfilling my job description.

The shock I feel hangs over me all weekend. I feel as if they shot me.

Ballistic
1983 Age: 21 Scotland

Sean Connery, who hasn't been the official James Bond for years, is part of a gang who acquired the rights to *Thunderball*, and now they produce a remake, *Never Say Never Again*. It's a rival to the official James Bond series, currently starring Roger Moore. I watch *Never Say Never Again* at the cinema in Stirling with my friend Martin. It's obviously a welcome distraction from the upcoming Honours Qualifying Exam!

But the film enrages me for several reasons.

There's really no need for a remake of *Thunderball*, which is a well-crafted, classic James Bond film. An ageing and obviously completely-bald-toupee-wearing Sean Connery doesn't have the eternal privilege of playing James Bond, just because he was the first actor to do so (the second, if you include Barry Nelson).

The film is blatantly prejudiced against Muslims.

The lovely blonde Kim Basinger is captured; she is placed in stereotypical 'Muslim-woman-in-veil' black clothes; she is tied to a post in a remote desert location; she is being auctioned off as a slave (obviously not for domestic chores), to an audience of very savage and unsavoury-looking tribal Arab men; a particularly grubby-looking Arab man with a fistful of gold coins is going to win the auction. Ms Basinger is rescued by James Bond, assisted by Felix from the CIA and courageous American naval personnel. Symbolically, the black clothes fall away just as James Bond pulls her onto his horse, revealing her skimpy, sexy clothes underneath – we admire her lovely legs, and get delicious glimpses of breasts and buttocks. [Is there no middle ground?]

One of the psychopathic, villainous characters is called Fatima, the name of the Prophet's youngest daughter —

although she displays not one iota of moral Islamic behaviour (she has sex with James Bond, before trying to kill him with a radio-controlled shark). [Killing people with radio-controlled sharks is completely un-Islamic.] There is really no plot justification for her to have a Muslim name, and for it to be that of the Prophet's daughter is very insensitive. Muslims in the film are depicted as savage, incomprehensible, barbaric, inhuman.

There are no positive Muslim characters at all, to provide some 'balance'.

But what really sends me absolutely ballistic is the unbelievable ignorance. There is a piece of jewellery which contains a map showing where the stolen US nuke is hidden. The pendant is called the '*Tears of Allah*', because apparently: 'The Prophet wept for the barrenness of the desert, and his tears made a well.'

Didn't anyone know how wrong this was? The writers, the producers, the directors, the actors, the hundreds of people who worked on the film? Sean Connery didn't know? Even the Cambridge-educated Rowan Atkinson didn't know?

Islam and the Western world have interacted for centuries, but Hollywood doesn't know (or care) that in Islam, *Allah* is God, and our very human Prophet is *Muhammad.* They may have a legal right to be disparaging, but can't they at least get the basic facts correct?

'Calm down, Imran, it's only a film.'

'Only a film? But this is my religion they are talking about. How can they be *so* clueless?'

Prisoner
1989 Age: 26 London

I am desperately unhappy in Unilever Internal Audit. I know it's a great career path and I'm lucky to have this opportunity, but I really don't fit in. It just isn't right for me.

And now, thanks to the very poor feedback from Patrick, the department is placing me under close scrutiny – I am a 'problem' employee.

I'm also finding it very hard to reconcile my new marriage with my Unilever career, and both of these with my true self. Unilever demands absolute dedication to the business, otherwise one is viewed as lacking the potential to make it to the ranks of the top leadership, to which everyone in Internal Audit is expected to aspire. (The Audit department considers itself a cut above even the prestigious ranks of all the other Unilever Companies Management Development Scheme recruits.)

Sabrina is very demanding of my attention and critical of the fact that I seem to spend much of my time in deep thought. She's not at all worried about whether the Universe will stop expanding and collapse again, the hole in the ozone layer, or whether only one man was involved in the shooting of Kennedy. We are expected to visit her parents' house every weekend and, in addition, her parents expect us both to accompany them to many tedious Pakistani gatherings – where dinner is served too late, there is too much cigarette smoke emanating from ignorant bigoted men with moustaches, and nobody has heard of Kennedy, let alone that he was shot.

Furthermore, my financial assumptions about this marriage were completely flawed. I had thought that having a second income would solve all my financial problems but, in reality, Sabrina spends more money than she brings in, most days coming home laden with shopping bags from Marks & Spencer, and forever buying household goods and worthless ornaments, and presents for everyone her family knows and their infernal offspring. Previously, I was able to live extremely frugally, with absolute control over my expenditure – this is completely beyond her. Any attempt by me to discuss this results in a torrent of outrage and abuse.

Also, her father does not really seem to be a millionaire, after all. That was all exaggeration by the middlewomen. There is always talk of business deals about gas wells and global commodities, but nothing ever seems to materialise.

I am a prisoner in a miserable life and slipping further into debt.

Old Man
1968 Age: 5 Pakistan

[This story was related by my mother. She did not tell me directly – I heard her telling it to other people.]

It was the summer that my mother took my brothers and me to Pakistan and was seriously considering remaining there permanently – life in England being miserable and humiliating, with little money and widespread racism. Our father stayed behind in London, continuing to work; he had no choice – there was a mortgage to pay and lodgers in the house.

We were visiting relatives in some village up north near Rawalpindi. My mother and I were sleeping in the same room – I was lying next to her on the bed. There was no one else in that room.

In the middle of the night, she woke up to see a man standing at the end of the bed. He was an old Asian man with a beard, dressed in traditional white *kurta pyjama*. He was watching me – standing absolutely still and silent, without blinking, without expression. He paid no attention to my mother – his eyes remained only on me.

Terrified, she hid her head under the sheet and began reciting verses from the Qur'an. She did this for the rest of the night.

When dawn came, she dared to look out from under the sheet. He was gone.

Skelly
1989 Age: 26 London

There's an unfriendly and somewhat abrasive Glaswegian who has joined the department; his name is Paul Skelly. The senior manager who now runs Internal Audit, faced with a shortage of Finance resources, has circumvented the centralised corporate selection process (with its challenging eight-page application form, campus interview and daunting Selection Board) and started hiring people directly, whose only qualification is that they are chartered accountants. Skelly is proud to be a chartered accountant; I resent him for this and because he is from Glasgow, the only part of Scotland that I'm not comfortable with (a city which I associate with drunkenness, cigarette smoke, and football violence). There's no way that he could have passed the full selection process, the way that I did.

Unfortunately for me, I am now assigned to work for Skelly, and find him so arrogant and difficult, that it becomes miserable to come to work. I think about taking time off-sick, but that would be frowned upon as weakness and be extremely career-limiting, especially after Patrick van Hoegaerden's awful feedback recently. I press on, but this is not the glamorous career that I had imagined.

One day I fall into a trap. I have never discussed religion at work, but Skelly makes a shooting gesture with his hand and says in a provocative way: 'Have you got your gun ready to kill Salman Rushdie?'

I am outraged. *How dare he make assumptions about me?* He knows nothing about me or about Islam, although he thinks he knows all about the latter. I am confused in my position, and end up attacking Rushdie and saying that he deserves to be punished. Skelly clearly has an issue with Islam that he needs to deal with, using me as his punch bag.

He attacks the cruelty of (apparently) Islamic punishments. I respond defensively, by criticising the state of the West; the prisons are overflowing, but crime continues to explode out of control. The victims of crime are treated as if it's their fault for being careless; the criminals are absolved of any responsibility. *'Why did you leave your car there?' 'Why didn't you lock your bicycle?' 'Why were you walking there at night?'* The victim is to blame. Burglary, robbery, rape, car theft, drug-dealing etc are all considered a 'normal' part of life. In Islam these are not tolerated, because they undermine society and people's sense of well-being. The punishments are necessary to totally curtail them, for the greater good.

Skelly asserts his *right* to drink alcohol and that Islam has no business telling him he can't. He demands his 'freedom of choice'. I state that alcohol is an addictive, mind-altering and harmful drug, and the opinion of an addict of this drug is of no consequence. What choice do those killed by drunk drivers have? What choice do terrified children have whose fathers come home drunk on Friday night and beat their mothers, after spending their entire week's wages on drink? What choice did we all have, when a huge oil tanker controlled by a drunken man unloaded its devastating cargo of crude oil into our beautiful natural environment?

Skelly gets agitated by my position and storms off.* I reflect on how miserable it is to work for these ignorant, arrogant, drunken people. But I take comfort in the fact that they are going to get such a shock on the Day of Judgement.

* Some years later, he accepted a job in a Muslim country (not one that prohibits alcohol) and has been living in the Middle East for over a decade now.

Cold
1989 Age: 26 London

I arrive in the car at Sabrina's parents one Friday evening in January, after another drab week spent on this audit in Essex. It is such a long drive, and conducted entirely in blackness. We agreed that I would take her home from here. There is some friend of her father's visiting from Pakistan, and we are required to sit in the living room with him. He's in procurement or something – I'm not really interested. He has a moustache.

My parents also drop in, so now it's an energised Pakistani gathering, with everyone talking in loud voices, except for me. (Apparently, Italians also do this.) I'm noticing the intricate designs in the big woollen rug, for the first time.

Sabrina whispers to me, 'You can go home yourself. I'm not coming.' I know this is because I have not met my on-going obligation to show an interest in other people, especially her parents' tedious friends.

'Fine!' I retort and I storm out, stopping in the hallway to sit on the steps to lace up my shoes, and retrieve my coat. Everyone is shocked by my sudden outburst and departure from the room – there is an awkward silence. My parents are particularly embarrassed, as they are responsible for me.

I step outside into the cold and dark, and close the front door firmly – not quite slamming it – behind me, and hurry to my Alfa Romeo. All of its windows are misted up. I get seated and fumble the key into the ignition. She starts okay.

There is a rule about Alfa Romeo Alfasuds – don't ever attempt to drive one when it's still cold. There's even a red light which only goes out when the engine is adequately warm. I always religiously warm up my Alfa Romeo before driving it – causing Sabrina to accuse me of being obsessive and compulsive and so *not* normal. Also, on this occasion, there's the issue of the condensation on the windows.

But the drama of my exit can only be maintained if I depart stormily without delay. Sitting here warming up the engine and de-misting the windows undermines my angry-young-man credibility. I have the fan running at full speed, but it's not having much effect on the windscreen yet – the blown air, of course, is still cold. I wind down my window, so that I can see out, and awkwardly pull off the driveway, painfully revving the engine to keep her from stalling.

This is crazy and irrational. I can't really see very well ahead of me (I have my head stuck out of the window) and the Alfa Romeo's engine is protesting that it's not ready to go yet. But we are going. Never have I treated my beloved Alfa Romeo like this, but I feel caught up in this performance and I have to see it through.

There is a traffic light junction, at which I will turn right, followed by a very sharp bend in the road where I will go left. I can see that the traffic light is green, so I proceed, but I can't really see the bend in the road to the left, because my head is out of the window to the right. So, I guess its position.

There is an untidy clatter of rusty car impacting government metal, as the Alfa slides into the wire panels of the crash barrier, comes to an unexpected and abrupt stop, and stalls. I am stunned by the sudden silence, and I fear the worst. After a moment, I step carefully out of the Alfa and go to the front.

Surprisingly, there's no damage to the Alfa, but a wire panel of the crash barrier has come loose and is a little bent. I am very fortunate, but it is best that I leave the scene immediately, before anyone in a dark uniform takes an interest.

Turning back, I am surprised to see my parents and Sabrina, all standing awkwardly in front of my father's Honda Accord, which has stopped just behind my Alfa. This is an unnecessary complication. I just want to be away from here immediately. I bark at them to 'Get back in the car!' I hurry back into the Alfa, start the engine and pull away as fast as I can, heading home, but still waiting for the windscreen to clear. My father's car follows me the whole way.

Back in my living room, my mother directs a making up between Sabrina and me – we have an awkward, stage-managed hug.

I thought I was going to have the place to myself this weekend. I could have done something interesting – I'm not sure what.

Picard
1990 Age: 28 UK

Star Trek: The Next Generation begins on BBC television (three years behind the US). It is extraordinarily good and gets better. Milton and I always discuss it with enthusiasm – we already began watching it a couple of years ago on VHS tapes rented from Blockbuster Video.

It often explores deep human issues, such as religious belief, the Middle East crisis, global militarism, cultural conflict, inequality, environmental issues etc, but in thinly disguised fictional scenarios. There is an episode obviously dealing with homosexual equality and rights. I'm very uncomfortable with this one, as God does not like gay people.

I tell Milton that I have a sure feeling that I will randomly meet Patrick Stewart one day. I've already decided that, when I do, I won't fixate on *Star Trek* — I will talk about his many other fine acting achievements. (He must get so annoyed that Americans only ever associate him with *Star Trek*.)

Paki
1989 Age: 27 UK

Apart from Paul Skelly's very specific Islamophobia, I don't consider the Internal Audit department to be racist; far from it. But this cannot be said for all the businesses which I visit out in the field, where I have to deal with a lot of mundane clerical people.

At one agricultural fertiliser company in Shropshire, there is a large open plan office. I am seated at one end, and a very overweight young woman is seated far across the room from me. There happens to occur a random moment of silence across the whole office, just when she whispers to the man next to her about me being a 'Paki'. I hear it loud and clear, and so must everyone else in between us – but I show no reaction and I don't look up from the fascinating financial documents which I am examining.

At a company in Hampshire, there is a spoof employment application form, allegedly from the HR department, on a staff noticeboard. It asks about the applicant's ethnicity, and then goes on to make assumptions about the applicant's model of car (if they are Black, it must be a Ford Cortina of some sort) and their lack of toilet training (if they are Asian).

Curiously, I find it both offensive and funny, as if I can exist on both sides of the fence simultaneously. As an Internal Auditor, I could easily make a fuss about it, have it removed and write a reprimanding memo (it contravenes both external laws and internal policies) – but I don't say anything about it (because people would think I was a spoilsport with no sense of humour).

Virgins
1996 Age: 33 Mexico City

'Welcome to CompuServe.'

Religion Forum
Author: Travelin' Man
Subject: Virgins

It is a generally accepted fact that the Bible is all about peace and love, whereas the Qur'an is a book encouraging violence and killing.

Take this example:
'... as God commanded the Prophet, and killed every man. . . . The ... women and children and all the herds, flocks and goods were taken as plunder. . . . The Prophet was angry with the officers. . . . "Have you allowed all the women to live?" he asked them. . . . "Now kill all the boys. And kill every woman who has slept with a man, but save for yourselves every girl who has never slept with a man." . . . So they did as God commanded the Prophet. The plunder remaining from the spoils that the soldiers took was 675,000 sheep, 72,000 cattle, 61,000 donkeys and 32,000 women who had never slept with a man. The half share of those who fought in the battle was . . . 16,000 people, of whom the tribute for God was 32. ...'

This tribute of 32 virgins for God? It means they were sacrificed on the altar by having their throats cut.

Now, on the face of it, this does demonstrate how barbaric and violent the Qur'an is. How can a Muslim possibly explain or defend this?

Well, we don't have to. These verses are actually from the Bible – **Numbers 31:7-40**

All I did was replace 'Moses' with 'the Prophet' and 'The Lord' with 'God'. If you had no difficulty in believing these verses self-evidently demonstrate how violent the Qur'an is, you now have to explain these as Bible verses.

Some Christians will say: 'This is Old Testament. We have a new deal.'

Indeed, but it is the *same* God, is it not? Quite a brutal character, and not really so eternally unchanging?

To conclude: *nowhere* in the Qur'an will you find anything like this, instructions to *kill everyone* and to keep virgins for yourselves and for some to be sacrificed to God.

In the Qur'an, the only even vaguely comparable directive is that it is okay to fight and to slay those who are oppressing you and fighting against you – but to make peace at any opportunity.

As for the notorious and well-known Islamic punishment of 'stoning to death' – it is not mentioned anywhere in the Qur'an as a punishment for anything. It is from the Bible. Be careful you don't gather fire wood on the wrong day of the week!

Not
1989 Age: 26 London

There's a lot of flurry around Audit department. The six-monthly salary review letters are being placed in the pigeon-holes by one of the secretaries. I retrieve my letter, at the same time listening to the others discuss their pay rises. It sounds like £1,750 is the norm.

I open my letter and nearly gasp with shock. It says £750.

My performance review is issued, and I am shocked to see that Paul Skelly was assigned to write it. It's actually signed by Paul Skelly's boss, Adriano Regondi, but I can hear Skelly's voice in the words. It is awful; it says that I lack commitment and competence. It's practically an invitation to leave. Now he's ticked a different box: *Not promotable.*

Because of the severe nature of this appraisal, John Cruickshank himself (the Senior Group Manager) conducts the review meeting. He seems remarkably calm, almost sympathetic. He explains that my consistently poor performance has become problematic. It's reached the point where resources from the year below me can be relied upon to do a better job.

I rally back with the perfect excuse: it's getting married that's caused the problem. The demands on my attention from both my new marriage and from Unilever are very hard to balance. I'm the only person in my year to have gotten married already.

He agrees with me that it is a challenge to live with such conflicting parameters – they all struggle with it. But, in my case, we need to do something about it. The way forward is for me to absolutely *focus* on doing a good job every hour, every day, on every audit. And the department will help me by giving continuous feedback, such as an appraisal after every single audit.

Brooch
1974 Age: 11 London

For this summer holiday, before I start at Hampton Grammar School, we are finally going to go somewhere that isn't Pakistan – we are going to Canada, which is almost America! (This will be a proper vacation like white people have – I've always been a bit embarrassed that we never go anywhere but Pakistan.)

All five of us – my parents, two younger brothers and me – will be gone for three weeks, staying with my mother's uncles in Toronto. (Obviously we wouldn't stay in a hotel.)

We've been living in our brand new semi-detached house in Hampton for just over one year. The other half of the semi is occupied by a young English couple, Mr and Mrs Turner, who moved in just a few days before us. They seem quite nice, and relations are friendly. My parents often chat with them in the front garden, and my brothers and I use a tennis ball to play 'fetch' with one of their dogs *Pepsi* (the other dog *Coco* seems too aloof for this).

Because we will be gone to Canada for three weeks, Mrs Turner offers to water our many houseplants while we are away. My mother puts all the plants together in the kitchen and leaves Mrs Turner the front door key.

Sometime after we return, an issue arises. My mother cannot find a precious brooch of hers – it is not in the drawer in the master bedroom where it is supposed to be. Her conclusion is obvious, and very troubling – while we were away, Mrs Turner must have rummaged around upstairs and taken it. This would go unnoticed for a long time, and then be impossible for us to be sure about.

My mother is very angry about this – it just goes to prove that, no matter how friendly they may appear outwardly, you just can't trust white people. This upsetting incident clouds our relationship with the Turners. No one says anything, of course – but we can't really trust them.

Some months later, my mother finds the brooch deep in the drawer where she had hidden it.

Boots
1989 Age: 26 UK

I have become disillusioned with this life and the business of Internal Audit. The fact is that when I really focus and make an effort, I produce the best audit documentation that exists in the department. This is occasionally acknowledged, but not widely broadcast. However, most of the time I am disinterested, just getting by without giving it my best. I have become very judgemental about others, live in my head too much and think about philosophical matters much too avidly. It is easy to see that I am sullen and not committed; there is a growing awareness that I am incompetent.

Mark Hemstedt wants a word with me at the beginning of the next audit. We sit in a conference room, and casually he puts his feet up on a chair – I notice that he wears boots, rather than shoes. I find this arrogant, and I resent the fact that he is self-confident, competent and highly regarded (everything that, apparently, I am not). He is also slightly younger than me; he reached his current seniority at this age because he didn't waste any years trying to do a PhD. *For all these reasons … I hate him.* What is it about him that makes him so successful, whereas I am drowning?

Mark wants to know what it is that motivates me. I tell him I want to be good at my job, be recognised for this, and be promoted in due course. It seems a futile expectation.

Proficient
1973 Age: 10 London

At the beginning of the school summer vacation, before we visit my grandparents in Pakistan, I attend the training programme known as the Cycling Proficiency Test. This is held in the playground of a school in Twickenham (nearly three miles away) and it takes three days. I cycle there every morning in the rush hour traffic – thinking rather smugly that I must already be proficient if I can do this without being knocked off my bike by a car.

The playground is laid out with various signs and markers, and we have to practise every aspect of cycling on a road: traffic lights, crossings, signalling our intention to turn with our arms, braking safely and so on. The hardest part is doing a right turn – you have to look over your shoulder, signal with your arm, stop in the middle of the road, and proceed when there's no car coming, without losing your balance.

On the third day we all have individual tests – just like a car driving test! I'm a bit nervous about the right turn part, but I manage it smoothly.

I pass!

We will receive our certificates and, most importantly, our Cycling Proficiency Test badges in the post. The badge is shaped like a red warning triangle and it's like having a driving licence you can show off by wearing it.

When we return from Pakistan, the envelope is waiting for me. It's an A4 size brown envelope, stiffened to protect the certificate inside. I open it eagerly and pull out the certificate, which has my name on it. But there's no badge! No matter how many times I look inside the big envelope … there … is … no … badge.

The person preparing these envelopes only had to do two things: insert a certificate and insert a badge. In my case, they neglected to drop in the badge. The reason is obvious. They saw my Asian name and decided to deny me a badge out of petty spite. This is how life is – we experience this all the time.

Back at my totally white school, everyone else who did the course is proudly wearing a Cycling Proficiency Test badge.

Grief
1989 Age: 26 UK

On the long road journey back to London, I come across an upsetting sight. There's a flattened and bloody mess which used to be a pigeon in the road – clearly it has been run over by a car. But there's another pigeon beside it, which is frantically and mindlessly pacing about without any obvious purpose, in a state of extreme agitation and distress. I recognise it as the dead pigeon's grieving partner.

I am deeply moved and saddened by this. I never thought of pigeons in this way – as having recognisable feelings and emotions, perhaps even love. And it also makes me think of Sabrina and I feel a twinge of sadness at the thought of something happening to her, and I know that, despite our hostile marriage and her chaotic inability to close drawers, I do love her in some way. *For a man … shall cleave unto his wife.*

Inquisition
1989 Age: 26 UK

I drive in a rental car to Norfolk with Colin Slater, who is actually from the year below me. I'm the only one from my year group who is still in Audit department at the moment – everyone else has gone on their traditional one-year secondments in the various businesses, but I haven't been placed yet. We are auditing an agricultural business and it's swelteringly hot as we drive there. We're staying in a village with a quaint hotel, and everyone at the company – which reminds me of a garden centre rather than part of a huge multinational corporation – is extremely nice. But the weather is oppressively hot; the sun beating down on us in the greenhouse-like office.

Patrick van Hoegaerden, the Assistant Group Manager of this audit, comes to visit for a couple of days, and then moves on.

Early the following week, we are winding things up at this site, before travelling to the next one. Patrick calls me on the phone and wants to debrief me on the Sales function audit I have conducted. I am reasonably happy that I have done a complete job, and that my working papers and systems notes are comprehensive. But what follows is a ninety-minute interrogation, in the relentless heat, in which Patrick deconstructs my audit and finds hole after apparent hole. There are so many questions he comes up with which I can't answer. (I remember what Gillian Blackhurst said: '*If I don't know the answer, I just make it up.*') It is an ordeal – and a relief when I hang up.

Colin and I travel on to the next site in Staffordshire, which appears to operate from offices in giant prefabricated cabins. Mark Hemstedt calls me on the phone and tells me he would like me to come into Unilever

House for a debrief at the end of the week, after I've completed my assigned audit in Wales. Then he asks to speak to Colin. I hand the phone to Colin and go back to work, but I notice him throw a strange glance in my direction, as he listens intently to Mark on the phone.

A day later, I arrive by myself in the rental car at the Carreg Mon hotel on the island of Anglesey in Wales, and I'm supposed to audit the small animal feeds and fertiliser sales business which Unilever has here. I so much want to impress Patrick after that very severe debriefing on the phone. Audit people please their managers by finding things wrong, so that is what I will do – I will conduct a severe audit and find as much wrong as possible, then write a very damning report. My problem all along has been that I don't like finding things wrong with how people are conducting their business. I have a *laissez faire* attitude, and that's why I'm such a terrible auditor (although the people I'm auditing don't seem to mind).

This is a beautiful island and a delightful hotel, but I don't have any time for that. I launch myself diligently and ruthlessly into the audit, not being as personable as I would normally be with these charming local people. I tap away at my computer while having dinner at one of the tables outside, and then continue in my room, into the early hours, producing the best systems documentation that I possibly can.

I do find something severely wrong. They leave stocks of fertiliser bags in huge piles outside the building, completely unguarded at night. The site isn't secured by a fence and anyone could come along with a vehicle and steal some fertiliser. When I ask about this, I am told that they know the neighbours will look out for any strange vehicles coming and going. Everyone around here knows everyone else apparently, and strangers always stick out. But this measure is totally inadequate. It completely contravenes Control Objective 401 in the Audit Manual – 'the assets of the business are safeguarded'. The business cannot expect its neighbours to perform a security function – the shareholders of Unilever require that we take much better care with their investments.

This is the big failure that I have discovered in this business (which will give me some kudos), and I decide that it is so important that I must tell Patrick in person. I will stop off at his current audit location, which is on my way to London. On Friday morning I make an early start (after again working into the early hours, whereas the true me would have spent some time walking around this beautiful island) and I head off in the rental car.

At the business in Gloucestershire, Patrick is a bit busy with something. He's on the phone to Mark Hemstedt, and apparently about to send him a fax, which he says is 'extremely sensitive'.

When he's free, I tell him about this failure to ensure that 'the assets of the business are safeguarded' in accordance with Control Objective 401 in the Audit Manual. Surprisingly, he doesn't seem that troubled by it. He asks me to write it up in the usual way and our meeting is over.

It's quiet in Audit department when I get to Unilever House – it's a Friday afternoon and most people will still be out in the field or just setting off homewards. That smug, arrogant fellow Mark Hemstedt is expecting me. He ushers me into an office and then has a quiet word with John Cruickshank, before joining me and closing the door. He is carrying a fax.

It goes even worse than I expected.

He places the fax on the table in front of me. It's to him, from Patrick, and it's about me. It's an evaluation of my performance on this last audit. It's NA – 'not adequate'. It says that 'Imran continues to perform his assigned audits superficially and without adequate concern for detail and the satisfactory attainment of all control objectives. This means that he cannot be relied upon as a resource for the completion of designated audits.'

Mark tells me that Patrick was so unhappy with the quality of the Sales audit, that they sent Colin back there to do it again. Hence the phone call and the strange glance.

Mark is surprisingly gentle, compassionate even. He asks me what the problem is, and he makes notes in his new leather Time Manager International personal organiser (a lot of the managers went on this TMI course recently and they've all been raving about it), as I explain that I don't know – there seems to be some mental obstacle that won't allow me to succeed. He continues to be gentle as he discusses the possibility that perhaps Unilever isn't right for me – perhaps I need a less demanding environment? Perhaps I'd like to go into public practice as an accountant?

But I retort that I don't want to be an accountant – *I never did.* I always wanted to work in Information Systems … and Audit was just my starting point in Unilever. I thought everyone knew that! *(This is so not my fault!)*

Mark says that my future is something we can discuss further when I return to Audit in three weeks' time – after my second Business Education Programme two-week course (which starts on this Sunday afternoon) and a week's leave after that. My next audit will be in Basingstoke and he will be the Group Manager – he will work very closely with me. By the way, if I was to find another job, he would be happy to provide a reference.

I leave this meeting knowing that I have absolutely no shred of credibility in the department. My dream career in Unilever is over. I spent so much effort getting into Unilever ... then what went wrong?

My life has been so completely out of my control: this huge mortgage for the house my parents made me buy; all the distraction from the ridiculous arranged marriage process; this idiot I've married who can't stop spending money; the awful people I have to work with, like Timson and Smiffy and Skelly; the list goes on.

I travel home in a state of melancholy. Sabrina can see my pain. I tell her that I have to find another job before I get fired.

Jinn
1996 Age: 33 Mexico City

My interest in Theology never wanes. I read a Christian fundamentalist article postulating that the Toronto Airport Vineyard Christian Fellowship (a fringe Christian sect) are misguided and their miraculous Holy Spirit manifestations are actually a satanic deception. In the article it is taken for granted that Islam is the result of a satanic plot, but the writer asserts that this is also the case with some Christian sects. *This is excellent!* Once we bring Satan into the picture, as the originator of other religions, then we have to be willing to explain why this is not the case for *our* religion. This writer has exposed his own Christianity to this test.

This validates my *Unified Theory of Supernatural Phenomena*, except that I also include regular Christian fundamentalist Holy Spirit manifestations and miracles under this umbrella. There's no mumbo jumbo or superstition in Islam – it's all very clear and pure. We don't believe in Astrology, psychics, reincarnation, past life regression, Tarot, palm-reading, Numerology, ghosts, modern day inspiration from God, mystical dead saints, helpful deceased people, religious 'miracles'. If any phenomena like these occur or appear to occur, there are sound scientific reasons why they should be disregarded. If something strange really is going on, then we know for sure it's not what it purports to be – it's actually Jinn having some fun. The Qur'an explains that Jinn are another creation alongside Man – they live in the same universe as us, but in a parallel dimension. Everything can be explained in terms of mischievous Jinn: ghosts, poltergeists, fairies, leprechauns, the flying witches of the South Sea islands, even aliens! Americans don't generally entertain 'old' superstitions like ghosts and fairies, so Jinn appear to them as scientifically plausible technologically-enabled aliens from other planets – it's science-superstition instead. Why don't alien ships land in Africa (where they believe in tree spirits) – why do they always land in Middle America? Why don't Americans experience tree spirits? Tree spirits in Africa and aliens in America have the *same* root cause – it's Jinn having fun. We experience them as what *we already believe in*, whatever is consistent with our culture.

So, everything is rationally explained. I can believe in Islam, without ignoring the strange phenomena associated with other religions — these are *all* caused by Satan and the Jinn.

I spend many evenings in my hotel room in Mexico City, immersed in the CompuServe discussion board about Religion. The threads about Islam seem to be frequented mostly by Christians, who are always trashing Islam and trying to prove it wrong. We have come to this, on both sides; we each need to prove the other's religion is *wrong,* in order to confirm to ourselves that ours is *right.* It's much easier to prove the other side is wrong!

If I can prove Christianity is wrong, then Islam must be right.

Opportunities
1989 Age: 26 UK

Katherine – my friend from Lady Eleanor Holles School, now a lawyer – comes to visit this weekend and I show her my CV. She says it's laid out all wrong. Instead of beginning with my education, I should be highlighting my experience first, then working backwards in time to my schooling – which is not my main selling point now. I take her point and rewrite the résumé.

I'm heading off to BEP 2 (Unilever's internal MBA) on Sunday evening – it's at a beautiful hotel near Peterborough, about eighty miles north of London. I pack my Unilever computer and luggable printer in the Alfa Romeo, along with a copy of the reference book *Graduate Opportunities*, which lists many companies that employ people with university degrees.

In my hotel room, I prepare a standard letter to accompany my CV, then work through *Graduate Opportunities* to select specific IT companies for whom I tailor and print out the letter. I work through all the obvious ones: IBM, Capgemini, Oracle, Logica. It's five in the morning when I decide to call it a day. I'm so exhausted – my head is pounding, and I've got BEP starting promptly at nine. *One more, maybe just one more.* This one, near the back: Strategic Systems International. I love the name.

I hand in a dozen letters to Reception in the morning, asking them to mail them out First Class and charge it to my room. Each one is addressed to 'The HR Manager' of an IT company.

By the time I'm home at the weekend, it is Strategic Systems International alone which has written, inviting me to an interview when BEP is over.

At the interview, Mr George Medd asks me how much I currently earn. I say £14,500, knowing full well that the true answer is actually £14,050. If this inconsistency is ever discovered, it will easily be attributed to a transcription error.

Two days later the job offer for Business Analyst arrives, at a salary of £17,500. I don't get invited to interview by any other company.

I tell Mark Hemstedt that I have a job offer, and he very kindly and graciously reiterates his willingness to write me a reference. All my negativity towards him is not reflected in how he behaves towards me.

I work out my one month's notice period at an animal feeds company near Basingstoke. It's very interesting.

Mortal
1989 Age: 26 UK

Ayatollah Khomeini dies in Iran and his funeral is a fiasco – we watch it endlessly repeated on television. The huge crowd is so traumatised, they are impossible to control. When his coffin passes by, some of the mourners grab it and rip off the lid, trying to snatch a piece of the shroud. Khomeini's body actually falls out of the coffin.

Once again, I am embarrassed by the unnecessarily dramatic and undignified behaviour of the minority Shias and how they present Islam to the world. Have they not read the Qur'an? Did they not know that Khomeini was merely a mortal man and must surely perish, whereas God is almighty and lives forever? Are they not behaving as if Khomeini was more than a man, which is offensive to God?

Am I the only one who actually understands anything about true Islamic belief?

Exit
1989 Age: 26 London

On my last day at Unilever, I wear my best suit – the dark blue Italian pinstripe I bought on Jermyn Street for my wedding – and go to Unilever House for my exit interview with John Cruickshank. I try to be upbeat, to show some dignity, as if this was my free choice – not a hurried exit before being fired. John says that as soon as I realised I didn't enjoy auditing, I should have let them know. Unilever would have found me something else, not shown me the door. But, once my performance appraisals began to nosedive, it was impossible to do anything with me.

I feel a strong twinge of regret at leaving Unilever, which surely was a privileged and exclusive opportunity, but it did not make me happy.

What went wrong? It was the stupid arranged marriage that ruined everything.

Strategic
1989 Age: 26 Basingstoke

My new place of work at Strategic Systems International in the converted trousers factory in Basingstoke perhaps doesn't have quite the grandeur of Unilever House – there being no stone columns or Greek statues or uniformed polite-but-imposing security officers – but at least no one knows I'm completely incompetent (at least not yet). The name is impressive though, and I quote it proudly in a letter I write to Janice, making it sound like a positive move I have chosen to make.

Also, the travel is much easier. I drop Sabrina at Hampton Station for the 7:53 a.m. train and then head out west on the nearby M3 motorway, a straight run of 36 miles – all the other traffic is on the opposite side, going into London. It's a pleasure to drive the Alfa Romeo in this way every day, although I'm in constant fear of a breakdown. I have no idea how I could get to work without a functioning car.

I am suspicious of everyone at SSI to begin with, assuming that they are all highly ambitious, career-focused alphas who will stab me at the first sign of weakness. The lessons I have learned in Unilever: never show weakness, uncertainty or humanity.

My boss is Chris Gavin – a bearded man who studied Political Science at university, then worked as a coach driver until he was able to find a graduate trainee job as a computer programmer. He is also a Labour Party volunteer. He doesn't have a typical Unilever-like management profile, and he seems strangely human – a ruse perhaps, to get my guard down?

In typical SSI fashion, although he is my boss, he had no say in hiring me. His boss George Medd, one of the

Directors, announced to him that a candidate had been secured to fill the vacant position. I do learn that George had been looking through a stack of CVs which had come in as the result of an ad he had placed for consultants, and my résumé – which coincidentally had come in at the same time when I applied purely speculatively – had caught his eye because of the words 'Sales Ledger' and 'General Ledger' under the Experience section on the first page. (Exactly how Katherine told me to arrange it.) He was looking for someone with an accounting background and I fit the bill.

The fact that SSI was the *last* company to whom desperately I wrote a letter that late night on my BEP course gives me a tingling feeling that, no matter how I stumble through life, I am being looked after. *Thank you, God.*

The work at SSI is actually very enjoyable. I have a shiny new monitor and keyboard on my desk, giving me access to the DEC VAX computer which is kept in the heavily air-conditioned computer room. On the DEC, I become familiar with the financial modules of SSI's PROTOS software, using a test system to set up and run a pretend company: making products, selling them, collecting the revenue, earning a profit and generating the reports. I make sure that the accounting makes sense and is representative of the real world – apart from the funny names I use to represent different people in my pretend company ('Napoleon Solo'). Soon I will be helping clients to implement and use this system.

It is strange to be enjoying work. It is also strange that people get up and leave at around 5:30 p.m. There doesn't seem to be an expectation that you work until 7:00 p.m. as a matter of routine, to show your dedication.

The one thing that is hanging over me is the accounting qualification. I have passed up to Stage 2. I have two more stages to complete, and I will need to find the time and motivation to finish this, as it will be good for my long-term career and credibility. SSI does not make the same provision of study leave as Unilever did.

I assume that in SSI there will be similar career and salary potential as in Unilever. It was certainly a promising start that my salary jumped to £17,500. With promotion and Unilever-like salary increases, I should be earning in the mid-twenties next year. (I found George's original ad for SSI in a back copy of *The Times* at the public library, and it said: *Consultants: 20K–30K, plus car.*) The other thing to look forward to is a company car. All of the consultants have one, and I will too, as soon as I make the step up from business analyst.

Despite this new salary, our financial situation is still tight. Sabrina wants to keep improving and redecorating the house, and Nigel Lawson, the Chancellor of the Exchequer, keeps putting up interest rates – he says it's to stop the economy overheating. Our mortgage payments keep going up. I never seem to have any actual cash.

Chore
1989 Age: 27 Derby

I drive to Derby on a business trip to visit British Rail Engineering, and I park the SSI pool car in a public car park near the client's office. Opposite the car park, there is a building that is unmistakably a purpose-built mosque, with a dome and a small minaret. I feel drawn to it. This means that I have no excuse to do the noon prayer in catch-up mode at the end of the working day – I should go to the mosque at lunchtime, when the prayer is due.

I go along and I think that the locals are surprised to see a man in a suit coming there, but I still feel a sense of belonging to this universal brotherhood. I make many trips to this client in Derby and generally go along to the mosque at lunchtime, and before I drive home to London, if I'm not staying the night.

One afternoon I go there to perform the mid-afternoon prayer. There is an imam sitting here, who looks like he's fresh off the boat from Pakistan, and he's chatting with another Pakistani man. A couple of Malaysian students show up and so, since there is now a group of us, it is understood, without any words being exchanged, that this will be a communal prayer led by the imam. Like RAF cadets, we align ourselves in a straight line and stand to attention.

The imam commences the prayer ritual and I can't believe what he's doing. He's racing through every stage, like it's a chore he wants to get over as quickly as possible. I don't even have time to finish each recitation to myself, before he's rushing into the next one, and taking us with him, as we have to remain synchronised. He's not savouring the moment, not immersing himself in the rhythm and allowing it to clear his mind of extraneous thoughts, not settling into a peaceful One-ness with God. I am so angry as we perform this farce, that I almost feel like breaking formation, as it were, and continuing at my own pace. But I don't – it would be divisive.

As I leave the mosque, I come to terms with my thoughts. I don't feel as if I have performed my *salaat* properly. But what disturbs me the most is the attitude of the imam. He treated the prayer as a burden. He didn't relish it, didn't show any appreciation for its spiritually uplifting and calming effect. There is something wrong here, very wrong. It's as if his Islam and mine are not the same. For him it's a chore and for me it's a precious gift.

I suddenly realise that there are two kinds of Muslim, and I don't mean *Sunni* and *Shia.*

Van
1990 Age: 27 London

I'm in the Alfa Romeo with Sabrina, heading to her parents' house, and a white van impatiently tries to pass – the implication is that I am driving too slowly, *but I'm not!* I put my foot down and he is not able to get by. He seems to be going in the same direction as us.

For the next few miles, I ensure that he can't get by, always managing to keep ahead of him at every light and junction. When I stop for a man on a pedestrian crossing, the white van pulls past (*illegally!*). I catch up with the van further down the road, where there are two lanes of near-stationary traffic. We are parallel with each other, each one trying to edge ahead. In a moment's inattention, he hits the car in front and breaks a light.

He is furious with me as he inspects the damage and, at my window, asks why I was racing him. I shrug my shoulders, pretending that I wasn't racing and turn off down a side road to get out of the situation.

Why did I behave like this? Because, as Mary Poppins so shrewdly observes, *men are stupid.*

Audi
1990 Age: 27 London

The new job is going well. Sabrina constantly insists that we visit showhouses on new developments (allegedly for interior design ideas), and eventually we buy a brand new detached house, with the help of a horrendously huge mortgage which Sabrina's father arranges through his 'business associates'. The monthly payment is so high, it takes literally all of my monthly income, leaving us to get by on Sabrina's salary for everything else. Her father says not to worry — this is only a temporary arrangement. As soon as one of his big business deals comes through, he intends to pay off our mortgage in full, as a gift. Then we will live mortgage-free and will be exceptionally well off. This is the only reason why I let myself get into this financially crippling arrangement. [This expressed intention of Sabrina's father never materialises and is never mentioned ever again.]

I am driving home later in the week, having recently completed the purchase. I am on the big roundabout near our new house, and about to move over into the exit lane. My left indicator is on. A red Audi 100 comes up rapidly and recklessly in the next lane and passes me from the left, forcing me to abort my manoeuvre in order to avoid a collision.

I stop behind him at the red traffic light. I mouth vituperative obscene abuse at him. I can see his bespectacled eyes in his rear-view mirror and he can see my mouth moving. He doesn't need to know every word – he gets the gist of it.

The light changes and we drive off. Inexplicably, the red Audi turns into my road, as I follow behind. Inexplicably, it slows down in front of our house.

Inexplicably, it drives onto the driveway of the brand new house next to our brand new house. The painful truth suddenly dawns on me. This is our new neighbour.

There are many moral lessons in this story.

(I think the most obvious one is that I should have been watching my left door mirror more closely and should have blocked his approach on the roundabout, or, failing that, should have rammed him off the road.)

John does a remarkable and very clever thing. He pretends that it never happened and greets me warmly. I follow his cue and do the same. Road rage should be reserved only for people with whom we have no other dealings.

Horseback
1990 Age: 28 UK

I love my new company car from KPMG Management Consulting – a metallic bronze Rover 216 GSi, with air conditioning! – and I treat it like my own, thinking I may buy it when the company lease runs out. I continue doing a lot of business travel around the UK – but going by car now, rather than second-class on trains like I used to.

I have learned something about the flexibility of Islamic rules, and one of these is around the daily prayers. Apparently, if you are travelling, you can perform shortened prayers, with fewer *rakah*s. Also, if you are on horseback, you can perform the *salaat* while remaining on the back of the horse. You merely approximate the bowing and prostration movements. The comprehensive ablution is also waived, if it is simply not practicable.

I extrapolate these rules to the 20th century and to the car (my equivalent of a horse). Now, when I'm travelling, I try to find a moment in the afternoon to go out to my car and perform my *salaat* here, sitting in the driver's seat and putting my face to the steering wheel. In so doing, I am able to capture a few minutes of peaceful, calm detachment from the worries of the world. As a management consultant, I am under far more pressure than I ever was as a postgraduate student (although I receive far more money than I ever thought possible).

Space
1990 Age: 28 London

I have my Stage 3 Accounting exams, which are very important to my business career. One of the exams is at 9:30 a.m. at a community hall in Surbiton (a suburb of London). I set off in the Rover in good time and immediately hit a horrendous traffic jam. The time ticks by, and my progress is very slow. I am desperately worried. If I miss this exam, or fail it by being very late, it will really hurt my career.

As I approach the hall, it is already 9:30 a.m. and the exam will be about to start. The problem remains that my plan was to use a public car park some distance away and walk down to the hall. Now I will have to park there and run, and arrive sweating and gasping, my concentration greatly affected and too much time lost.

I have to stop at a red light immediately in front of the hall. I see something unbelievable. There appears to be an empty parking space in the road, immediately in front of the hall. This space is between the crossing and the first parked car, so I could literally drive into it without even any parallel manoeuvring. There doesn't appear to be any yellow line or other restriction. This simply *cannot* be true. It *cannot* be a legitimate parking space, *not* right in front of the hall, *not* in this area of London, *not* at 9:30 a.m. on a weekday.

This is a pivotal moment. I am reluctant to believe that this could possibly be true, that I could possibly be so fortunate, so blessed. I am afraid to accept the gift, and I almost drive past the miracle space. Fortunately, I pull in, and run straight into the hall. I have only missed a couple of minutes and I *do* pass the exam.

[Today that space no longer exists. Our mean government has put double yellow lines there.]

Aloe
1996 Age: 33 Mexico City

'Welcome to CompuServe.'

Religion Forum
Author: Travelin' Man
Subject: Aloe

How the facts related *in the Bible* makes it absolutely clear that Jesus did not die on the cross.

- His companions Joseph of Arimathea and Nicode'mus were in on it. (How they were going to get Jesus through this ordeal was pre-planned.)
- They brought in advance 'a hundredweight' (112 pounds, 51 kilograms) of aloe and myrrh. (These are healing herbs, soothing, antiseptic and anti-inflammatory, not embalming herbs – in any case, Jewish burial does not involve embalming. The companions knew in advance that they would have to treat Jesus' wounds.)
- They gave Jesus something strange smelling to drink (obviously not water).
- After drinking this, Jesus gave a 'loud cry' immediately before appearing to die (which is impossible if about to die from asphyxiation – death by crucifixion is through asphyxiation).
- Jesus was up there for about three hours and there is specific mention that *his legs were not broken*. (Roman crucifixion typically took three days – unless the legs were broken so that the victim could no longer push himself back up onto the little seat which provided temporary relief to his abdominal muscles, but cruelly prolonged the process).
- Blood gushed out when he was pierced with the spear.

- Joseph went *immediately* to Pilate to request the body.
- Pilate (who had ordered and overseen many crucifixions) '*was surprised that he was dead already*' and asked the centurion.
- The centurion confirmed it. (The same centurion whose servant Jesus had healed!)
- Gospel of Peter (banned by the Church) reports that three men were seen walking away from the tomb, *two of them supporting the third*.
- Mary did not recognise Jesus; she thought he was the gardener. (He had covered his face to not be recognised. He did not want to be caught and put through this ordeal again – and the second time they would make absolutely sure he was dead.)

Jesus told his followers that he was leaving Jerusalem for now, but would try to come back in the future. Of course, he never made it back. This stated intention evolved into the 'Second Coming'.

Throughout human history, and *even today*, there are literally countless accounts of people who were thought to be dead and yet returned to consciousness. Many skeletons excavated from old graves (and some even in relatively modern times) are found to be in positions which indicate that the unfortunate individual regained consciousness *after* being buried. They obviously must have seemed to be dead when they were buried.

The Qur'an says that Jesus did not die on the cross and *people with no first-hand knowledge of what actually happened fell into speculation – causing much confusion.* This perfectly and rationally explains what happened, entirely consistently with the individual events as described in the Bible.

The confusion about Jesus apparently dying and yet being seen alive again (always discreetly and only to a select few) created the 'Resurrection' myth – which was later used by Rome to construct a complex blood redemption theology (a 'mystery religion') including confession and absolution, which was exclusively the path to Salvation and resulted in eternal damnation if the Authorities (the priests) were not followed unquestioningly.

Is any of this not clear?

Doctors
1991 Age: 28 London

Sabrina decides that we should now have a child. I'm not entirely sure how she expects us to afford this, as my entire income is swallowed up paying the mortgage on our expensive new house, and we barely get by on hers. But her parents get into the loop, assuring me that they will take care of everything.

The truth is that – while I'm working in Gloucestershire as a management consultant at the nuclear laboratories; living in the paid-for rented country cottage during the week; receiving additional allowances; driving around in a brand new lynx bronze Rover (with air conditioning!) – I'm feeling flush with wealth, privilege and status. My dire situation back in Unilever Audit, when I had neither money nor respect of any kind, seems like a lifetime ago. So I agree, and Sabrina stops taking the Pill (or already did, for all I know — she's never very honest to me).

I'm only home at weekends, and always very tired, and then getting ready to go back to Gloucestershire (ironing shirts and so on), as well as mowing the lawn, and going to visit her parents every Saturday, and look in on my parents occasionally. We perform the necessary textbook act perhaps once a month. (There is no passion in it whatsoever.)

Despite the infrequency of the necessary event, Sabrina become anxious that we need to see a gynaecologist who specialises in such matters. She tells me that there is an Indian woman named Dr Verma, whom some of her parents' dimwit friends advise is 'the second best in Europe'. Confused by how such a ranking could have been established (i.e. what is the definition of 'Europe' and what organisation is able to determine such a fact across that specific geography – *is it like the Eurovision Song Contest?*) I nonetheless agree (as if I have any choice in the matter).

Using our private health insurance from KPMG (another privilege of recent times), we arrange to see Dr Verma at her consulting rooms in the private Parkside Hospital in Wimbledon. Sitting in the waiting room is a youngish Indian woman, about our age, with either her parents or her in-laws sitting with her. It is obvious what is going on. She has failed to produce a child, and has now been dragged along to see the famous Dr Verma, to have her barrenness put right. I seethe with anger. Does it not occur to them that the pressure they are putting her under is probably the number one factor preventing pregnancy? – it's the stress. Also, where is her husband? *He* should be sitting here with her, not the potential grandparents.

Dr Verma spends a little time with us, and the scientific investigation begins. She wants me to provide a sample – which I do one Saturday morning. The result comes back for this – it is much too high and can't possibly be right (I know why, it's because it's been so long since …). So, I have to do it again. This time the results come back within a normal range.

Next, she wants to check that Sabrina's tubes are clear, by performing a laparoscopy. This is scheduled and I take time off work to be there. Sabrina has a private room and I'm sure that the nurse is very impressed when my cell phone rings – I must be very important. It's Clive from the team at Nuclear Electric. He says that he found a problem in the new invoice payment software, which implies that my own testing of this has not been comprehensive enough. I take shelter in the fact that I'm in a hospital right now, for 'my wife's procedure' and 'I'll look at it when I get back'. Inwardly, I tiredly acknowledge that this was inevitable – I am incompetent and eventually must be found out. This life of privilege suddenly feels tenuous.

The procedure takes place under anaesthetic, while I wait in the private room, and Sabrina's tubes are declared to be clear. The next step must be determined.

Exactly fourteen days later, I'm overseeing some user acceptance testing at Nuclear Electric's headquarters in Bristol. Actually, it's not going very well. I haven't been as thorough as I should have been in my preparation. *Do I really enjoy this? I'm not sure.* I think the answer is the same as it was at Unilever. I enjoy the peripheral stuff – travel, hotels and dinners – but the actual work doesn't seem to enthuse me enough.

My cell phone rings and it's Sabrina. She's in acute abdominal pain and has managed to get an appointment with Dr Verma at short notice. She will have to make her own way to Wimbledon, but can I meet her there? This sounds really serious. I call Paul Connew on his cell phone and tell him that my wife is having some post-operative complication and I have to go. He agrees readily. I kick myself that I left the laptop at the cottage – I need it if I am to be able to do any meaningful 'working from home'. I drive back to the cottage, grab the computer and then head for London.

The traffic is bad and I miss the appointment, but I'm waiting in the hospital car park when Sabrina comes out. Dr Verma called her a 'silly girl' – when she screamed on being poked in the belly – and prescribed painkillers for her 'heavy period'. She also asked her to call some other private place the next day, to arrange a scan.

Sabrina is in pain all night, and extremely weak. She also bleeds a lot more than is usual. There is something very wrong here, but I have no idea what it could be. The next day, I try calling the number for that private scan, but keep getting the answering machine. Eventually, in the afternoon, I call our GP's office and explain to the nurse what is happening. She tells me to bring Sabrina in immediately and gives us an appointment with Dr Lewis.

The good doctor is extremely patient, asks searching questions, and is sympathetic when Sabrina gasps in severe pain at the slightest prod to her belly. He instructs us to proceed *immediately* to Kingston Hospital, giving us a sealed letter to take with us.

They seem to be expecting us, when we hand the letter in at reception. After a very short wait, Sabrina is ushered into an examination room and a Polish woman doctor begins some tests. Not long after, she announces that the pregnancy test came back 'strongly positive', but that there are clearly complications. Sabrina bursts into tears, and I wonder what these complications could be.

A consultant arrives and tells us that there is strong evidence of an 'ectopic pregnancy'. He explains what this means: that the fertilised egg has become stuck in a tube – instead of making it to the uterus. Not only is the foetus not viable in this situation, but the mother's life is in severe danger.

I'm sitting in the waiting room this evening, while Sabrina is in surgery; both our mothers are here too. My cell phone rings and it's Paul. He tells me to take all the time I need. The thought occurs to me that no one is going to chastise me now for not doing a comprehensive enough job in the software testing. The team will pull together to cover for my shortcomings, and I will be off the hook.

The consultant calls me to his office, still in his surgical scrubs. His trousers, shirt and tie are hanging on the back of the door. He tells me that they found an embryo of about four-to-six weeks of age in one of the Fallopian tubes. They had to remove this tube and the associated ovary. There were no complications and he expects a full recovery.

However, given Sabrina's recent history, he questions why this ectopic pregnancy was not spotted at the laparoscopy, just fourteen days ago, and also why an experienced gynaecologist failed to recognise the symptoms (including acute abdominal pain) in her patient, just yesterday.

So much for 'the second best in Europe', I think bitterly.

Sabrina spends some time at her parents' house getting her strength back, and then, as soon as she's well enough, I bring her to the cottage to rest there. She spends the days reclining on the sofa in the living room. Whenever I drive back from the client's offices, it's nice to see her face looking out of the window: expectant, welcoming, beautiful, vulnerable.

Master
1991 Age: 29 Nigeria

KPMG Management Consulting has done a lot of work in Nigeria in the past. Before I depart, I hear nothing but negative criticism about the country, from colleagues who have been there before. I am to leave in September and Sabrina is to join me later (having given up her job to come on this adventure). We rent out the house and move to our respective parents' homes.

For the first time in my life, I travel Business Class, and it's a confirmed seat too. I feel very privileged. I travel with an American colleague named John Bannert, who is from our Dallas office.

The arrival in Lagos is not as bad as we have been told it would be. A Customs official discreetly demands a five pound 'facilitating payment' from me to let me through. John's passport is discreetly stolen from his sweat pants pocket when we are surrounded by men insistent on carrying our luggage.

We are met at the airport and taken to our accommodation. On the way there, our car is stopped at an unofficial police roadblock; another facilitating payment enables us to proceed. The corporate apartment in its own secure compound is comfortable, with hot and cold running insects, but the water is intermittent. Lagos is not unlike Karachi, so it's not so much of a culture shock for me.

The next day we go to the American Embassy to try to replace John's passport. The middle-aged American man at the desk is humourless and stony-faced. He interrogates John to establish if he really is American. (John could not be more Texan than he obviously is; perhaps only a Stetson hat would help.) The man insists that John must bring a police report about the theft of his passport.

We go to a police station to report the stolen passport. We are ushered into the office of the Inspector. He listens patiently, then tells us that he cannot help; the airport is outside his jurisdiction. At the airport police station, the Inspector informs John that he requires a sworn and notarised statement. A visit to a lawyer's office follows. John dictates what happened; the lawyer's assistant types it out on an ancient manual typewriter. The lawyer notarises the statement and his fee is paid. This statement is taken to the airport police station, where a police report is obtained on payment of another fee. This police report is taken to the American Embassy, which agrees to provide John with a replacement passport.

What worries me is that if John was a visitor travelling alone, without the benefit of a company infrastructure to support him, without all of us, and if he was robbed and left penniless, to what extent would his embassy help him to get home? I wonder what the British Embassy is like. Fortunately, I am not placed in a position of needing such help.

There's a small group of us living and working together in Lagos, mostly British. We live like kings. Our expense allowance alone is a fortune every month. What we spend on a single restaurant meal approximates to one month's average wage. Nigeria is an apartheid country – money is the divider. We surround ourselves with poor and humble staff: drivers, cooks, guards, general stewards. They all address us as 'Master'.

There are rich Nigerians as well, of course. This country is one of the world's largest oil producers. But unlike Saudi Arabia for example, where money has been spent visibly on infrastructure – roads, hospitals, schools, stadiums – here there is no such common benefit. The wealth has clearly been funnelled into a relatively small number of private hands, much of it secreted abroad. A fraction of it is channelled into mainstream society by the prevalence of 'facilitating payments', these being requested by anyone in a uniform or performing an official function. But the majority of Nigerians have no access to the oil wealth.

Foreigners, non-Africans, are all perceived as being rich. To a large extent this is true; they would not be there other than for employment or business.

There are many fine houses in the neighbourhood where we live, always set back behind high walls and iron gates. The architecture is also reminiscent of Karachi, to me. Behind the gate of one such house, I catch sight of a red Jaguar XJ-S; how privileged and wealthy the owner must be, to have such a dream car here in Nigeria. But, on closer inspection, things look different. The XJ-S has no wheels; it is resting on bricks. Perhaps, they were stolen by a gang. Or, worse, perhaps this XJ-S is a major 'project' – what a struggle it must be to get parts and expertise, here in Lagos. An endless financial and administrative and bureaucratic heartache for its owner. A dream car turned into a nightmare.

Despite the huge gulf in our relative wealth, the Nigerians that we employ are cheerful, respectful and without resentment. By contrast, I am very uncomfortable with the attitude of some of my colleagues. They treat the country with contempt and laugh at Nigerians. They joke about the religious humility of the Nigerians, saying that they *have to* believe in an Afterlife, because this one is so miserable for them. They refer to Nigerians as 'chimps' and 'monkeys', and occasionally (when they are frustrated by inefficiency) as 'niggers'. Always in private, of course. It is only the English ones who use this language. John, the American, never does.

They also call John a 'loud and fat American' behind his back. I wonder what they say about me, when I'm not there.

(This racism doesn't apply to me, does it? I'm not one of the Africans – I'm very light brown, almost white.)

I don't fit into this group. I understand the paradoxes, the difficulties of Nigerian society, and I feel respect for our employees, because of their humility and faith. Levinus is my steward. He is a trained and experienced chef, but his duties here go beyond just cooking. He works hard, on his own initiative, without complaint. He is a wonderful, kind, cheerful, humble man. I ask him not to call me 'Master'. I don't deserve it. 'Sir' is fine.

Fire
1993 Age: 30 London

Milton, who has never flown and is afraid of the concept, has finally been persuaded by his family to join them on a trip to Switzerland. He comes to visit us in London and, on the dreaded day, I take him to Heathrow Airport for the rendezvous with his family.

At the airport, Milton is drinking water constantly, from a bottle of mineral water. I warn him to stop for a while because, once he boards, he will not have access to the lavatory for at least half-an-hour, until the plane is airborne. He thanks me for this insight; never having flown, he has no idea of what to expect.

A few days later, he tells me what happened on the flight. His brother was looking out of the window and said, 'That engine's on fire.' Milton thought that he was joking, but he looked and indeed the engine *was* on fire. The pilot eventually noticed this and shut down that engine, telling the passengers it was under control and there was nothing to worry about. The flight was able to proceed safely. Milton can't understand why this scary incident had to happen on his first ever flight. I have flown many times and nothing untoward has ever happened.

Notepad
1992 Age: 29 Nigeria

Chris Gant, the Partner from KPMG London, is staying in the guest room, but he's disappeared from Lagos. He never mentioned whether he was going to Abuja or Port Harcourt. He really should have said something. Looking around the room, to get some clue as to where he's gone, my eyes fall on a notepad on his desk. The top page seems to have notes from his meeting with Richard.

Express concern about Imran Ahmad
- Competence
- Confidence
- Credibility
May need to replace resource

I feel physically sick. I return to our bedroom and Sabrina knows immediately that something is wrong.

Before we leave, Alex, one of the guards in the private compound where we live, tells me a story he wants me to hear. He knows that I am unhappy about leaving Lagos. He shows me an old black-and-white photo of himself in an army uniform. He says that when he was in the army, there was an excursion being planned, in which he wanted to participate. However, he was forbidden to come along, being required to stay in the camp and perform some mundane chores. He was very upset by this and wished that he could go.

Later, he learned that everyone who went on the expedition was killed in an ambush.

Alex tells me something which, over the years, I learn to be profoundly true: 'Every disappointment is a blessing.'

Riverside
1993 Age: 30 London

Leslie Hancock, my favourite client – who is very grateful for the work I did to prevent DHL from implementing a very poor accounting design for their new Oracle system – takes me to a meeting with some other DHL people. It's at the DHL facility in Brentford. There's a softly spoken man with a gentle South African accent, named Michael. Leslie introduces me and the three of us go to a business lunch at a pub, sitting outside by the river. Leslie and Michael appear to be on good terms and are chatting casually. I'm usually a listener.

Michael says, 'My divorce has come through.'

Those words resonate with something inside me – they trigger such a longing. I feel envious of Michael and helpless in my situation. *'My divorce has come through.'* How wonderful that would be, to be divorced. It feels like a fantasy, like winning the lottery. Something you can yearn for, but you're never going to have it.

I can't have a divorce – I love my daughter too much and I want her to grow up with two parents in a nice house, the way it's supposed to be.

Red Light
1992 Age: 29 London

We return to London from Nigeria and stay at our parents' homes. Our big house remains rented out; with Sabrina no longer working and now pregnant, I cannot afford the mortgage payments anyway. It's funny to drive the Rover again, after six months of being chauffeured everywhere.

I am in the London office for a while, my reputation having taken a setback within the Firm. Since I joined KPMG, I've always been working flat out, but this enforced idleness is very uncomfortable.

Finally, I am assigned to an in-house project, working for an American woman named Cathy, on part of a huge internal systems development effort. I have already heard things about Cathy from other employees of the firm – apparently, she can be very difficult. The nightmare begins at once. Cathy and I just don't seem to be on the same wavelength. Nothing which I do is good enough or quite right. From my perspective, it seems that she keeps changing the parameters of what is required, moving the goalposts. From the Firm's perspective, I begin to look incompetent again, and this clouds my self-view. Maybe *I really am incompetent?*

One day in a memo she conveys something that simply isn't true. I *didn't* fail to meet a deadline; she moved the due date, so that it was no longer achievable. I don't seem to have any options. There's no question of complaining to a Partner; that would be pathetic. I slip easily into a victim mentality.

Every single day is absolutely miserable; either being at work on weekdays, or thinking about returning to work, at the weekends. I have a pregnant wife, a reduced income, a house I can't afford to live in, an employer who is taking a dim view of me – nothing is going right. I hate this life. It's a horrible summer.

I finish my agonising two-month assignment with Cathy and return to the London office. This coincides with an economic depression which has now hit the consulting market. Many of the 'Big Six' firms are laying off people.

I, and many of my colleagues, find ourselves in the office without chargeable client work to do. In the consulting industry, hourly utilisation is everything – otherwise we become an expensive overhead.

One afternoon, Steve Langridge, our Resource Manager, tells me that Brian Clarke, the Senior Partner, would like to see me. I go to Brian's office, but see that the red light ('Do Not Disturb') is on outside his door. I go back to Steve's office to tell him this, and Steve replies: 'I think he's waiting for you.'

Inside, Brian is sitting at his conference table, along with a bald man I don't recognise. Brian says that Leonard is from Human Resources. There's a white envelope on the table – it has my name on it!

I am not entirely surprised when they send me home. The feeling of imminent doom has been very heavy. Leonard actually escorts me out of the building, taking my photo ID.

Although I am worried and upset as I travel home, I also feel a sense of relief; I did not enjoy the last few months at all.

This quickly turns out to be one of the best things that has ever happened to me. Two weeks later I have a fresh start as a consultant in Oracle Corporation, which is doing well, unlike many of the consulting firms. I also get a slight pay rise and a red Nissan sports coupé as a company car.

My Oracle career begins with three wonderful weeks at the Paris office, learning about their software products. *Thank you, God.*

Random
2004 Age: 42 London

We attend Prize Giving Day at Lady Eleanor Holles School. Aleena has won a prize for science. She cannot take all the credit for this; surely I gave her the scientist genes?

The guest of honour is Gail Rebuck, the Chief Executive of Random House, the most powerful woman in publishing in the whole world, perhaps the most powerful *person* in the publishing world. Is this a coincidence, just when I want to write a book? *I think not!*

After the ceremony, we have tea and scones (*'skons'*) in the dining hall, but my mind is on one thing only. I am going to tell the world's most important publishing executive about my planned book.

I see Gail Rebuck in the crowd, moving purposefully across the hall. I rapidly move to intercept her, pushing unceremoniously past many little clusters of parents and teachers. I thrust myself in front of her with almost expert casualness, introduce myself modestly, and engage her in a conversation about how interesting her job must be. Gail Rebuck shows only the faintest flicker of surprise and remains absolutely civil and gracious, amiably agreeing that her job is indeed very enjoyable. I then mention, almost as an aside, that I am writing a book. Gail Rebuck expertly retains her poise. She must often be confronted by gibbering idiots who all think they've written a bestseller, and has learned to distinguish the authentic ones like me. Politely and with apparently genuine interest, she asks me what it is about. *I have my moment to pitch my book to the most powerful person in the publishing world!* The book is very hard to explain or summarise, but it's a great read and will be a bestseller; this is what I convey. I give her my business card and say that I will write to her. She courteously says that she looks forward to it and resumes her interrupted exit.

Well, I think that went quite well.

Naked
1992 Age: 32 London

It's just past 5:00 a.m. on Wednesday morning when we get on the road in the little red Nissan sports car with the removable hardtop roof panels, that Oracle Corporation has given me as my company car. Fortunately, there is absolutely no traffic and, when we get to the hospital, there is plenty of parking. This is a huge relief for me. I was totally stressed out by the thought of having to drive to Queen Charlotte's Hospital in rush hour and then, on arrival, finding the car parks to be full (which they usually are). For this reason, I had prepared a couple of signs for the inside of the car windows, which read: *Having a baby. Queen Charlotte's Labour Ward.* These were to both facilitate the drive and to serve as an excuse if I had to park somewhere that wasn't actually a recognised parking spot.

The first nurse to examine Sabrina confirms that it looks like the baby is on his/her way. We are moved to a delivery room, which is quite spacious, and even has a television. The room is large because it contains a lot of emergency equipment, and just the sight of this causes me great anxiety. I hope and pray that we won't need to use any of it.

Around 9:00 a.m. I call the office on my cell phone and relay the exciting news to Barbara, our departmental secretary. Later, David Greenwood calls me and says there's no hurry, not to come back before Monday. These people are so supportive, I am truly blessed. I was so lucky to get into Oracle Corporation last month, just two weeks after being laid off by KPMG.

Despite the early start, the baby seems in no hurry to come, and the day passes mostly uneventfully. The BBC News advises that the UK pound has gone into freefall against other currencies and during the day the Chancellor raises interest rates *by* 5%. (This day comes to be known as 'Black Wednesday'.) This huge rise would have caused me a heart attack if I hadn't already got us a rate that is fixed at 10%, not variable with the Bank of England rate like many mortgage deals. At 6:00 p.m. *Star Trek* is on BBC2, and it's that famous episode *The Naked Time*, when all the crew go crazy, some running around the ship waving swords, generally behaving irrationally – even Spock.

Finally, around 7:15 p.m., it seems to be happening. There's no doctor, just an Indian midwife and a couple of nurses.

As the baby finally emerges, the midwife declares: 'It's a girl!'

The most extraordinary thing happens. The baby quite deliberately (it seems to me) looks around the room and then locks her eyes on *me* and gives me a most intense and disparaging look – as if to convey: 'What have you got to say for yourself?' She's looking at me as if *she* is the reprimanding adult and *I* am the delinquent child!

But this doesn't make any sense. I thought newborn babies couldn't focus more than a few inches in front of their eyes – and I'm a couple of feet away.

She stops holding my gaze and the moment passes and the baby begins to behave as a baby is supposed to behave.

Obviously, I was mistaken – it must have been how I *perceived* her random head and eye movements.

Levinus
1992 Age: 31 London

I receive a letter from Levinus. He has been fired by the person that replaced me as his 'Master'. Apparently, this American couple brought their baby to Nigeria and the husband got it into his head that they didn't need to buy *Pampers* (which are readily available in Nigeria) – the steward would wash the soiled cotton diapers. Levinus, a skilled pastry chef, complained that this was not within his normal duties ('Masters' should either buy *Pampers* or get the nanny to wash cotton diapers), and they fired him.

I am outraged. Just because Levinus is a poor Nigerian, it doesn't mean that he should do whatever demeaning work his 'Master' demands, in exchange for his meagre one thousand nairas per month salary (sixty dollars).

I write back to Levinus and I put a twenty pound note in the envelope with the letter.

When Levinus writes back, his letter is joyful and uplifting. He had been travelling around, looking for a new job. He had run out of money and literally could not even pay for bus fares around Lagos. He desperately needed some cash, to continue his search for a new job. My letter came, and in it was a half-month's salary. With this money, he was able to travel, and he almost immediately secured a new position.

He is grateful to me, but I am even more grateful to him for telling me this. I feel joy and humility. I am thankful that I was able to help in such a small way. We both were able to find new jobs when we needed them.

Rome
1996 Age: 33 Mexico City

'Welcome to CompuServe.'

Religion Forum
Author: Travelin' Man
Subject: Rome

It is commonly believed that there are three Abrahamic religions: Judaism, Christianity and Islam.

In fact, only Judaism and Islam are Abrahamic religions. They both worship an invisible, formless One God who is omniscient, omnipresent and omnipotent. They never use anthropomorphic imagery to depict Him. The idea of a bearded old man God (called Deus, who looks like Zeus!) having a physical son is utterly repugnant to Judaism and Islam. They differ primarily in that Judaism is specifically for one particular tribe of people, whereas Islam is intended to be universal.

Christianity is a Roman religion. It was formulated and crafted by Rome, hijacking the known events in the life story of Jesus, forcibly displacing the many groups who followed Jesus' teachings authentically, and imposing Roman components into the story. Also, making this 'mystery religion' exclusively true and threatening eternal torment for those who did not follow it ***unquestioningly***. This does not sound much like peaceful, compassionate Jesus. It sounds like a ruthless system of controlling people through fear.

December 25th is the birthday of the Roman Sun God. It is that point in the year when you begin to notice that the days are getting longer again. There's Christmas.

Ēostre was the Goddess of sex and fertility, her symbols including eggs and rabbits. There's Easter.

As explained in an earlier post, crucifixion took place on a T structure, not a cross. The vertical part of the T (the *stipes*) was fixed permanently in the ground. If it wasn't fixed permanently into the ground, imagine how much effort and time it would take to dig it into the ground at the time of each crucifixion, deep enough to take the weight of a man without keeling over. Consider also how *long* it would have to be to take the weight and remain steady. The poor victim carried only the horizontal part, the *patibulum* – which would have been heavy enough by itself. To drag the whole structure through the streets would have been literally impossible.

The adoption of the cross as a Christian symbol does not come from the authentic crucifixion process. It comes from some earlier use of the cross as an icon: the Egyptian *ankh*, the Chaldean *tau*, the Celtic cross. (The Chaldean *tau* is the most likely candidate.)

The crucifixion is manufactured imagery and the cross is manufactured symbolism.

No credible historian takes the Nativity Story as literally true. Why would the otherwise super-efficient Romans actually require people to *return to their villages of origin* for a census? How impractical and absurd is that? What if Joseph and Mary had been from different places? What are shepherds in Palestine doing watching sheep in the middle of winter? How do you follow a star? How far did these 'wise men' have to walk? The Romans only marched twenty miles in a day and they were fit!

It is outrageous that this story is programmed into children as literally true.

Rome spent centuries brutally killing the authentic followers of Jesus and then manufactured the new religion of 'Christianity'. Ponder that statement.

Turmoil
1994 Age: 31 UK

My business career with Oracle Corporation is progressing well, with lots of travel around the UK and mainland Europe. I enjoy being a management consultant, specialising in Oracle systems. But I am conscious of the fact that my reserve of money from my KPMG severance package is running low. If we are to remain in the house, with Sabrina not working, I have to boost my income in some way.

Right on cue, I receive a call from a headhunter, who tells me that the 'Big Six' are all hiring again and urgently looking for people with Oracle experience. I am likely to get a very significant pay rise.

Interviews are arranged and, after a lengthy evaluation process which includes psychometric tests, a job offer results from Touche Ross*, a 'Big Six' firm. There is more money, but an inferior car. With a new child rapidly growing her way through the most fashionable and elegant infant outfits to be seen in Surrey, it's money that I need; the ordinary car will be quite adequate.

However, I really enjoy working with Oracle Corporation, which is an upbeat company and does appear to be going places. It has recently hired a new Director of Consulting, and his job is to take Oracle UK into the more upmarket consulting space occupied by the 'Big Six' firms. I make an appointment to see Mike Powell, make a short presentation about myself, and tell him that I want to move into something new; I need a fresh challenge. He says that I would be perfect for the new Business Process Re-

* The British firm was known as Touche Ross; its American partner was known as Deloitte & Touche. Eventually, all entities in the group became known as Deloitte.

engineering (BPR) group, which will provide general consulting in how businesses can radically improve their internal processes. There is much talk of BPR in business school circles; it is the latest industry fashion. Mike also says that I will receive a significant pay rise for this new position.

My happiness could not be more complete. I am to receive more money, keep the same car, and will have an exciting new job in a growth area for Oracle. I can turn down Touche Ross. Their offer is open for a while, so I just leave it unanswered.

Just before I start with the new BPR group, the head of that unit resigns and leaves (to join a 'Big Six' firm). *Not to worry*, the Director of Consulting will personally oversee the group, until he appoints a replacement.

A few days later, after an alleged argument with the UK Managing Director, the Director of Consulting resigns suddenly; I never see Mike again. This new consulting business unit is falling apart. But I cannot go back to the group I came from; my excellent boss there, Debbie, was unhappy after a clumsy reorganisation; she resigned and left. Oracle UK is going through extreme turmoil. I am a nobody in what's left, and I don't know where to turn.

The offer from Touche Ross is still on the table. I pick up the phone and call Peter Catchpole, the Partner who offered me the position, to tell him that I *will* be joining.

Wind
1994 Age: 31 UK

Milton makes a trip to Spain, involving another dreaded flight – his second ever flying experience. He tells me later what happened.

It was a very windy day and, as the aircraft was coming in to land, a sudden strong gust pushed it violently to one side. The pilot aborted the landing, suddenly powering up the engines again. He apologised for this and circled around for another attempt. Milton says he noticed the flight attendants looking very afraid as they made their second approach. Passengers were vomiting and running to use the lavatories – even though they weren't supposed to be out of their seats. As the plane dropped down to the runway, there was another sideways lurch and again the sound of the engines being powered up; the plane jolted up as the landing was aborted again.

The flight was diverted to Gibraltar and the passengers were brought to their destination by buses – a two-hour road trip.

Milton can't understand it when I tell him that flying is perfectly safe.

Jazz Café
1994 Age: 32 Minneapolis

One day in early December, I am relaxing at home in London with flu, when I receive a phone call from David Williams, who is a Manager. I am to leave for Minneapolis within a week. There is a project there at Honeywell which needs my input.

Apparently, Minnesota is quite cold, so I pack a sweater and gloves. I manage to get everything into one suitcase, and I will be carrying just my attaché case and a bag for the laptop computer which Touche Ross very recently gave me. (It has a colour screen!)

It is wonderful to fly Business Class to America. I arrive in the early evening at Minneapolis-St Paul Airport. It is dark, shockingly cold and snowing.

My taxi driver is African. In the course of the conversation, he relates that he moved from Ethiopia to the US via Greece. While in Greece, he had a specific economic strategy. Whenever he had money, he always ensured that the rent for his apartment was paid well in advance. He also maintained stocks of dried food; he kept sacks of lentils, beans and so on. He figured that as long as his rent was paid and he had this store of food, he would always be able to survive for at least a couple of months, no matter what disaster befell him.

I am touched and humbled by this completely different philosophy of personal physical wellbeing. Here was a man who did not assume that the global socio-economic system and supply chain would always work and provide for him; he took responsibility for his own welfare. If there was a total breakdown of the system, our university degrees and share certificates and credit cards would be worthless in ensuring our survival. We would be looking for people like this man, holed up in his apartment, from whom to beg, borrow or steal.

My hotel is the Luxford Suites, in downtown Minneapolis. Downstairs it has the Café Luxford, a jazz club. The sound of smooth jazz music coming from there, blending in with the dark, moody anticipation of winter and Christmas and America, creates in me a cosy and warm feeling of excitement and wellbeing. There is something really sexy about America – I can feel it in the air.

I call Moira Berman from my suite; she is staying in the nearby Hilton. She explains that she gets Hilton points, so always stays in one. I find her voice, with its soft South African accent, to be quite attractive, and we have a long conversation about this project.

My body clock awakes me early. America feels different – even though I'm in a hotel room, I can just feel it. Anticipation. Something wonderful, exciting, is going to happen to me in America. Perhaps that Passion I always yearned for.

Downstairs there is a team of five professional-looking American men and women in dark suits, waiting for me. It's the team from Deloitte & Touche, including Moira. We have a business breakfast. It's now lunchtime in England, so I am ravenous. I have a vegetarian omelette (a 'Café Scramble'), with wheat toast, liberal amounts of tomato ketchup and black pepper, orange juice and coffee. I love America already!

Everything seems exciting and upbeat. There is a real sense of energy in the air, of a 'can do' attitude. I have never felt this in the British work environments.

Jim Rea, the Senior Manager, reminds me a little of Fred Flintstone, with his thick black hair and generous build. He takes me in his car and leads the fleet of vehicles from the hotel's underground car park to the corporate headquarters of Honeywell, a couple of miles away. In daylight, I have a greater appreciation of the immensely thick blanket of snow which covers the landscape. Unlike London snow, this won't be turning to slush anytime soon. But the sun is bright in the sky, creating a dazzling vista – I wish I had my sunglasses.

I spend a very interesting day at the client's offices and meet the various team members (an attractive older woman named Penelope particularly catches my attention). Afterwards, Tom Berquist of Deloitte drops me back at the Luxford Suites in his sporty coupe. He's young, smart, good-looking and very pleasant to chat with. He shakes my hand and welcomes me to the project and to America.

I love Minneapolis. The sky is blue, the sun is bright, the snow is deep and *Star Trek: The Next Generation* is on the local Minneapolis TV station, two episodes every night, in a continuous chronological cycle. I watch it from the sofa of my hotel suite, with my feet up (although sometimes I sleep through it). This is paradise on Earth.

My long love affair with America begins.

This trip is for three weeks, but the clients love me, and I am to return after New Year for further involvement in this global project – a worldwide implementation of Oracle software. It is great to be wanted. I am *not* incompetent. Sabrina and Aleena will be joining me, and I find a comfortable apartment on the top (34th) floor of an elegant apartment block on Marquette Avenue, on the edge of downtown. It even has skyway access (the skyways are a network of enclosed glass walkways connecting the public areas of various buildings, which means that you don't have to step outside). It is possible to leave the apartment and walk all over downtown, without needing a coat – even in these sub-zero temperatures.

Power
1989 Age: 26 London

One night in January, there is to be another of these miserable Unilever Audit social gatherings; this time in a Mexican restaurant. I'm going because I feel I have to – to not go would be like an *admission* of an irreconcilable gulf between this department and myself. I am driving back to London from an audit site in Essex – so far from home, it really should have been an 'away' assignment, requiring a hotel. The sun disappeared hours ago; it is pitch dark, raining heavily, and a gale is blowing. The Alfa Romeo is being buffeted by gusts of wind as I drive in the blackness on the M25 (the long motorway that encircles London).

The sound of the engine fades and the car loses power, beginning to slow down. I am able to get into the emergency lane before the car stops altogether. I sit here in the darkness, thinking that I can't even look under the bonnet in this weather. I turn the key and the car starts; the engine sounds just fine. I set off again, wondering what caused this.

A couple of minutes later, the engine fails again. As I'm sitting in the emergency lane, I decide that I am *not* going to this restaurant; I just want to get home. *Please God, just let me get home.* I turn the key and the engine starts without a problem. I get back on the road, but turn off the motorway at the next exit and head in the direction of home, hoping to get there while the car is still running.

I reach home without any trouble. The problem does not occur again, this night or any time subsequently.

I hear about the restaurant event next morning at the office. There is much merriment about how wild it was and how many margaritas were downed by all. I'm glad I didn't go; it would have been an ordeal for me – especially if they made me pay the same amount as everyone else, when I only drank Diet Coke.

Milky Way
1968 Age: 5 London

Rehan, who is three years old, is asleep on our parents' bed. I am reclining beside him. Our mother has bought each of us a Milky Way chocolate bar. She gives me mine and places Rehan's next to him on the pillow.

Milky Way is a lovely treat. I rip open the wrapper and dig my teeth into the delicious chocolate and the soft, sweet interior. I love the way the gooey inside stretches as I pull the bar away from my mouth, and then it tears without too much resistance. I chew appreciatively and gobble down the bar.

It was so delicious, and now it's gone.

I am left contemplating my loss in the empty bedroom, Rehan still obliviously asleep beside me. His Milky Way is right there, under my gaze.

If I took *just one little bite* of his Milky Way, he wouldn't even notice.

Sneakily, I unwrap one end of his bar and take a little bite. I fold the wrapper back over the open end of the bar and place it back on his pillow.

Stillness.

Contemplation.

I unwrap the end of the bar, take another little bite, fold the wrapper over the end of the bar and place it back on the pillow.

By the time our mother returns, the bar is mostly crumpled wrapper and not much chocolate. She reprimands me and Rehan wakes up – he takes in the situation, observes what is left of his Milky Way, comes to understand that I have eaten most of it, and starts crying.

I smile at my own naughtiness.

Hugo Boss
1994 Age: 32 London

At Heathrow, I check in at British Airways to fly Business Class to Chicago, and then to Minneapolis with American Airlines. The BA Business Class lounge is arranged in numerous clusters of sofas and armchairs, bordered by lines of exotic plants to create a sense of intimacy and privacy. I enter one of these enclosed areas, which is fully occupied except for an empty sofa immediately opposite me. As I approach the seat, an arm appears from between the plants behind it, and deposits a leather case onto the sofa. *I don't believe it!* Some idiot, seeing me going for that empty sofa and unable to reach it first, thinks he can reserve it by throwing his briefcase on it through the partition. I won't be cheated like this. *Who does he think he is?* Someone walking up to an empty seat has precedence over someone who can only throw an object on to it. *Everyone knows that!*

Stubbornly, I sit down on the right side of the two-seater sofa, leaving his case untouched on the left. The handsome, smartly dressed jerk looks like an Italian model for Hugo Boss or something. Perhaps he's surprised to see me sitting here, but stubbornly he comes up to the sofa, retrieves his case, and then sits down on the left side of the sofa, which he has claimed as his.

We sit here awkwardly, our warm thighs too close for comfort. I open my attaché case on the coffee table in front of us, and busy myself with my important-looking papers. I could show off my laptop computer – *I don't think he has one* – but I can't be bothered to get it out and start it up; it takes forever. Finally, I finish the important business of shuffling my papers, look thoughtfully at my Gucci watch, and realise I must be going – my important life is very busy. I slowly and deliberately close my attaché case, stand up, reach for my computer bag, and slowly and deliberately walk away.

At the furthest end of the lounge, I find an empty seat, get myself some orange juice and peanuts, and flop down on the sofa, drained.

Earth
1994 Age: 32 Austria

At Christmas, we are making a now rare trip to Pakistan (Sabrina's parents have moved back there and live in a big house with servants — although electricity and water are not completely reliable). We persuade Milton to come too, citing *carpe diem.* If he doesn't *seize the day* now, when will he ever get such a chance? He thinks about it a lot and finally concedes. His fear of flying should not stand in the way of such an opportunity. He comes down from Edinburgh to London by train, and then we all head off to Karachi via Dubai, on Emirates Airlines.

On the flight, somewhere over Austria, we receive our dinner trays. Suddenly, violent turbulence rocks the aircraft, and our stomachs leap as the plane drops towards the earth for what seems an eternity (in reality, it must have been less than two seconds). The flight attendant, who was handing out trays, looks shocked and frightened, losing her balance and falling over. My bread roll flies away, never to be seen again (and not replaced by the airline). I have flown quite a lot, and this is the worst turbulence I have ever experienced.

I can't stop laughing. Milton is afraid of flying, and every time that he does fly, something happens. It means that *God has a sense of humour.*

Rapture
1996 Age: 33 Mexico City

'Welcome to CompuServe.'

Religion Forum
Author: Travelin' Man
Subject: The Rapture

I have studied the *Rapture* in detail, consulting many sources. The concept as it is presented did not exist in Christianity until it was constructed by John Nelson Derby in the 19th Century, under the Plymouth Brethren.

The belief was popularized by Hal Lindsey in the 1970's. His book, *The Late Great Planet Earth*, effectively gave birth to the *End Times* industry, which has exploded amongst the ignorant masses, without any due regard to Biblical scholarship or the teachings of Jesus.

Part of the belief system requires the fulfilment of expected events from their interpretation of Biblical prophecy, such as the return of *all* Jews to the historic land of Israel (including the Jewish Ethiopian *falashas*, hence the extraordinary concern for their relocation in the late eighties). This belief system requires certain parties to fulfil the roles described in Revelations, as the legions of the Antichrist and the great Empires of the Earth.

The seductive attraction of this belief system is that it makes its followers the *winners* over the non-believers; the Believers are a cosmic elite who will avoid the horrible suffering in this world and enjoy the highest status and comfort in the next world. It doesn't matter if they bring about environmental catastrophe, nuclear destruction, disease, famine and global misery (due to a complete breakdown of the world's socio-economic infrastructure, caused by a Middle East conflagration); they will not be around to suffer the consequences. It is hard to imagine a more selfish position and a less loving God, who would set it all up this way.

Rapture can be a legitimate religious belief; I do not deny this. But, once it influences global politics and US foreign policy (through the Christian voting blocs), then it becomes a danger to us all. These are people who don't need to worry about the environment, since they believe that they will soon be leaving the Earth *en masse*, and for them a global conflagration is part of the process. If someone succeeds in bringing about world peace, that person (whether it be Prince Charles, the Dalai Lama, the Pope, or the Head of the United Nations) is the Antichrist.

According to these beliefs, world peace is a bad thing, orchestrated by Satan, intended to unite all non-believers in the oppression of true Christians!

I am deeply concerned by this. Rapture politics will hurt us all.

Silk
1996 Age: 33 Hong Kong

I have now reached Gold status in the *Sheraton Club*. I pay a return visit to Hong Kong, after an absence of many months. When I check in at the Sheraton and present my *Sheraton Club International Gold Card*, the man at Reception apologises that there are no Club Level rooms available, and would I mind having a suite? *Of course I don't mind.*

The suite is magnificent. It has a study, as well as a living room, and the shower cubicle is virtually a room in itself. A wall of glass looks over Hong Kong's dazzling harbour. I sit for hours staring out at the captivating view. (I wish Penelope was here to share this – it's even better than that suite she was given last year!) This is the essence of Hong Kong for me; a magical place where it's always exciting to be. It never becomes ordinary.

On this trip I buy a Chinese silk carpet. It is about five feet by two feet. It has a pleasing geometric pattern and depictions of the Emperor's warriors, horses and chariots. The colours are muted and elegant, and the silk is so smooth, it is a pleasure to run my fingers over it. I like to kid myself that it is several thousand years old. One thing is for sure; this silk will never be stepped on by a shoe. I will always keep it pure and unsoiled, so that running my hands and bare feet over it is a sensuous delight.

Hell
1994 Age: 31 London

This marriage is a living Hell. There is nothing normal or 'to be expected' about it. My parents totally ruined my life with their insistence that they could only be happy if I married a Muslim Pakistani girl. And the justification for the arranged marriage process – that it follows a rigorous and careful procedure of matching, vetting and validation – is all bullshit. All Pakistanis know that all Pakistanis are endemic liars – so why should we believe anything that we are told in the information gathering phase?

I do share some of the blame. The truth is that, once we had engaged in some conversations, I became aware that Sabrina wasn't very educated, informed or bright. Some of the things she said reeked of total ignorance and superstition. Her use of English was fluent – but unsophisticated. Her so-called 'degree' (from a 'computing school' above some shops on Oxford Street) wasn't worth the paper it was printed on. Her job was two orders of magnitude less prestigious than my senior management fast-track position at Unilever.

I chose to overlook these niggling details because of her father being a 'multi-millionaire'. But this turned out to be more bullshit. At best, he was a formerly successful businessman who had now completely lost his marbles and his money – sitting around in his pyjamas all day sending and receiving faxes which spoke of major transactions that never actually materialised. Because of his bragging, he attracted criminals who were hoping to get a cut of some of these imaginary deals. His criminal associations attracted the interest of the Metropolitan Police, who confiscated his British passport to prevent him fleeing abroad, pending further investigations.

As the net closed in on him – and we could never be sure what this was actually about, as he never told the truth about anything – he took his wife and Sabrina's brother (newly married to a girl from a Pakistani family who had spent their entire time in England living on social security) and fled back to Pakistan, using his expired passport to do so (don't ask me how).

Despite all this, Sabrina treats me as the boy from a poor family who was so lucky to marry a rich girl. She constantly refers to her 'rich family' and her 'powerful and wealthy father'. Her position is without one iota of validity – but the rage which it ignites within me is impossible to control.

I am so angry with my parents. I got into Hampton Grammar School, and they sent me there on the first day without the proper sports kit – despite everything being clearly explained in all the detailed correspondence which they never read. I was humiliated. My parents took my brothers and me on a trip to Mecca and Medina for the two weeks immediately before my first-year exams, when I should have been studying (but I still managed to do okay). From that experience I learned that you don't need to prepare much for exams (which belief caused me some severe problems later). I got myself into the prestigious Unilever Companies Management Development Scheme, and my parents insisted on initiating the arranged marriage process just when I was preparing for my first accounting exams – with all the chaos and distraction that ensued. Then they shepherded me (willingly, I admit) into a nightmare of a marriage with an arrogant, uneducated, frigid dimwit whose deranged *faux* millionaire father was getting himself into shady dealings with African criminals. The demands of this self-entitled family of losers made it impossible for me to devote the necessary full attention to my Unilever career, which promised high rewards in exchange for absolute dedication. The stress was unbearable.

So much for the arranged marriage process. Would it really have been so bad if I married a woman who wasn't Muslim and wasn't Pakistani? That would be more 'normal' than this nightmare. Every time I think about what my parents did to me through their prejudice, ignorance and stupidity … I'm so full of rage that I imagine taking care of them with a machine gun.

If ensuring my happiness and everyone's happiness was the main justification for the arranged marriage process, it clearly hasn't worked.

Miles
1995 Age: 32 Minneapolis

In the new year, I make several trips to Minneapolis and spend quite a lot of time there. The Siberian winter eventually transforms to a gorgeous, hot summer. Sabrina and Aleena also come for a couple of trips.

My first impressions of America are that it is upbeat, optimistic, organised. People are friendly, emotional, compassionate, not afraid to live life, not ashamed to do well. They are nice to me and I really enjoy being here. The shopping is also much cheaper than in London, and it makes a change to deal with store staff who are friendly and want to help me shop, unlike the indifference in London. This American attitude may be a simple matter of good business sense, but it obviously works; I feel a lot better parting with my money in the US.

Nick Pribus, one of the Honeywell staff, tells me that I *must* join Northwest Airlines' frequent flyer programme, called *World Perks*. I am somewhat cynical about these schemes; in Europe they are more trouble than they are worth. You get lots of junk mail and, after many paid flights, you may just scrape a free trip between London and Paris – on the airline's terms. However, he seems quite adamant, so I fill out the application and achieve *Blue* status.

Now Life is all about the Miles!

Balcony
1995 Age: 32 Minneapolis

It's a sunny day in March, quite mild compared to the last couple of months, and I'm standing out on the balcony of our 34th floor corporate apartment on the edge of downtown Minneapolis. In my arms I'm holding my beloved daughter Aleena, now two-and-a-half years old and beginning to be quite articulate. She calls me 'Daddy'. I tell her stories about Thomas the Tank engine. I love her more than anyone or anything. I love her more than I ever thought it was possible to love.

Sabrina is standing just inside the glass doors and is at it again. She is berating what a useless man I am and that because of my job we all had to move to this stupid apartment in this miserable country. (The apartment in Marquette Place is spacious, light, elegant, comfortable and secure – but it's only temporary, and Deloitte & Touche flew her and Aleena in Business Class to join me.) Apparently, Sabrina's friends have amazing husbands who run their own businesses and they don't have to do anything like this. They have loads of money without having to be a 'management consultant'. She also reminds me how incredibly wealthy her renowned father is and that 'my father will clean you out' if I try to divorce her (she means 'take you to the cleaners' obviously).

I am not a bad person – I've always been generally kind and thoughtful and well-intentioned. I am not a criminal or a psychopath. I know this for sure. But I don't deserve this and the anger seething through me is toxic. This person is so ignorant – she has no idea how ignorant she is.

I can end this quickly and give her the painful shock she truly deserves. I visualise what to do. I can drop Aleena over the railing to hit the ground 34 storeys below. Then I have to quickly climb over and let myself go. It will be quick and painless for both of us. If I throw Aleena, but don't follow – then I'll be the most reviled man in America. Probably it would mean life imprisonment without the possibility of parole. But, strangely, even that might be better than this. Aleena would be gone to Paradise, so she wouldn't have to suffer her parents' utterly vitriolic relationship. I could make a big story about how arranged marriage ruins your life. People generally have no idea that it isn't always the woman who suffers at the hands of a brutal man – it can be the other way around. A mild-mannered, gentle man can be driven to insanity by an abusive woman (who, to be fair, did not want to marry him in the first place, but was forced to do so by her idiotic and deceiving parents). Everyone who knows me from school, university, work – they would all be totally stunned by this. Maybe some good would come of it.

I stand here on the balcony 34 storeys up in the sky, holding Aleena to my chest, gently pressing my lips to her forehead, the cool air whispering around us – deep in this imagined scenario. The pain inside is unbearable. I am trembling at where my thoughts went.

Modem
1995 Age: 32 Minneapolis

At the office in Minneapolis, Nick Pribus and Greg Uhlenhopp are raving about some new service called CompuServe. Apparently, you install some software on your computer and connect it to the phone line. The computer dials a number and connects you to CompuServe, which is like a global community. You can read the news, e-mail other subscribers (all over the world!), 'chat' with them by typing, and access the worldwide public computer inter-network.

This evening in our corporate apartment, after Sabrina and Aleena have gone to bed, I sit at the dining table. I connect the phone cable into my laptop, insert the floppy disc Greg gave me, and install the CompuServe software. It wants my credit card details, to charge twenty dollars per month – I give them gladly. The modem makes all kinds of beeping noises, then a steady sort of quiet static, then a beautiful American female voice says: 'Welcome to CompuServe.'

My identity is 76031,2003 and with this I enter a new world. There are people here, rooms where they chat, subjects to talk about, places to meet. It's exciting, arousing, compulsive.

I wonder who else has joined? For hours, I sit typing in names to the 'Member Search'. I am able to find Julian Hamilton-Peach from Stirling University, and Douglas Adams, writer of *The Hitchhiker's Guide to the Galaxy*. Well, I don't know if it's him for sure, but I send him an e-mail anyway, saying how much I enjoy his work.

In the early hours, I tiptoe to the master bedroom, which is where I sleep alone, and quietly pull the door closed behind me.

Suits
1995 Age: 32 Hong Kong

In July, I have to go to Hong Kong for the first time ever, with some client staff from Minneapolis. In order to bond with them, I voluntarily fly Economy Class. We leave Minneapolis on Saturday morning, fly to Seattle and then have a twelve-hour flight to Hong Kong. Crossing the International Date Line, we come into Hong Kong on Sunday night, so I spend practically the whole weekend in 57H. Aircraft landing in Hong Kong fly very, very low over the apartment buildings – I can almost see into people's homes.

We reach the Sheraton at about 9:00 p.m. I agree with the exhausted clients that we will meet in the lobby at twelve noon to go to the office, and we retire for the night. My room is comfortable and has an excellent view of a construction site.

I awake early the next morning and swim in the rooftop pool of the Sheraton, taking in Hong Kong's fabulous skyline, in the brilliant sunshine, under a clear blue sky. I reflect that this is a dirty assignment, but somebody has to do it. I enjoy an exquisite buffet breakfast in the Sheraton restaurant, consisting mainly of smoked salmon which I pile shamelessly on to my plate, since I want to get my money's worth. Despite my best endeavour, I'm sure that the hotel still manages to make a profit on my meal.

After breakfast, I set out to explore the vicinity of the Sheraton. Hong Kong is an exciting and vibrant place, with people of all cultures shoving and pushing past each other. I establish the location of many restaurants which the clients and I must frequent in the days to follow (*what else is a consultant expected to do?*), as well as a large air-conditioned shopping mall. My last assignment for the morning is to find a tailor shop. I go into a few and have preliminary discussions, but nothing really feels right. It's interesting that most of the tailor shops in Hong Kong are run by Indians, although the actual tailors are Chinese.

I am walking down Hankow Road in Kowloon, having passed the *Bottoms Up Club* featured in the James Bond film *The Man With The Golden Gun* (a fact that is now proudly displayed on the outside, although that film was made over twenty years ago), when I come upon *Anukay Tailors*, with a bearded Indian man standing outside. Careful not to let on that I am an eager buyer just looking for somewhere to stretch my credit card, I pause to look in through the window. It is a narrow but long shop, and from floor to ceiling the walls are covered in rolls of fabric.

The proprietor invites me in with an enthusiasm that is impossible to resist. I enter and observe under the glass counter row upon row of business cards, mostly from western corporations, many from IT companies. There is one from Unilever Internal Audit in London, although the name is not one that I recognise. The tailor invites me to take a seat on a stool, and then goes through an amazing sales routine that involves twisting and crumpling and stamping on a piece of cloth, and then showing me how it has refused to crease, which is true. There isn't a wrinkle in it.

He shows me his order book full of orders from people in Europe and the US, and letters of recommendation from around the world. I am beginning to succumb.

I have the intention of buying *one*, dark blue business suit but, after I have selected that fabric, he is able to persuade me to choose a second (a blue/grey) and, after that, six business shirts in a wrinkle free cotton/silk fabric with my initials stitched on the pockets.

He measures every single one of my dimensions (one particular dimension has become worse than I have let myself believe) and he asks me to return for a fitting the next day.

I return to the Sheraton, shower, dress in a suit and meet my clients in the lobby at noon. I ask them what they have been doing. They have just gotten up. They ask me what I have done this morning, so I tell them. They look amazed at how much I have achieved already.

The next day they all come with me to observe my fitting ceremony, in which the lining of my suit is fine-tuned to fit me precisely, and the day after that my two suits and six shirts are ready. I try them on and they are superb. Inside both suits are labels which read: *Specially made for Mr. Imran Ahmad 7051*.

The dark blue suit becomes my instant favourite, and I wear it to many important meetings that I attend.

Suzanne Vega
1995 Age: 32 US

I love being alone in America, on an extended business trip. Being away from Sabrina, the sense of freedom is intoxicating. Spring is coming to Minneapolis, and I enjoy working with my clients at Honeywell – they have become friends.

I spend the late evenings in my hotel room, going to chatrooms on CompuServe. It's compulsive…

… Samantha tells me on the phone that she's faxing me the requested picture of herself. I stand anxiously by the fax machine in the office, to intercept it. (Obviously, to any casual observer, I must be receiving some dull administrative document from Touche Ross in London.) It comes through and I take it back to my desk. It's a group shot, taken at a company training course. It's black-and-white and the resolution is dreadful. I can barely make out the people. She tells me that she's in the back row, second from the right. I can just make her out – I think she looks like Suzanne Vega. *I love Suzanne Vega!*

Samantha and I talk for hours on the phone every evening. I recline on the sofa, with *Star Trek: The Next Generation* playing on the television, and experience paradise on earth – the joy of communicating with this amazing woman, who thinks I'm wonderful too and really appreciates me. We talk about our lives and how we've led them.

The American way is that you go to college to study something you really enjoy; date some people to get an understanding of relationships and personality types (and validate your sexual preference); get a job; share an apartment with a friend; date some more people; enhance your understanding of relationships; save some money; do an MBA; date some more people; get a really great job in a major corporation; get your own place and establish a life and independence; then, and only then, begin to consider if you might like to settle down with someone; then give it a try before you commit to doing it legally and permanently, if at all; and children – they can wait until you have significant financial assets.

The Muslim or South Asian way is that you study subjects which are respectable, but not necessarily the ones you enjoy or have any natural aptitude for, and then, as soon as you get a job – before you even have a chance to know if you're any good at it or if it's really what you want to do for a career – you get mortgaged and married and reproduced, so that by the time you have any faint glimmering of who you really are and what you might want to do in life, it's too late. You are set in concrete. You can only dream of what you might have done, how it might have been. (It's even worse if you are gay.)

This is a magical day – the day I'm going to meet my destiny of true love and personal fulfilment (and great sex, for sure). I leave the office a little early; I've told my clients I'm visiting an 'old friend' in New York City. I'm trembling with excitement and anticipation as carefully I drive the rental car, which Deloitte & Touche has given me, to Minneapolis-Saint Paul International airport and leave it in the multi-storey parking garage. I check in to Continental Airlines just like an ordinary person – not a business traveller – carrying only my meticulously packed Touche Ross holdall. But the 'ordinary' life of America – where I am guaranteed the right to pursue my personal happiness – is just so wonderful. *How lucky they are here – do they know that?*

The flight is slightly annoying. I have an aisle seat, and there is an arrogant looking American man, perhaps my age, sitting next to me, wearing shorts. He keeps saying 'Ta' to the flight attendant, instead of 'Thank you', as if he's trying to speak impressive, cultured British English. But who the hell says 'Ta' these days? – and that was never cultured anyway.

The flight attendant offers us a soul-less cheese roll, wrapped in plastic. I hesitate, thinking that I want to be in my best condition when I meet Samantha and don't want to risk undesired abdominal turbulence, but my usual greed for sensuous pleasure triumphs and I take the roll. It's like being on drugs. Afterwards, you wonder why you did it (I imagine that's what drug users think).

All the usual clichés apply as I wait impatiently to exit the plane at La Guardia airport – my heart is pounding; I'm out of breath; I'm hot; nervous with excitement and joy. This is too good to be true. At the gate, I take a moment to visit the restroom, to splash cold water on my face and comb my hair. Then I take up my Touche Ross holdall – with its distinct, prestigious logo – as if it's my knight's shield, and I stride out into the terminal, to meet my true love.

It doesn't go quite as I expected.

There's an escalator which takes arriving passengers down into the area where people are waiting to meet flights. I stand perfectly still and composed (stomach pulled in), holding my Touche Ross bag (which clearly identifies me) with great poise in my right hand, surveying with an apparent (but fragile) confident dignity the waiting crowd in the arrivals area – who are all looking up at the passengers descending on the escalator. There's an African-American family (clearly waiting for their grandparents who are immediately in front of me); an old white couple; a frumpy white woman in a straw hat; a Korean family; a late middle-aged bald white man; a white family; an Indian family; a middle-aged white couple …

I look back and forth, with a slight sense of panic. *Where's Samantha? Maybe she's not here? Maybe she didn't come?* My eyes run over all the waiting people. The frumpy woman in the straw hat is looking towards me and smiling. *Surely not at me?*

I try not to look concerned as I realise the awful truth, and I smile with fake joy – but all I want to do is run back *up* this 'down' escalator and back to Minneapolis and back to my old, flawed-but-comfortable life, which wasn't so bad after all.

In the limo to New York City, which she has arranged, I'm sitting next to her in an apparent state of euphoria – trying to mask the mutual tension which we are both feeling – but my mind is running over the Instant Message exchanges, trying to recall what was said about weight and build. And how did I get it into my head that she looked like Suzanne Vega? *She doesn't look at all like Suzanne Vega.*

Her apartment, only a few blocks from Times Square, is wonderful, cosy, Parisian. There are shelves of intelligent books, tasteful ornaments, a clean kitchen, the sound of the city coming in through the open windows. It's incredibly erotic … except that it isn't.

I'm an awful, awful person. I'm a really shallow man, no better than all the other shallow men. I had no problem communicating with this woman when in my mind she was really attractive – but now that I see her, I can't get past her skin to the inner beauty, intelligence and spirit. I just see someone I'm not physically attracted to. *I'm an awful person.*

We pass the weekend civilly, talking somewhat, and she takes me around New York City. We visit the World Trade

Centre; it has many escalators. We eat sushi and walk in Central Park. We do the things friends do.

On Fifth Avenue, Samantha tells me something strange and uplifting.

'Imran, America needs people like you. American corporations are desperate for talent like you, and American women are crying out for men like you. You don't have a mean bone in your body.'

I'm enjoying this trip; Samantha (and America) are radically shifting my perception of myself.

In another, more abstract moment, she says, 'Imran, you are going to go through life meeting women that will make you wish you were divorced already.'

The weekend draws to an end and I fly back to Minneapolis, feeling emotionally and physically drained. I think I walked all over Manhattan.

Eden
1995 Age: 32 Minnesota

Honeywell offers me a job and full relocation to Minneapolis. We were not expecting this; it comes completely out of the blue. We have really been enjoying our trips to America and have found it all very eye-opening. But this is a big decision. I consider whether I really want Aleena to grow up in America, and not go to Lady Eleanor Holles School.

We evaluate the implications of living in America. One of these is that we can live in a really BIG house, which Sabrina really wants to do. She buys a big, thick, illustrated book entitled '50 Best Places to Live in America'. By looking through real estate newspapers she finds a new residential development for us to look at. It's in Eden Prairie, a planned city which has very recently grown out of the flat prairie lands bordering Minneapolis. In the development, the builder sells you a parcel of land and then builds on it a house to your specification. You choose the basic model of house that you want and then add all the optional extras which customise the house to make it your own, including the colours and finish.

We look around the showhouse, which is cheap by London standards. It has five bedrooms, four and a half bathrooms, a formal living room, formal dining room, family living room, family dining room, massive kitchen, playroom, study, cinema room, laundry room and triple garage. Sabrina asks the salesman if they have any bigger houses for us to look at. I can see her mind working overtime on the interior design possibilities.

Where will the money come from? I'll just get an enormous mortgage, of course – which means that I will always be under pressure to earn a high salary under great stress, while in a miserable marriage. But surely living in a big house with three garages will make me happy.

Sheep
1996 Age: 33 San Francisco

I'm sitting in one of the many restaurants at Oracle Corporation's magnificent headquarters beside San Francisco Bay. Mike Wilson, my colleague from Honeywell, and I are here on a training course. Not only are the sunshine and sky magnificent, as always in this area, but there is a confident, upbeat energy around Oracle headquarters, about the future and technology's role in defining it. Mike and I are discussing the American economy, and this allows me to practise my well-thought-out rant about how it all doesn't make sense.

It goes like this.

When I was in Unilever, we were taught the following. You invest some money in a business that has a viable proposition, by buying shares to give it startup funding. The business makes a product or provides a service – adding value in some way – and generates an honest sustainable profit. You get a return on your investment by being given a share of the profit in proportion to how much money you invested – through a dividend. So, if you buy a share for $100, you might consider an annual dividend of, say, $10 to be a good return.

But some people decided that this was not good enough. They wanted *more* money, *sooner*. They found a different way of making money – by selling the share on the *expectation* of a higher share price in the future. They had to find someone who would buy the share from them, for a higher price than was originally paid. And the buyer is acquiring the share on the expectation that he too will find someone later who will buy the share for *even more* money. And that person will buy the share because he thinks he will be able to sell it to someone else for even more money. And so it goes on …

But what has this to do with the company adding value and generating a genuine profit? *Nothing at all.* The company itself, and what it does and how it's doing, have become detached from the share price – the ticker symbol has acquired a life of its own. Information about the company can move the share price, and that information may be about future growth. The actual value adding activity of the company is no longer how the shareholders make money – it's through the movement of the ticker symbol.

So now we have a herd of sheep all moving together in the same direction, driving the share price up and up, sometimes steadily, sometimes like an out-of-control rocket.

But then some of the sheep start to pull away from the herd and, if we look closely, we see that they are not sheep, but wolves in sheep's clothing. They sell their shares and drop out of the herd, going back the other way. As more of the sheep notice this, there's a panic and the herd stops its concerted drift and falls apart. Now the share price is dropping, and the wolves are making money on the way down, as well, by 'shorting' the stock – making commitments to sell shares at a fixed price at a fixed date in the future, fully expecting that by that time the market price will be even lower.

The wolves make money when the share price *moves* – up or down, they don't care, as long as it moves. They buy and sell the same shares within a day, an hour, a minute, even a few seconds – riding the waves of movement, using superfast computers to predict the behaviour of each wave, each herd of sheep. By encouraging the masses to participate in this game – by making them believe themselves to be shrewd, informed and responsible investors – the wolves make money from the sheep. Some of the sheep do make money sometimes, of course – this is necessary to keep all the sheep interested.

Any piece of news or information can be used to move the ticker symbol, one way or the other, and through the movement, the wolves can make money.

This is not investment. The market value of the company generates money which isn't real, because it has no foundation in the growth of true value – one hundred bags of wheat have not become two hundred bags of wheat.

The tragedy is that even if a healthy company continues to make a profit in difficult times, that is not good enough. A profit which is lower than the previous year's figure deflates the stock price. So-called 'investors' lose imaginary money, even though the company has a healthy business model and continues to generate genuine value. The 'market' determines how well the company is doing, based on factors predominantly outside the company's control. So, the CEO panics, because he's measured on share price performance, and the company announces lay-offs, which will result in cost savings – which he hopes will move the share price upwards, because that will show he's doing a good job.

It's madness and it could collapse at any time, and the wolves will still make money when it does …

And a greater tragedy is that this *growth*-based model of 'making money' drives further out-of-control consumerism, pollution and depletion of the Earth's resources. There is no profit unless we consume *more* than we did last year.

But every executive and senior employee in America is getting rich on stock options right now – the value of shares in companies like Dell has increased literally a hundred-fold. I could get rich too, the same way.

What I don't say to Mike is that I feel very strongly about this, because of how un-Islamic it is. It is completely *haram* to make money simply by moving money, without creating any tangible value. People who dig raw materials out of the ground, who make useful things, who transport goods, who teach children – these are all creating or adding value. But people who just trade pieces of paper to make more and more theoretical money are dragging us all into a grand illusion – and I know that one day it will all collapse. But for now, it means that farm workers growing food for us all to consume live in abject poverty, whilst bankers trading in paper assets without doing anything useful enjoy lives of enormous and conspicuous wealth.

I feel uncomfortable that I'm a part of this system, when I know it's wrong, but I don't want to think about it too much.

Mike disagrees with me completely. I know that he is a shrewd investor and is making loads of money.

Windstar
1997 Age: 34 Minnesota

Weekends in our enormous house in Eden Prairie are bittersweet. Any extended period of time in which Sabrina and I are together carries a high risk of conflict. However, if Aleena (now four-and-a-half years old and articulate) is with us, we are able to function as a family, and I love this time. Aleena is the only reason why I work such long hours in stressful situations, in which a 'highly experienced' management consulting team with hardly any practical expertise in Oracle ERP is ripping off yet another clueless corporate client with inflatedly expensive billable hours and reckless advice, and I am conflicted between saying the right thing and loyalty to the Firm. But I need the job to pay for the house, and we need the house to provide a safe, comfortable, happy environment for Aleena. So, I keep quiet and soldier on.

Saturday mornings, we usually go to a mall and eat, loiter around, spend money. This could be Eden Prairie Mall, or Galleria in Edina, or very occasionally Mall of America – where all the tourists go. Today we are going to Galleria, in the Ford Windstar minivan – I am driving, Sabrina is upfront, and Aleena is just behind us in the middle row in her child seat.

Unfortunately, Sabrina is in an abusive mood and starts saying what an inadequate man I am, compared to the other husbands and fathers in the neighbourhood. Nothing she says actually makes any sense. For example, she blames *me* for taking jobs in which I have to travel all the time – but I need to be in this kind of high-paying job to pay the mortgage for the huge house which she wanted to buy (and in which I was complicit). Inexplicably, she mentions a particular person in the cul-de-sac whom our

Indian neighbour Dipak Shah has convinced us is racist, and says: 'She's better than you.'

My self-control evaporates as a monstrous rage erupts inside me. I cannot take it anymore – this is going to end *now*. I reach over and press the release on Sabrina's seatbelt, which slips free and retracts. The idiot says: 'What are you doing?' Then I put my foot down and the Windstar lurches forward terrifyingly. I swing from lane to lane, manoeuvring past cars, hurtling towards the next traffic light junction – which I intend to cross even if it's red.

From behind me, Aleena's sobbing voice calls out: 'Daddy, please don't hurt us.'

… I cannot do this. Before it's too late, I hit the brake and bring the minivan under control, back to normal speed. Just up ahead, there's some kind of a track leading off the highway. I pull over onto it, stop the car, jump out, run towards the woods, without my jacket, in the freezing cold – my blood boiling with anger and hatred and grief and self-pity … completely broken by what Aleena must be going through right now.

Cholesterol
1997 Age: 35 Minnesota

I read that Pakistani men living in the West have a much higher likelihood of early mortality, due to genetic factors combined with an affluent diet. Well, I'm not so sure about this. I feel in pretty good shape and I'm very fit. Milton always says that I'm one of the most naturally fit people he's ever known. I can go for months without formal exercise, and then still out run him. He says this is also due to my stubborn determination, which is quite powerful when it's turned on.

I understand what they are saying about the diet. Pakistani food is the best, but maybe not the healthiest. My mother's cooking, when I'm lucky enough to occasionally enjoy it still, is fabulous (and it's funny that I took it for granted when I was growing-up), but it is very high in cholesterol. Milton and I laugh about how he grew up on a strict and bland regime of 'meat and two veg', like most of our contemporaries in England.

Still, my father is in great shape. He looks at least ten years younger than he really is, he has all his hair and it's still black – which bodes very well for me, since baldness is significantly hereditary.

My parents occasionally come to visit from London and, when they do, I always arrange for my father a guest membership at my fantastic Flagship Health Club. He really enjoys it and spends hours there, mainly swimming lengths in the deserted indoor pool.

Left Behind
1997 Age: 34 Minneapolis

I absolutely *love* living in America, and I'm never made to feel unwelcome or a foreigner, except in a nice way, as a quaint Englishman. But I am disturbed by the high profile of 'Christian fundamentalists' and their *end of the world* philosophy.

On various television channels, preachers are interpreting global events in the context of Biblical prophecy and saying that this is the time to harvest as many souls as possible for Jesus, before the Rapture, which is coming imminently. Their *absolute certainty* (they would call it *faith*) troubles me.

Those who *believe now* will be taken away straight to Heaven at the moment of Rapture, and will never have to suffer any of the subsequent Tribulation on Earth.

Those who are *left behind*, but subsequently believe, will be admitted to Heaven when they die, but will have to suffer all the horrors that befall the Earth (war, famine, pestilence etc), as well as torture and suffering at the hands of the resolute non-Believers.

Those who remain *always* non-Believers will suffer the horrors of Tribulation on Earth, will attempt to wage a war on Jesus when He returns, will be utterly vanquished and destroyed, and burn in Hell for all eternity.

I can understand how having this system of beliefs would impact one's attitude and conduct in life. I just hope it's not true, because I would definitely not be in the first category.

Ishmael
1996 Age: 33 Mexico City

'Welcome to CompuServe.'

Religion Forum
Author: Travelin' Man
Subject: Who Was Abraham's 'Only Son'?

The issue of Isaac and Ishmael has long been a matter of dispute between Islam and Judaism/Christianity. Abraham had two sons; Isaac and Ishmael. Isaac was the father of the Jews, Ishmael the father of the Arabs. Abraham's wife Sarah had not borne him a son, and was not likely to, so she gave him her slave girl Hagar, who bore Abraham a son, Ishmael. About thirteen years later, Sarah produced Isaac.

Ishmael was thus the first-born and Isaac was born second.

There is no disagreement on the facts stated thus far.

The Bible says that God asked Abraham to sacrifice *Isaac*, whereas in Islam we believe that it was *Ishmael*. The Islamic belief is that the story was deliberately altered with the insertion of Isaac's name to elevate his status over that of Ishmael.

For a long time I have grappled with this issue. I am uncomfortable being asked to believe by Islamic advocates that the Bible story has been distorted in such a fundamental way. But all I have to do is study the Bible to see the answer.

In the Bible, God asks Abraham to sacrifice 'your son, *your only son* Isaac….'

Later, when God cancels the order, He reveals that he was only testing Abraham.

'By myself I have sworn, says the LORD, because you have done this, and have not withheld your son, *your only son*, I will indeed bless you, and I will multiply your descendants as the stars of heaven and as the sand which is on the seashore.'

When one reads this, it is another point scored for Islam. It is so obvious that Isaac was *never* the *only son* of Abraham, whereas Ishmael was his *only son* for thirteen years, before Isaac was born. Reading the text with an open mind and a critical eye, it is obvious that the name Isaac was deliberately and blatantly inserted after the *only son* reference, even though it is fundamentally illogical.

Furthermore, God says that he will reward Abraham for his willingness to sacrifice his *only son*, by blessing him and multiplying his descendants. The arrival of Isaac by Abraham's *proper* wife Sarah is most obviously this blessing. Because Abraham showed willingness to sacrifice his *only son*, Ishmael, born of a slave girl, God was pleased and rewarded him with *another son*, Isaac, born of his actual wife.

The more one studies Islam, the more sense it makes.

Number
1997 Age: 34 Minneapolis

I finally join Ernst & Young in Minneapolis, after a long recruitment process and some hesitation caused by another job offer (from KPMG).

Whenever I submit a timesheet or expense form, I need to enter my four-digit Ernst & Young employee number. I haven't memorised it, so I keep asking my secretary to remind me what it is.

Then one day it suddenly dawns on me that I don't need to keep asking her; I always have the number on my person. Two years earlier, my tailor in Hong Kong thoughtfully placed it where I could easily refer to it, on the labels inside my suits, which read: *Specially made for Mr. Imran Ahmad 7051.*

Halal
1996: Age 33 Mexico City

'Welcome to CompuServe.'

Religion Forum
Author: Travelin' Man
Subject: Halal Meat

There is a lot of confusion over halal meat, because some Muslims insist that (as with kosher meat) pre-stunning must not be applied before the animal's throat is cut. Halal and kosher slaughter are thus considered to be cruel and to cause unnecessary suffering.

I can only speak for halal, but I believe that the same principles may apply to kosher.

The true meaning of halal meat is that the animal is treated humanely. It lives a good life, is looked after, kept in pleasant conditions, and – when the end comes – it is so sudden and swift that the animal had no idea it was going to happen. It shouldn't even see the very sharp blade, distracted perhaps by being given a piece of fruit or some other treat. The carotid artery, the jugular vein and the windpipe are all swiftly cut, so that unconsciousness from the sudden drop in blood pressure follows in moments. All the blood is drained out, as Muslims do not eat blood. To seal the process, it is ritualized with a blessing in Arabic as the cut is made.

Another requirement is that the animal must be perfectly healthy when slaughtered and shows no negative symptoms.

The Western industrialized process for slaughtering animals is hideous and barbaric – driven by our insatiable appetite for consumption and profits driven by growth. We have to process as many units as possible, and more this year than last year. In this system, the animals are lined up and they *know* what is happening; they can smell the blood and sense the terror of those animals ahead in the queue.

Bizarrely, many Muslims accept this process as halal if the blessing in Arabic is recited at the moment of slaughter. The ritual becomes more important than the humane process. This is often the case with people who hold narrow-minded, 'fundamentalist' religious views – the ritual becomes more important than anything else, rules supersede values.

In the normal Western process, the animal is pre-stunned, by a variety of methods. Some Muslims (and Jews) reject this, because the stunned animal is no longer healthy *at the moment of slaughter*. So, a literal and rigid interpretation of the need for the animal to be healthy (obviously intended to prevent consumption of diseased meat) is applied to reject pre-stunning.

Anti-halal activists then denounce the halal process as cruel, because there is no pre-stunning and so the animal suffers unnecessarily. The perception is that the halal process is cruel, whereas the entire *intention* of halal is to be humane. (They should remember that the method was formulated before there was any electrical killing technology.) Even Salman Rushdie gets it wrong – his 'Muslim' background is a little blurred. In *The Satanic Verses* he states that Muslims believe that the animal must die slowly to allow it to reflect on its own life. This is completely untrue. The animal must die as quickly as possible!

In reality, it is the Western industrialized process which is cruel, and the pre-stunning is intended to make the already traumatized animal suffer just a little less. This process can *never* be halal just because the Arabic prayer is recited – regardless of whether pre-stunning is used or not.

So it's *only* organic meat which has the potential to be halal, with animals living a good life and then being dispatched swiftly and unexpectedly, and not in a barbaric queue. Whether the Arabic is recited or not is less important than the rest of the process. So I believe that organic meat with no Arabic blessing is actually *more halal* than industrialized meat with the Arabic blessing.

Some Muslims will denounce me as not a proper Muslim for saying this.

It is impossible for the organic process to be applied to the huge volume of meat which needs to be produced – the real problem is that we humans consume far too much meat.

Dallas
1997 Age: 35 Dallas

I'm in Dallas for two days of recruiting interviews for Ernst & Young. I am known as one of my division's most active Oracle recruiters – always willing to travel wherever the interview sessions are being held. This is indicative of my selfless dedication to the success of our Firm.

In reality, I travel as much as possible to get away from Sabrina's endless verbal abuse and the utter chaos of our home environment. Each hotel room becomes my *home* – predictable, clean, tidy, ordered. And, as an executive business traveller, I get a certain level of respect which I am not given at home. It is horrible being away from Aleena – but being at home for too long always leads to some form of tension which inevitably causes an explosion of some sort. That is worse for Aleena to deal with than her father being absent.

I cannot help but associate Dallas with the television series of the same name. A series with so many unattainably beautiful women that it set my blood on fire when I was a teenager and continued to do so throughout the wilderness of my marriage. I check in at the Omni Hotel this evening and proceed up to my elegant, tidy, deliciously cool hotel room – the faint hum of the ventilation system providing a soothing calmness of sorts. Of course, the very fact that I'm in a hotel also makes me restless with that bittersweet longing that burns deep within. I long to hold a beautiful woman in my arms, to kiss her and taste her and inhale her. It's been nearly two years since my last intimacy, and that was in Hong Kong. Now being in a luxury hotel in Dallas is unbearably erotic.

I can't help it. I start looking through the phone book. Prostitution is illegal in Texas, but massage and escort agencies clearly are not. I've looked in phone books before, even made a call to inquire — but I've never actually gone through with it.

There's no shortage of advertisements for escorts and private massage. Arbitrarily, I select one and make the call, fingers trembling. A man answers, very matter-of-fact, and takes my hotel name, telephone number and room number. He says that one of the ladies will call me shortly.

The phone rings and it sounds like a young woman with a delightful-but-not-too-heavy Texas accent. I deliberately play up my British accent, which will help to convince her that she's lucked out with a real gentleman tonight. We both skirt around the subject of what service will be provided – she mentions 'dancing and conversation'. It is somewhat bizarre that I would pay 200 dollars cash for these services in my hotel room, but it's clear that she's as worried about entrapment as I am about soliciting illegal services.

I do ask her to describe herself and she says that she is 'blonde and real pretty'. Well, that sounds okay.

Imagining a lingering erotic experience as if in a movie, I run the bath with hot water and plenty of scented foam, and lay out the two white towelling bathrobes from the closet.

The knock on the door comes about thirty minutes later, just as I'm on the phone to Sabrina, checking in as usual. I hastily say that room service has arrived, close with the ritual 'love you', and hang up.

I'm relieved to see that she is slim and attractive, but my delusion that she would follow my directions of getting into the bath and using the robe soon evaporate. She takes charge immediately. After counting the cash, which I've put in a hotel envelope, she orders me to undress and sit back on the bed, the pillows propped up behind me. She herself undresses to her underwear, and then kneels on the bed beside me, at the same time issuing a clear directive that I am not to touch her with any part of my body, including the lips and tongue.

She then makes small talk while indifferently massaging my male member with one hand – *are you married? what do you do? where do you live?* Of course, I'm not married, and I live in England. I would rather not be having this conversation, which detracts from the desired eroticism of this interaction.

She does have attractive breasts, which are a few inches in front of my face.

'Will you take your bra off?'

'If you tip me.'

'How much?'

'Fifty dollars.'

My silence is indicative that I don't want to commit any further funds to what is proving to be a disappointing and very poor value experience. I had wanted to hold a woman in my arms, to embrace and kiss her – and that's clearly not going to happen. But nor can I complain to any authority in Texas (consumer rights, perhaps?) about this poor customer service.

Her cell phone rings and she stops to answer. It's clearly a call checking on her location and well-being. As her attention returns to me, bizarrely she asks me if I came (which I thought would be self-evident) and then resumes to get me there as quickly as possible … so that this nightmare can end for both of us.

When it's over, she goes to the bathroom and it's almost an insult how long she spends washing her hands. I remain on the bed, not daring to move. She returns, throws me a hand towel, gets dressed quickly and is gone with barely a word.

I feel like such a fool. She got 200 dollars cash from me to make me feel unsatisfied and humiliated, and of course there's absolutely nothing I can do about it – *this is Texas!*

During the night, I lie awake hot and sweating. This is Texas. What if the police come? If I'm arrested, it will be the end of everything – my job in Ernst & Young, the work visa, cash flow, Aleena's education and well-being. I feel sick to the stomach at the stupidity of what I have done.

When morning comes without a pounding on the door, I consider myself very fortunate. I can't wait to check out and get away from here.

Conversations
1997 Age: 35 Minneapolis

In a bookshop in Galleria mall, I pick up a copy of a book called *Conversations with God* by Neale Donald Walsch and I skim through it. It makes me so angry. These are transcriptions of his alleged conversations with God, conducted in such a casual manner. He talks to God, and God talks right back. *Who the hell does he think he is?* Weren't Moses, Jesus and Muhammad good enough? Did God forget to tell us something and He needed to converse with this man, many centuries later? Who would believe this nonsense? How does it even get published?

Here is another stupid, gullible, greedy individual who is participating in this global masterplan of Satan's to keep people away from worshipping only the One, true God. He's either making it up, getting it from his own subconscious, or getting it from Satan. Both Islam and Christianity would agree on this. This is evil!

Hey, Neale Donald Walsch! I know a great way for you to have a conversation with God for sure. It requires a few bullets.

Billable Hours
1997 Age: 35 Minneapolis

There's news of the Imation project, the one which I was 'concerned' about. It has overrun by many months and many millions of dollars. The 'go live' is rescheduled to next year. It was so obvious to me that this was going to happen. *Why was I the only one who could see it?*

There is a dark side to my time at Ernst & Young. I seem to keep finding myself in these situations where people really don't know what they are doing, but they will never admit to this. (Everyone is afraid; there is always so much at stake.) There seems to be little genuine knowledge of Oracle software, or of the principles of software package implementation, including the fact that you should avoid modifying the software if possible. The clients don't understand this either, of course. Exactly the opposite seems to be what happens. The clients request endless changes, and the consultants don't argue; they are happy to oblige, generating many billable hours of revenue in the process – but leaving the client with a system which will be expensive and clumsy to maintain, forever. (Of course, we use relatively cheap Indians to write the customisations, but charge them out at high rates.)

My problem is that if I express my honest opinion about what is really best for the client in the long term, it will result in less revenue for the Firm, and the client may not believe it either, because I'm the only one saying it. This makes it impossible for me to function effectively. I analyse the situations earnestly, then end up not rocking the boat for E&Y, but also not really driving forward the process which I don't believe in. My reputation starts to get a little checkered. I obviously know Oracle well, but *do I have what it takes to be a Partner?*

Ecumenical
1997 Age: 35 Minneapolis

Idly flicking through the hundred-plus television channels we have, I come upon a smartly dressed young pastor explaining that the Founding Fathers definitely meant for America to be run as a Christian country. By 'separation of church and state', they just wanted to ensure that one Christian church did not oppress another. They would be horrified at today's trend to secularism and equality of rights for non-Christian religions in America, he says.

On another Christian channel, I see a congregation of evangelicals having a musical gathering in church. A group of teenage girls are upfront, playing guitars and singing a song that is disparaging to inter-religious respect and dialogue. It goes something like:

'Hindu, Moslem, Buddhist, Jew,

I guess they'll want the Devil too…'

The song goes on to say something like '*I know for sure that I'm going to Heaven, so I don't need any Ecumenical Movement, so you can shove it*' or words to that effect.

These people really make me angry. They are so convinced that they are right – they don't have a clue about the evidence and rationality that Islam is based on. They are going to get such a shock when they arrive in the Afterlife. And these kinds of Christians don't even show any compassion or humility – all they project is arrogance and contempt for people who don't believe as they do.

Partition
1998 Age: 35 Cleveland

One day in the project office in Cleveland, there's a sudden buzz of excitement going around. Someone just read some news on the Internet – India tested nuclear weapons today. *I don't believe it! How could they be so stupid?* This is going to get them roundly condemned by the world, and especially by America. Pakistan gets to be on the moral high ground for once. Apparently it was underground testing and it was less than 100 miles from the border with Pakistan. *That is so provocative!*

The office is full of Indians, on work visas like me. I'm the only person of Pakistani origin. I remain impassive and don't join the chatter. Even though I'm British – and I think of Pakistan as a corrupt and backward country where no one has any sense of social responsibility – when that country is threatened, it tugs at my loyalty as if it's programmed into me.

At least this should get Pakistan back into America's good books again.

A few weeks later, Pakistan completely blows it, by testing its own nuclear weapons. Like children, they just couldn't resist – they had to prove to India: *we can do it too!*

Now tensions are running high. Kashmir, the ancient problem, is rearing up again – people are spoiling for a fight.

In Eden Prairie, our Indian neighbour Dipak Shah is acting like an idiot. Being Minnesota, there are no fences between the backyards, just markers to show where the property lines are. Dipak has a community drain in his backyard. The land around is graded so that the water from our other neighbours' backyards flows across our land, joins our water, and it all flows into the drain on Dipak's property. That's the theory. But Dipak seems to object to this and builds a vegetable patch on the edge of his property, in the path of the water, and surrounds it with an impenetrable wall of concrete slabs dug into the ground. The water flows to this point and then stops – our backyard begins to flood.

I notify the United Nations … I mean the City … and their man Randy Slick comes to take a look, and then they order Dipak to remove the offending concrete slabs. I watch him from our back window as he is humiliated by having to dig up the slabs.

An icy hostility now exists between us – we ignore each other completely.

Trains, Planes, Automobiles
1998 Age: 35 Atlanta

Despite the project dilemmas, I love working for Ernst & Young management consulting. I do a variety of things for Ernst & Young: I work on projects; I perform recruitment interviews; I give training; I participate in business development. All of this involves a lot of travel. I am what the Americans call a 'road warrior' (*Gold* with Northwest airlines, *Gold* with Sheraton.) I don't mind this at all. I enjoy the travel and all the hard work has a purpose: I want to make Partner in the Firm, which will mean success, wealth and status.

For example, one typical week in June, I spend Monday to Thursday in Cleveland working on the Eaton project, and then Friday at the Atlanta office of Ernst & Young, doing management consulting recruitment interviews all day. By 4:15 p.m. we are having roundtable discussions about the candidates – but most of the other interviewers are focused on the fact that they have to rush to the airport to catch airplanes, some as early as 5:30 p.m. Of course, being a seasoned traveller, this unnecessary stress does not apply to me. I have a First Class seat on the 7:50 p.m. flight to Minneapolis, and I have not a worry in the world about making it.

After the others have long gone, I nonchalantly complete a few administrative tasks in the office I am using, until Carolyn, the (very attractive) Atlanta recruitment manager comes to get me. She has kindly agreed to give me a lift to the airport in her red convertible sports car, since she is also flying out this evening. As she weaves the car through the horrible Atlanta traffic, we are mostly discussing my exciting lifestyle (okay, I am discussing it while she is mostly just driving).

It is true that I have come to take First Class for granted. With the number of miles that I fly on Northwest, I have been Gold for four years in a row, and virtually always get upgraded to First Class. I enjoy visiting new cities, and favourite old ones like New York and San Francisco. I enjoy staying in fine hotels and eating in splendid restaurants. I impress her with my tales of the mysterious Orient, and of exciting Latin America, and she laughs when I say that the women I meet are mostly flight attendants (I don't mention being married, of course). Yes, it's a good life (and helps me to avoid the misery and tension of my domestic existence).

We have plenty of time to park the car and get into the terminal and, since my flight is an hour after hers, I have plenty of time to join her for a drink. Once she is on her way, I stroll down to my gate to check in. I always have an e-ticket, of course. A quick flash of my Minnesota driving license and a smile and I'm all done. My luggage is a model of efficiency as well. An expandable leather attaché case has my laptop computer inside, and my clothes and toiletries fit snugly inside an elegant green sports bag with our company logo.

I note with approval that the airplane is at the gate, always a good sign. Generally, if there is no aircraft at the gate, it is an indication that one won't be leaving for at least a few minutes. I line up to check in … and am told by the gate agent that, because of bad weather in Minneapolis, the crew has not yet arrived. In fact, they have not yet left Minneapolis. This means a minimum three-hour delay. I consider offering to fly the plane myself, since I flew Chipmunks (and an elastic-launched glider) with the Royal Air Force cadets in school, but I assume that this offer would be ungraciously declined. Actually, flying a Chipmunk is harder. These modern pilots don't have to do anything except read scripts to each other and check lightbulbs.

I sit in the gate area and wait. I observe the 150 people waiting with me; fellow travellers across the sea of life. A couple of hours pass. Then the gate agent makes an announcement, and all hell breaks loose. The flight is cancelled, and we are individually going to be re-routed, and none of us will get to Minneapolis tonight. A queue a mile-long forms at the gate, for re-routing, whilst every telephone in the vicinity is taken. More ominously, people are staking out seats on which to spend the night.

I telephone the Gold Line on my cell phone and secure my favourite seat on the 8:45 a.m. flight tomorrow morning. They give me the telephone numbers of airport hotels to call. Since this delay is weather-related, the airline is not responsible for overnight accommodation.

But wait. Before I book into a hotel, don't I need Bruce's permission (as my Director), according to all those new expense guidelines? It is Friday evening, but I have his home telephone number. Should I call him at home to ask for approval for this unexpected expense? What if he says NO?

I observe a late-middle-aged man stretched out on a row of seats, already sound asleep, his luggage laid out around him. This is not looking good. What about the security of my computer while I am asleep? I figure that I can secure it to my ankle with the security cable. But, if I am in a really deep sleep, someone will still be able to steal it. I decide to take the initiative of booking a hotel room without troubling my Director at home.

The voice at the Crowne Plaza is attractive. She's never heard of Ernst & Young, but she is going to give me a corporate rate of $105, because I sound like a Corporate Man. I wait fifteen minutes in the Atlanta heat and humidity for the shuttle to take me to the hotel. Life is glamorous.

The face at the Crowne Plaza is attractive. I have no membership privileges with Crowne Plaza, but she gives me an executive-level room, because I'm good looking, charming and have a cute English accent (she doesn't say this, of course). I need to use my room's key card in the elevator to convince it to stop on my floor. Life is privileged.

The room is fine. It looks like a hotel room. I take a cold shower and order a room service dinner. I have a 16 oz peppered steak, with a baked potato, butter and sour cream, and a large slice of chocolate dessert. It all comes with a salad, which is good, because I like to eat healthy.

The remote control for the television does not work, so all I can watch is the menu channel. I eat my dinner listening to music from the CD player in my Dell laptop computer. I reflect that it was really considerate of my company to equip me like this out in the field. Idly, I wonder if the CD player can also read software CDs, as well as audio CDs. That might be useful too, sometimes, I think.

I finish dessert and try to loosen my belt, but there are no more holes left. I contemplate my navel and consider the dilemma of Partnership. I am doing everything possible to make Partner in my Firm, which will make me rich. In order to *make* Partner, you have to become *like* a Partner. There are two kinds of Partner in the Minneapolis office; thin Partners and non-thin Partners. Unfortunately, my Director is a thin Partner, so if I am going to be more like my mentor, I will either have to go on a diet or change Director. I wonder which is easier.

I update my expense report and put in several lines of explanation about bad weather and computer security to explain this unauthorised night of unrestrained hedonism in a luxury hotel.

The next morning, I take the 7:30 a.m. shuttle to arrive at the ticket desk in good time for my flight. It has been cancelled. Northwest gives me a ticket for Delta, and tells me to get my seat assignment at the gate and, by the way, this will not be First Class on Delta, since I am holding an Economy ticket, and my upgrade is a Northwest privilege.

On the way to Concourse B, the airport train breaks down, so we all have to get off the train and use the moving walkways. Some of these are not working, so I have to walk.

What basically depresses me (as I carry my stuff in the heat and humidity) is that not only will I not be in First Class, but I will not get priority boarding of Economy Class, which Northwest always gives me on those rare occasions when I am not in First (once this year, out of 37 flights so far). The reason this depresses me is that I will have to hurry on board to ensure overhead space for my modest carry-on luggage, otherwise it will be in front of my feet throughout the flight. The reason this is possible is because some people persist in having ludicrously large carry-on luggage. Fortunately, as a Northwest frequent flyer, I am spared from all of this stress. But to Delta, I will just be some damn upstart who 'ain't from around here'. I am going to be a regular Economy Class passenger, the prospect of which scares the heebie-jeebies out of me.

Well, there is a crowd of Southerners at the Delta gate, along with a few anxious-looking displaced Mid-Westerners. I line up at the desk and await my turn. I am attended to by a friendly man in his fifties. He looks at me: trembling, sweat on my face, terror in my eyes, my voice shaking as I explain that my two successive flights have been cancelled. He must also notice from my accent that I am most definitely *not* from around here. Then he looks at my Northwest boarding card from last night, and notes that I would have been in 1B (my favourite seat, and unmistakably First Class on any aircraft except the Wright brothers' *Flyer*), and he says, 'I'll put you in First Class.'

The flight attendant gives me *Special K* for breakfast. Is this a sign from above to guide me in my Partnership dilemma?

I arrive at Minneapolis-St. Paul International Airport at mid-morning on Saturday, and exchange greetings with the airline staff on duty. Walking through the car park, I reach into my pocket and use the remote control; my Camry's engine gently purrs into life as I approach (just like James Bond's car would).

After a tolerably short weekend, in which I am able to spend some time with my beloved daughter (but not too much time arguing with my totally incompatible wife), I return to the airport the next evening and park in the exact same spot. *It's a great life.*

Disappointed
1998 Age: 35 Minneapolis

From what I have witnessed on many of our Oracle projects, I have developed a number of ideas about how Ernst & Young can really improve its competence in this area and deliver even better client service. I write all of these in a carefully composed e-mail, a proposal of sorts, and send it to Brad Callahan, the Minneapolis Partner who heads the national Oracle practice. His reply comes back and is very promising. He would like to meet with me to discuss them.

Because of our busy travel schedules, we organise this meeting in the Northwest Airlines World Club lounge at Minneapolis-St Paul airport. We collect bagels and coffee, and settle down. Brad launches immediately into the discussion. It is not quite as I expected.

He is very disappointed with me to date. I have not been performing as he would expect from a Senior Manager. I don't have a reputation for assertive leadership – rather, for quietly plodding along. He needs to see a dramatic improvement, or my time at the Firm may be limited. All of this he conveys very sympathetically, in the nicest possible way.

I am speechless, stunned. I thought that he'd understood, whenever I'd discussed an issue with him, that I always seemed to be stuck between a rock and a hard place. In every one of these projects, the *right* thing to do for the client was the *wrong* thing to do for Ernst & Young, in terms of its revenue and reputation. Because client service is so important to us, these situations always caused me to lock up, to freeze like some piece of faulty software.

Brad tells me that when I have genuine concerns about the conduct of a project and what E&Y is doing, I *must* have the confidence to communicate these up to Partner level. (*But what if the Partner is the idiot responsible for the situation?*)

Brad is quite clear. I must make sure that on my next assignment, when I find one, I perform like a Senior Manager, like a true leader of the Firm.

I leave this meeting to catch my plane, with a deep worry inside me. He has triggered off many deeply buried anxieties. *Perhaps I really am incompetent?*

Choice
1998 Age: 35 Minneapolis

Ever since I was old enough to understand these concepts, my parents (in particular, my mother) emphasised to me that romance and love were 'bad things' (which only the white people do), and they would be taking care of my marriage, and it would be to a Muslim girl of Pakistani origin. That was always clearly understood and it hung over my life – the weight of the misery was always there. There was simply no possibility of objecting to this – it would cause a huge conflagration in our family and demonstrate ingratitude to our hardworking parents who provided everything for us. But, on the plus side, they would also ensure that I was set up with a house (and accompanying mortgage). That was a benefit that my white friends would never have.

So when I was presented with options, I chose the *best* from what was presented (reasonably attractive, father a millionaire), and she did seem like a good candidate, and I even felt the liberty of free choice. But I was fooled by the fact that I was choosing from a controlled and limited subset of the women in the world (the other candidates in the subset were woefully inadequate in every department). And as for 'free choice' – that only applied to me, not her. She didn't have free choice. She never wanted to marry me, and her parents forced her – if I'd known this I would never have gone ahead with it.

Now we are locked in this Living Hell, making each other miserable – failing to hide our misery from our beloved daughter.

I know one thing – when Aleena grows up, she can marry whoever she wants to. I don't care – it will be *her* choice. Preferably a liberal progressive white man with no primitive cultural baggage. (And with a good degree and a proper job – not a hippie.)

Feather
2000 Age: 38 London

It seems like everyone in the UK is watching *Who Wants to be a Millionaire?* It's exactly the same as the show I used to watch in the US, except that it's in pounds instead of dollars, of course. Everyone plays along to see how far they can get; everyone dreams of being on it. I phone the number occasionally, to apply. Eight-year-old Aleena gives me earnest advice: 'Daddy, if you get to half-a-million and you don't know the answer, then *walk away ... walk away*!' She seems anxious that I would foolishly take a risk and drop back down to only £32,000. I have to pay her school fees and college expenses for years to come.

I discuss the show with Milton. Apparently, there was some chap who was *sure* he would succeed at getting in the hot seat, because he found a mysterious feather somewhere in his home. He took this as a miraculous sign that an angel had been there. We both laugh at this. Some people are so ignorant, they take backward religious beliefs as literally true. The idea that Heaven is actually in the clouds and angels have feathery wings which they flap to ascend and descend between Heaven and Earth is primitive Christian imagery, and to accept it as literally true is just plain stupid. But apparently some people really do believe that a feather means an angel has visited.

Milton says the guy didn't do very well: 'I think he left with a thousand quid or something.'

We both laugh.

Survival
1998 Age: 35 Austin

Ernst & Young is bidding for the new project to implement Oracle software at Dell Computers in Austin, Texas. I really want to be involved in this, but Ridley Juergens is leading the bid and doesn't want me anywhere near it. The project involves a big effort in Europe and revolves around how the system will deal with the new euro currency when it is phased in. I offer as much help and advice as I can to the team by e-mail, but I am largely ignored.

E&Y does not win the project; it is awarded to Price Waterhouse, a rival 'Big Six' firm. But the matter does not rest there. An E&Y executive learns of this and flies down to Austin, to tell Dell senior management that if they will not use E&Y for management consulting, then E&Y will no longer feel it necessary to buy literally hundreds of Dell computers every year; it may buy IBM laptops instead. Apparently, the innocent Price Waterhouse team is suddenly asked to leave the Dell premises one day, two weeks into the project.

Now, Dell's project team responds angrily to this interference from their own senior executive level, by insisting that they will personally interview (by telephone) any E&Y consultant being presented to the project, to determine if they have the right skills and experience. This is a painful process, with all of the initial E&Y candidates being rejected for lack of experience. Eventually, for one of the key roles, I seem to be the only suitable and available candidate in the Firm who has not yet been rejected. I undergo the telephone interviews and I am accepted by Dell. Based on my meeting with Brad, this will be my last chance to prove that I am a competent Senior Manager.

The E&Y team members fly to Texas from all corners of the United States and assemble at a hotel in Austin. The Principal in charge is Lucy Mingam, who comes from a West Coast office and has a formidable reputation within the Firm. From the outset, I am troubled by Lucy. I am not entirely sure, from what I hear her say, that she knows anything about Oracle or what she is doing – but this is the exact opposite of her reputation, so I say nothing. I have heard Partners speak enthusiastically of her.

On our first morning at Dell, we are being led to a conference room. I pass a stunningly beautiful dark-haired woman in the corridor and smile at her. She smiles right back. The initial briefing takes place and we consultants are then dispatched to meet our respective client teams, the people with whom we will be working closely. My client team has four people; *the beautiful woman is one of them!* Her name is Lucretia, and she is from Louisiana. Okay, I don't have time for any frivolous distractions; I must prove my worth on this project, or I am finished (but she *is* beautiful). I dive right into a discussion about Oracle, and the client team seems to be suitably impressed.

The E&Y team is assigned the same meeting room which was used by Price Waterhouse. Those poor guys must have left in such a hurry; their project plan is still on the whiteboard. This is an extremely tense situation for us. Because of the acrimonious way in which E&Y forced itself onto the project, the Dell project team is looking for any sign of weakness and incompetence, any excuse to have us thrown out. Our position is very tenuous.

A couple of E&Y consultants arrive from Europe: Sean Wheeler and Martin Kaas. Sean is an American, from Connecticut, but he actually lives in London and works for E&Y's London office; Martin is from Denmark. I pick them up at the hotel one morning, after they've flown in from Europe, and we go to Burger King for breakfast. We become good friends. Sean and I, in particular, have a connection. It's subtle and intangible, but it's clearly there. We are energised by each other's presence and cannot stop talking.

At Dell, the E&Y team is doing okay, except for the one person who counts the most. Lucy Mingam continues to say things which make no sense – both to us and to the client. We hear about a disastrous private meeting between Lucy and the client's project manager. Lucy was asked questions about the project approach and apparently she was clearly making up her answers, spinning things and weaving painfully tangled webs as the client challenged some of her responses. We hear about this from other members of the client team, not from Lucy, obviously. A dark cloud of anxiety hangs over our E&Y team.

I am deeply concerned and do some investigating. Lucy's previous project was at a client in California, and apparently the E&Y team had been thrown out. A Senior Manager was blamed, rather than Lucy herself.

From a discrete and secluded conference room, I call around a few people who had been on that project. One of them agrees to speak, under condition of anonymity. E&Y had been thrown out because of Lucy; she was completely clueless and made the firm look totally incompetent to the client. But she had saved her ass by spinning the blame on to the next person down, a Senior Manager. The Partners had believed her, because she has this amazing reputation, and that poor guy got the axe. Lucy had bullied all other members of the project team, using their Performance Reviews as a threat; if they did not support her, she would screw them in their Reviews.

I hang up the phone and absorb what I have just heard with a deep sense of foreboding. *Exactly the same thing* is happening on this project. E&Y is on the verge of being thrown out, because of Lucy. And the next most senior person, the only Senior Manager here, is … *me.*

We, the E&Y team excluding Lucy, have secret meetings at which we air our concerns and worry about what to do. We are all on the same page: Lucy Mingam is clueless; the client can see it; Lucy is going to get us thrown out. There will be fallout within the Firm (and guess who will take the brunt of it and be fired for sure?). I am totally stressed out.

One afternoon, I am conducting a client meeting, talking with them about Oracle, when Lucy comes in and asks me to accompany her. She takes me to a private room, where Tom Kramer from E&Y is sitting.

She says, 'Tom is concerned about how I'm running the project, and he says that you agree with him.'

I am totally unprepared for this. *Gee, thanks Tom.* I am forced to say that I do share his concerns: that there are some things which she has said and done which are questionable, and that we can all see that the client is also raising an eyebrow.

Lucy is visibly angry, but we conclude the discussion, as I must return to the client meeting and Lucy has to head out to the airport, to attend a company meeting in California.

It is a relief for us all when she is not on-site. Sean, Martin and I agree to meet for dinner, at 7:30 p.m. in the hotel lobby.

In the evening, at 7:26 p.m., Lucy calls me in my hotel room, from California. She is subtle, but not subtle. She reminds me that she will be doing my Performance Review for this project, advises me bluntly that she won't do anything to hurt my career, *if I do nothing to hurt hers*, and says, darkly, 'I would hate to see you leave the Firm.'

I join the others a few minutes late. It is a beautiful, hot evening in Austin, and we drive downtown to the very lively Main Street, which is bustling with students and young people, many of them extremely attractive women, of course. We have a table on the roof of a Mexican restaurant, enjoying the sights and sounds of the street below; there is a pleasant breeze to lighten the heat.

I say barely a word. There is a dark foreboding in me, a realisation that this is yet another situation which is not my fault – but I have to deal with it, and the most likely outcome will be a personal disaster. I will seem incompetent. There is no way that my reputation can survive such a hit – I will be fired. It's even worse for me; I'm a foreigner in the US, with a work permit that allows me to work only for Ernst & Young. Even if another employer is willing to offer me a job, they would also have to be willing to sort out the paperwork for my new H1B work visa. This can take weeks, months even. We could be deported. What about the house, and Aleena's education?

I dare not say a word to the others. This is an extremely volatile situation. Lucy has already found out once from Tom that I have been guilty of disloyalty. I can't say anything about this

Sean challenges me: 'You're extremely quiet, Imran. You haven't said a word all evening. That's not like you. What's up?'

How transparent am I? There are two options: keep it to myself or share it with my friends. Suddenly, I choose the latter. On the roof of the Mexican restaurant, I spill the beans! I tell them everything! *What a relief.* They are shocked and supportive; *this is war!*

This is an incredibly difficult situation. I have to deal with Lucy, a dangerous loose cannon and, at the same time, keep E&Y from being thrown out by the client. The consequences of failure do not bear thinking about.

Over the next few days, there are a few incidents. Lucy leaves me a voicemail message, copied to a Partner, and in it she offhandedly attributes blame to me for a staffing conflict which was absolutely and unambiguously her fault. She is doing what she does best, spinning blame. I let Sean hear the message. He is staggered: 'That's a real shot across the bows.'

Lucy operates in a way that is alien to me. She is like the worst kind of politician – everything is spin, spin, spin. Always trash the other party, make yourself look good, with every breath. I find this enormously difficult to deal with; I always think about what is best for the team – the extended team, the consultants and the clients together. But this is a deadly situation and, to survive, I must be more like her.

On another occasion, Lucy has the entire client team in a meeting room and is demonstrating something about Oracle on the whiteboard. It's complete nonsense; she's making it up as she goes along. Obviously (to me), she knows *nothing* about the software. The client team don't know this, but they are very bright; they will see the inconsistencies later on and will conclude that the E&Y consultants are completely clueless. I have no choice – I must act. I go to the front and speak to Lucy in a low voice. I say that I have already prepared a training course on this subject, and I can deliver it to the clients on Friday, when she is away – this is not a good use of her valuable time. Lucy is relieved that she doesn't need to remain on the spot now and agrees that this is a good idea.

Being in charge, she tells the clients: 'I've asked Imran to deliver this training to you on Friday.'

Lucretia goes for a business lunch with me one day. There is something that she wants to tell me. The Dell team is very disappointed by Ernst & Young so far. The Firm has not shown the clear expertise and leadership which Dell is expecting. We are on very thin ice now. This is a delicate situation, but I do what I think best. I tell Lucretia that many of the E&Y team share her concerns, and that we request that the Dell people do not treat us as a unified whole – but consider the value which they are getting from each team member individually, and act accordingly. If Dell wants to take action, we strongly recommend *focussed* action, rather than general action. In fact, we would be very supportive of that! I think that she gets the message – I can see it in her face. The spicy Chinese chicken is delicious and, if this was a date, I'd be the luckiest man alive.

I provide outstanding client service, and so do the rest of the E&Y consultants. They gravitate towards me as the only Senior Manager, and the true leader of this team; I become a shadowy alternative to Lucy's irrational command. Word is getting around the Firm that something is not right, and the Partners are beginning to hear about it. Lucy, now in a state of panic, buzzes around the project like an angry wasp trying to find a way out of a glasshouse.

Sabrina gets Aleena to leave me a voicemail message one evening. Aleena's cute five-year-old voice says, 'Don't worry about your job. We love you and we will always support you.' It's wonderful, but it won't pay the bills.

One day, it finally happens, *thank God.* Lucy is asked to leave the project. The client communicates this to the executive level in E&Y, and a Partner calls Lucy to tell her that they want her off the premises. Lucy is like a raging bull – but she has not a leg to stand on. The client management has conveyed that they are *entirely happy* with the rest of the E&Y team, and a Senior Vice President even tells Brad that *Imran's contribution*, in particular, has been outstanding. *What a relief! I am not incompetent.* It's almost too good to be true.

The project takes on an upbeat, almost festive atmosphere after this. We fly to Austin on Sunday nights, work hard at the client, have wonderful dinners in the evening, fly home at the end of the week. These are halcyon times.

Later, I hear about Lucy's latest spin. Apparently, she said that the Dell people were completely irrational, that the client's project manager was impossible to work with, that she tried to lead them in the right direction, but they were stubborn and clueless. Her Partners on the West Coast tell her not to worry; with her amazing reputation, it can't be her fault. Clients are often unreasonable; these things happen sometimes.

Brad does my Performance Review and it is brilliant. It is all 4's and 5's (on a scale of 1 low to 5 high). I even get to hear, from more than one Partner, that on the Dell project I have been described as 'the glue that held it all together'.

But most importantly … I survived.

Sabbath
1996 Age: 33 Mexico City

'Welcome to CompuServe.'

Religion Forum
Author: Travelin' Man
Subject: Which is the Sabbath Day of Christianity?

Which is the Sabbath Day of Christianity?

According to the Bible, the Sabbath Day is the seventh day, Saturday, which of course is the day still observed as such in Judaism.

How did the Christian Sabbath get changed to Sunday? It's not in the Bible. It was ordained by the Church of Rome, as a demonstration of the Church's absolute authority.

Of course, if the Bible is the absolute, infallible Word of God, then such changes made by Man have no authority. Some Churches acknowledge this and observe Saturday as the Sabbath. Others just ignore the issue, unable to contemplate that Sunday isn't the special day; what a huge upheaval that would cause.

According to some theorists, those that observe Sunday as the Sabbath will receive the mark of the Beast, in the End Times, and are not candidates for being saved in the *Rapture*. They will be *left behind*, along with the rest of us Heathens.

Lucretia
1998 Age: 35 Austin

At Dell headquarters, the lovely Lucretia and I often converse freely, and she recommends that I read *The Celestine Prophecy* by James Redfield. I go to Barnes & Noble in Austin to buy *The Celestine Prophecy*, and the woman at the sales counter raves about it.

I take the time to read it. The book has some interesting concepts, talking about synchronicity, energy fields and holistic living. It postulates that mankind is going through a process of accelerated spiritual growth that is happening right now. It's not Islamic, but it's not particularly un-Islamic, so I guess it's okay. However, its overall significance and the context are completely lost on me.

In another conversation, Lucretia also mentions Deepak Chopra. She says something about Chopra writing that Religion is how the Devil keeps people *away* from God. (*Well, that's true of course, except in the case of Islam.*)

I think: '*Deepak bloody Chopra, that bloody charlatan faker. He comes from India with that Hindu mumbo jumbo nonsense and these ignorant Americans buy into it, because it seems oh-so exotic. I hate Deepak Chopra!*'

However, Lucretia is too breathtakingly beautiful for me to say any such thing, so I just mumble something non-committal.

Trees
1998 Age: 36 Minnesota

One day in October, I am planting fruit trees in my backyard in Minneapolis, when my new neighbour comes to speak with me. He starts raving about the company he works for, Whittman-Hart, Inc, and how they need someone like me to build an Oracle practice in their new Minneapolis office. We talk for over an hour. I am really not interested in joining any other company, as I love working for Ernst & Young – but he insists that I should at least consider the opportunity. He asks me if it's okay for a recruiter to call me and, out of politeness, I say, 'Sure.' I'm in a hurry to finish the planting; my legs are being attacked by mosquitoes. I was supposed to get these trees into the ground by evening, before catching my flight back down to Austin to get to Dell.

The recruiter does call, but it's not me that she calls – it's Sabrina, at home. For about one-and-half hours, she talks to Sabrina about what a great opportunity this is, how I would be a great person for the role, how family-oriented Whittman-Hart is and, most importantly, how I wouldn't have to travel every week – my work will always be around Minneapolis. By the time that I get home, Sabrina is selling me the job.

I have meetings with Whittman-Hart, and there is one thing that does catch my attention: the *stock options*. There are so many people in America today getting really rich with stock options – why should I be left out? If I become a Partner in Ernst & Young, I will be wealthy … but that is a big *IF*. These people are offering me huge stock options *now*.

I am hesitant, but one thing clinches this. Sabrina sees an analyst appearing on CNN Financial, who is asked what her number one stock recommendation is. She says, 'My number one stock pick is a company you've never heard of, but it will be a household name in two years' time. It's called Whittman-Hart, Inc.'

I accept the offer, but it takes Whittman-Hart three months to sort out my work visa. I continue with E&Y at Dell during this time. The project is challenging and fun, the team dinners are enjoyable, the camaraderie is wonderful. To have colleagues and friends in one package is a joy. Many times during these three months, I cannot believe that I'm really going to leave my beloved Ernst & Young. But the work permit finally comes through in March, and I tell Brad that I'm resigning from E&Y. I never thought that this day would come – that I would resign voluntarily, when it's finally going so well. I have a heavy heart, but it seems that this is the logical thing to do. The day that I leave Ernst & Young I am deeply sad, but I'm going to become *very rich* in Whittman-Hart.

I start with Whittman-Hart, which does seem a very upbeat place, but it goes downhill almost immediately. I discover on the first day that my neighbour 'left the company' during the time my work permit was being processed, but never told me. The recruiter leaves the day after I join, presumably after collecting some kind of hiring-target bonus. The branch manager is fired ('pursuing other opportunities') very soon after I join.

Within two weeks I realise that I have made a big mistake in joining Whittman-Hart. I had been suffering from 'grass is greener' syndrome. Whittman-Hart is an illusory company, built on a tissue of hype and spin. The Minneapolis office is in deep despair. The Yahoo! site has a whole board conveying the message of what a terrible company Whittman-Hart is, and of how miserable people are there. Some of these posts allegedly are written by current and past employees. I wish I had seen this *before* I left E&Y! The alleged stock options and bonuses are all theoretical and completely unattainable (therefore a lie), due to the company's unrealistic revenue targets. This is a body shop (programmers by the hour), without much credibility or strategic commitment. There are some decent people here, but executive management is running a house of cards.

A few weeks after leaving Ernst & Young, I go to see Brad again. He is as amenable as ever. I tell him that I made a mistake, and that I would like my old job back. He is extremely accommodating. He tells me not to worry, he will take care of it, *and* he'll match my current pay, since I was due for a pay rise anyway. He says to leave it with him; he'll sort it out and will give me a call.

I leave his office with a great sense of excitement and relief. *I made a mistake, but it's going to be fixed, thank God.*

A couple of joyful days later, I get his voicemail. It's not quite what I expected. The executives of the Firm have just announced a hiring freeze on Senior Managers, except for those with a strong sales history. Since I'm not really a sales person (I'm a project delivery person), there is no way that he will be able to convince them to rehire me, especially as it will require an H1B work visa, and they are clamping down on those as well.

I am completely gutted. I hate working for Whittman-Hart.

But I'm stuck. I can only work for a US company that really wants me enough to get me an H1B work visa. I cannot move jobs freely in the US. Worse, my H1B status can only last until 2001. If I haven't got a Green Card by then, I cannot work again under H1B status until I've been out of the US for 365 days. Ernst & Young was getting me a Green Card, but I surrendered that process when I quit. Now Whittman-Hart is working on my Green Card (allegedly) and it *should* come through before the deadline in 2001. But if it does not, we would have to leave or be deported.

The worst part about returning to London in 2001 is that we would have missed the opportunity to get Aleena into Lady Eleanor Holles School. She would have to start in September 2000, *if* she was going to go there. If we miss that date, she'll never get in.

We love America and want to become citizens eventually. But my options are limited: stay with Whittman-Hart until we get the Green Card and get settled in America permanently (and Aleena remains happily in the International School of Minnesota), or my next job must be back in London (and we have to get there in time for the school).

There is no job waiting for me in London; we sold our house there (and the London property market is now out of control again); we made a huge investment in living in America. We don't have a choice. I *have to* stay with Whittman-Hart, although I hate it.

Kathleen, the new branch manager, is very attractive (and single), but somewhat implacable (and clearly under pressure). She expects me to cold call companies on the telephone, to try to sell them Oracle consulting services. This is unbearable; it reminds me of a long, hot, summer years ago, when I was selling worthless advertising on the telephone. It wasn't supposed to be like this. They told me before I joined Whittman-Hart that I wouldn't have to sell, that our professional Account Executives were the sales people, and they would bring me the hot project opportunities. I was only supposed to manage the staff and make sure that the projects were delivered to the satisfaction of the client. It was supposed to be fun.

My little Oracle unit is not making its revenue targets. I have hired some good people, but it's a struggle to get them billable work. The consulting market has just taken a dive; no one is starting any major new projects this close to the year 2000, with its potential computer problems. That's why there was so much work a few years ago; everyone was getting the new systems in *before* 2000. Now, no one will have a project in progress over the turn of the century; they want to see what happens with the so-called 'Y2K bug'.

Sure, I'm at home a lot now – not travelling every week like I was in Ernst & Young – but paradoxically that makes me more stressed and unhappy, as Sabrina and I are forced to spend more time together.

The prognosis in my new job is not looking good. What happens to senior people whose business units don't reach their revenue targets?

Norman Keith, who got me into Ernst & Young, calls me out of the blue and asks if he can help me with another move. I tell him: 'Norman, I'm really only interested in working for an American company with a job based in London. Otherwise, I'm staying where I am.' (I don't give him a long explanation about H1B work visas, Green Cards and 365-day exclusion periods.) Norman is completely US-based, so there's nothing he'll be able to do.

I try to convince myself, brainwash myself, that Whittman-Hart is fine, and will do well, although the signs are otherwise. But I have no choice and will continue on this path.

I even use a form of Islamic rationalisation. In Islam, planting trees (and especially fruit trees) is officially a good deed. I remember something like the Prophet said that planting trees was one of the roads to Paradise. Man is responsible for the Earth and is supposed to take good care of it (although this doesn't seem to be on the agenda of any so-called Islamic government). Well, I joined Whittman-Hart as a direct consequence of planting fruit trees, so no harm can come to me because of it. My motives were good, and God will look after me.

It's a tenuous hope, given what I see going on around me.

Knives
1999 Age: 37 Orlando

Tired of the relentless heat of the Orlando theme parks, we have ended up in a shopping mall – which is welcomingly cool and less frenetic. Sabrina and Aleena are in a shop somewhere, while I am wandering about by myself.

I come upon a large concession stand with many glass cabinets – I stop and stare, mesmerised, fascinated. In the voluminous and illuminated glass display cabinets are many collections of knives. I never imagined there were so many kinds of knives, so many sizes and colours: serrated, vicious, terrifying.

If I had such a knife, Sabrina would never dare to speak to me as she does, never dare to be so abusive. I imagine her yelling abuse at me and then the look on her face as I pull out my knife ... *the look on her face!*

Any normal man would have killed her by now. She is lucky that I am a decent, rational, gentle man who cares about his daughter – she doesn't appreciate that she could never get away with her behaviour with a regular man. She is so full of self-importance and superiority because of her *faux* wealthy family, and too stupid to realise that this pretension no longer has any credibility.

One of these exquisite knives would put an end to her abusive arrogance. (Angry men with guns kill their wives every single day in America.)

But I know that I cannot do this, because the whole point of persisting with this miserable existence and fake marriage is to give Aleena a safe and secure upbringing in a loving family and a comfortable home – a happy childhood.

Sabrina always ensures that divorce cannot even be *discussed* in a calm and civilised way, without dragging Aleena into it and making her aware of what is going on.

And when Aleena throws herself around me and pleads, 'Daddy, please don't talk about this', I totally crumble.

Sabrina appears out of nowhere and finds me staring at the knives. I can see from her face that she knows what I am imagining.

Q
1999 Age: 37 US

My *Platinum* status at Northwest Airlines is in jeopardy. In 1998 I easily accumulated the necessary 75,000 actual flight miles to reach this new status, making *Gold* seem very passé. But in 1999, things are looking dire, because I don't travel as much with Whittman-Hart as I did with Ernst & Young. It is already December and I am about 3,000 miles short, leaving me with the prospect of facing the New Millennium as only a *Gold* member.

I have no further business trips planned for 1999, so I decide to make a personal one. I buy the cheapest ticket that I can find for a long distance trip that involves a Saturday night stay (to get the lowest rate) and will provide the necessary miles. This trip is Minneapolis-to-Seattle return and costs around $400; not a lot to pay for the benefits of being *Platinum* for another year, including 125% bonus miles and being upgraded ahead of the *Gold* and *Silver* people.

So, on the cold, dark evening of Saturday, December 18th, 1999, I drive my Camry to Minneapolis airport, park in the usual area, check in with no luggage, and head off on the last flight to Seattle, which leaves at around 9:00 p.m.

I have a few peanuts and some apple juice on the flight, sitting in my usual 1B, in a mostly deserted First Class section.

We arrive at Seattle Airport around 10:00 p.m. local time, and I go to the World Club lounge, which is where I have my 'Saturday night stay' – around three hours in total, sipping coffee and juice, and eating nuts and cheese.

At 1:00 a.m. on Sunday morning, I am again in 1B, heading back to Minneapolis. First Class is even more deserted this time.

Yes, my life as a Frequent Flyer is extremely glamorous and privileged.

I arrive in Minneapolis at around 6:00 a.m. – the airport is as quiet as I have ever seen it. I walk back towards my Camry, remotely starting the engine with the control in my pocket (just like James Bond in *Tomorrow Never Dies*).

Very tired, I reach home and crawl into bed around 7:00 a.m., sleeping soundly.

I have a vivid and poignant, bittersweet dream.

'Q' from the James Bond films is there with me, and he is saying goodbye.

I ask: 'Does this mean that I'm not going to see you again?'

He nods and says, 'Yes, this is *goodbye.* You won't be seeing me again.' And with that, he disappears slowly into a hole in the floor, via a descending platform, just as in *The World is Not Enough*, when his parting advice to James Bond is: 'Always have an exit strategy.'

I wake up around noon and reflect on this dream. It appeals to my ego, because I was clearly in the role of James Bond. I have always admired 'Q', although he has never appeared in a dream before. I often watch old James Bond films like *Goldfinger* and I admire Desmond Llewelyn's acting – marvelling at the fact that he seems 'old' in *Goldfinger* and that was nearly 40 years ago. His appearances in the nineties in *Goldeneye*, *Tomorrow Never Dies* and *The World is Not Enough* are superb. He has kept himself and his talent in good shape.

The next morning, at the office, I check the news on the BBC website, as usual.

Desmond Llewelyn was involved in a very severe car crash on Sunday afternoon, in England. He was seriously injured and was airlifted to hospital, where he died at 5:20 p.m. local time.

5:20 p.m. in England would have been 11:20 a.m. in Minneapolis (Central Time), about forty minutes before I woke up.

The significance of this never leaves me and I am deeply touched by it, whatever the mechanism involved.

Did he actively take a moment to say goodbye to me, while he was passing over and I was in the dream state that allows us to be receptive to information from beyond our material world?

Or was it a more passive interconnectedness that exists between everyone that allowed my subconscious to know what was happening, somewhere else in the world?

Either way, there wouldn't have been many people in the Western world asleep at that specific time and I am grateful that I was, in order to experience this extraordinary and very uplifting synchronicity.

But this is also slightly confusing because, according to Islam and Christianity, dead people are *asleep* until the Day of Resurrection and have *no interaction whatsoever* with the living – there's nothing mentioned about them getting some free time before the long sleep.

As it turns out, a couple of weeks later we make a trip to London just before New Year, which gives me more than enough miles to reach the *Platinum* threshold before the deadline and makes the Seattle trip unnecessary in retrospect. But I am very glad that I made that trip.

Girl-Child

1996 Age: 33 Mexico City

'Welcome to CompuServe.'

Religion Forum
Author: Travelin' Man
Subject: Treatment of women in Islam

The pre-Islamic Arabs treated women very badly. They had a preference for male children, so if a baby girl was born and was unwanted, it was common to dispose of her by burying her in the sand.

Islam not only condemned this barbarity (and threatened severe punishment by God for it), but actively pushed an agenda of women's rights and respectful treatment that was unprecedented in the world at that time.

And when the girl-child that was buried alive is asked,
For what crime was she killed?

The Qur'an 81: 8-9

The Prophet was unpopular among his people because he challenged everything.

Unfortunately, the behaviour of (some/many) Arabs today regarding the treatment of women is completely contrary to the spirit of Islam at the time of the Prophet.

Rushdie!
2000 Age: 37 Minneapolis

In a Barnes & Noble in Minneapolis, I pick up a copy of *The Ground Beneath Her Feet* by Salman Rushdie and start reading it. I am compelled to buy it. The story is wonderful; it's complex and captivating. Rushdie is a brilliant and intelligent writer; he wields language and imagery breathlessly.

Surely there aren't many people who can understand this fully? It has so many diverse references and requires knowledge of English, French, Latin and Hindi. *He must have written it for me!*

And have you seen his latest woman? She's gorgeous. It's true: the best women prefer men with brains! It doesn't matter what they look like.

Brussels
2000 Age: 37 Europe

On my first trip to London in my new job with GE, I fly there overnight by Northwest Airlines and, laden with luggage, take a cab to my new office near Piccadilly Circus.

This evening I am to head to Brussels on the Eurostar train that runs under the English Channel, for some meetings about a project that is based there. I have a few hours to settle in to my desk in London, so I give Sean Wheeler a call, to tell him that I am now back in England. (He is still with Ernst & Young, based in London.) Sean is happy to hear from me, but tells me he is heading for Brussels this evening. I burst out that I'm going there too.

'Where are you staying?' he asks me.

I check my travel itinerary, which my new (and invaluable) administrative assistant Emma has prepared for me.

'It's a place called the Montgomery Hotel.'

'That's where I'm staying,' replies Sean, implausibly.

We meet for dinner this evening in Brussels. There is so much to catch up about and this is an *amazing* coincidence.

Penny
2000 Age: 38 London

The stock price of Whittman-Hart, now improbably renamed marchFIRST, continues to slide steadily downwards, from 60 dollars to about three cents (a 'penny stock'), over the course of this year. By the end of the year it ceases trading and the company collapses. I have lost a huge investment.

There is an on-going accounting scandal over dubious practices of inflating earnings by invoicing related companies for services not yet provided.

My dream of becoming wealthy in America through stock options had actually been a complete delusion.

Thank God (and Norman Keith, the headhunter) that I was hired by General Electric – which moved us back to London in time for Aleena to get into her excellent school. That was nothing short of miraculous!

India
2001 Age: 38 Hyderabad

I routinely travel from London to Connecticut on business, always staying in the Stamford Sheraton. The programme I am running in Europe is going reasonably well, but there is an unexpected development. GE Capital Corporate wants me to get involved with our new software division in India. I'm not at all happy about having to make a trip to India (I have never been there).

Besides my natural contempt for people who worship many false gods and believe in reincarnation, there is also the problem of India-Pakistan relations. There has been much Indian oppression in Kashmir, the Muslim-majority state that was supposed to have joined Pakistan at Partition. I have heard stories about both Kashmiri freedom fighters and Pakistanis (who have been visiting India for some reason) being taken away by the authorities and subsequently being killed in what the Indians call 'cross fire' incidents. This is their thin excuse for extra-judicial execution. Both countries recently tested nuclear weapons, there have been cross-border clashes in Kashmir, and India-Pakistan tensions are running high.

I know that I have to go there, but my attitude is hostile. We may have to work together, but I don't have to *like* them. I am expecting hostility from everyone, as they will know that I am a Muslim of Pakistani origin. Muslim Pakistanis and Hindu Indians can tell each other apart on sight – don't ask me to explain how.

Of course, the Indian embassy in London immediately kicks back my business visa application; in my British passport they can see that my place of birth is Karachi and they demand to see my Pakistani passport. The Indians don't want to acknowledge me as British, *the bastards*, clinging to tribal identities. I have to write them a respectful letter, stating that I don't maintain a Pakistani passport, and I'm going to India on business for *General Electric.* It makes me sick having to be so reverential, but I can't allow this to interfere with my career – GE would see me as a less effective employee if I cannot visit India, where it has so many operations. The visa is grudgingly granted.

The GE travel system offers me the lowest fare to Hyderabad, which involves an eight-hour layover in Mumbai, during the late night and early morning. I refuse to take this option. Sitting around in an Indian airport overnight would leave me extremely vulnerable and exposed. I insist on taking a more expensive direct flight.

From the moment of my arrival in India, everyone I meet is wonderful and friendly. The Immigration Officer is cheerful and welcoming. The hotel desk clerk at the Taj Residential welcomes me warmly and gives me an upgrade (despite the fact that she can see from examining my passport that I was born in Pakistan). Everyone is warm, friendly and *human.* This is an enlightenment for me. Since childhood I have dehumanised India, but I did not know the people personally. I assumed that they would be hostile to me. But now these wonderful people are treating me with such open, joyful, friendly humanity, that I cannot continue to view them with cold hostility, no matter how much I think that I should. Of course, I'm still uncomfortable about their religion, but it seems that we can put that aside in our daily, human interactions. I begin to love India. I'm quite sorry to return to London.

But Hinduism is still nonsense. Islam and Christianity are the only contenders for the one true religion (and it all depends on who it *really* was that gave the Qur'an to Muhammad — Gabriel or Satan).

Shoes
2001 Age: 38 London

My parents come to visit us one day. Inexplicably, my father does not remove his shoes in the hallway as we all habitually do, and then I watch in horror as he enters the living room and unexpectedly walks over my pure Chinese silk carpet. *Pure*, in the sense that no shoe had ever been on it. I am angry and upset. I always loved running my hands over the smooth, sensuous silk, knowing how pure it was – and now shoes have defiled it.

I berate my father. *How could he do such a thing!* He is taken aback and hurt. He asks why I keep it on the floor then. But that is not the point, I respond. In our culture, we never wear outdoor shoes inside the house; *why did he suddenly choose to do that now?*

I take the rug away and gently wipe it with a damp cloth, cleaning it of the invisible, *imaginary* dirt that is on it now. But it will never feel the same again; I will never again delight in its joyful purity, knowing that shoes have been on it. I find myself thinking angrily of my father every time that I lay eyes on that carpet.

Towelheads
2001 Age: 38 London

Monday September 10th is an exciting day in General Electric. The new Chairman, Jeff Immelt, is finally taking over the reins from the legendary Jack Welch, who has run GE for decades. There is to be a global all-employee meeting to launch this new era. I gather with Duncan, Claire, Hayley, Dawn and James, and we walk – in a leisurely fashion on this lovely day – to the Sheraton in Piccadilly, where a vast room has been booked. The meeting itself is shown on a big screen, with a live satellite link to New York.

It's very upbeat and enjoyable. The new Chairman is young (compared to Jack Welch), dynamic and optimistic. He reminds us that GE is a world leader in energy, healthcare, financial services, aircraft engines, transport and many other things. This is the best place to have an exciting global career in the 21st century. The future looks very bright. I feel very smug and upbeat – everything turned out great for me after the nightmare of Whittman-Hart and the dot.com crash.

The next day, I'm in the Strand office as usual, working on whatever I feel like, as usual. This is the best working life I've ever known – Heaven compared to Internal Audit Hell. Soon after lunch, Hayley mentions to me that there's some news about an aircraft crashing into the World Trade Centre. I look at the BBC News on the Internet. The story is there, but it's very unclear. *This is just a light aircraft, isn't it?*

We watch the horror unfold in the Boardroom, on the big television screen, with the discreet speakers pumping out surround sound – as if we're at the movies. It seems surreal. Claire puts her hand over her mouth, as I've noticed she does when she's uncomfortable. A young woman from Finance sobs. Duncan, the most senior person present, a sort of corporate father-figure, maintains a quiet dignity. My heart is heavy, my mind is racing around. There's a sickening inevitability in my gut that this is going to be about 'Islamic' terrorists. As the story progresses, I am thinking in many directions. This is a disaster for the world. How will it affect us all? In particular, I'm thinking, '*How will this affect me?*'

The train home is totally sombre, almost silent.

I walk in the front door and Sabrina says, provocatively: 'Why are you so glum?'

Trying to contain my rage at the utter stupidity of this ignorant imbecile, I reply: 'Because of what happened today.'

Inexplicably, she retorts: 'It doesn't affect us.'

I swear, if there was a gun in the house, I would shoot her now.

There's a young American woman named Christine who works for me. She was not in the office on Tuesday, the 11th. She comes in on my birthday, September 13th. I ask her if she is okay and she says that she is fine. (I don't think that she blames me personally.)

The tragedy continues, beyond the terrible loss of life on the day. This one event has caused the gates of stupidity to be flung open, and people all over the world are rushing headfirst into the 'tribal trap'. Dehumanisation, anger and hatred run riot all around the globe.

Many in Third World and Muslim countries seem to rejoice, as this is 'one in the eye' for the country they blame for all their woes. They may have good reasons to be resentful (some US foreign policy has been selfish, hypocritical and self-defeating for decades), but there is no excuse for the dehumanisation that is necessary to applaud this tragic event. Some of these people have no concept of what actually happened that day, in human terms. And why are they so quick to forget US humanitarian intervention in Bosnia, Somalia and countless other places? It isn't *always* about oil.

Americans are at a loss. Why would anyone do this? How could they do it? *Why do they hate us enough to be willing to die killing us?* Most Americans are compassionate people; many are generally unaware of some of their many Administrations' foreign policy errors. America was always so friendly and laid-back; there was no concept of hostility like this. The hijackers took advantage of this easy-going attitude – so unlike the fear, darkness and paranoia that grip their own countries.

There is a dilemma here, over which I have no control. On the one hand, Muslims around the world apparently are not doing enough to condemn the atrocity. On the other hand, to do so would imply an element of responsibility, of connectedness to Islam – whereas this was not an Islamic act, regardless of what the perpetrators and their opportunistic masters claim so cynically. But the very implication of Islam in this is enough to get crowds in a frenzy on both sides; all intellects are cast aside.

There are many worrying news stories, although given the size of the United States, I try to comfort myself that these are relatively insignificant in number.

In Arizona, a Sikh gas station owner is shot dead, his murderer believing him to be Muslim. Of course, there's an outcry, *Sikhs are not Muslims* – the killer was ignorant and stupid. The bizarre logic inferred from this is that it would have been a lesser crime, more understandable, if the victim *actually was* Muslim.

In San Antonio, Ashraf Khan – holder of a Green Card, Frequent Flyer status and a First Class boarding pass – is on the first leg of a long journey to his brother's wedding in Pakistan, when the pilot of the Delta Airlines flight forces him off the plane, because he does not feel safe flying with him. This particularly disturbs me; that could have been *me* on that flight. I worry about my next business trip to the US. Joyful anticipation has turned to fear.

The pilot's attitude is not about safety. It's about needing to exact vengeance in some way. This desire for group retribution, and assigning of collective guilt, is one of the lowest forms of human behaviour, and a betrayal of American values. It's what happens in primitive and savage places, surely not in America.

Shakespeare describes this in *Julius Caesar*. After Caesar is murdered by a number of conspirators that include Brutus and Cinna, a crowd goes in search of retribution. They come upon *Cinna the Poet*, and even though it is patently clear that this is not *Cinna the Conspirator*, they lynch him, trying to find any justification to do so, because he shares a name with the true culprit.

The Internet is teeming with hatred. On the message boards of America Online, Yahoo!, and other places, the postings could not be any uglier.

Now we should NUKE Mecca Mavrik700
Make 'em eat pork! PatriotEd
Great new toilet paper - the Koran! BradTx
Kill all the towel heads MikeinNC

And these postings can be read all over the world, so the hatred and the fury are being fuelled even more.

This is not the America I know and love; the America I feel great elation at visiting. What the hijackers have done goes beyond the murder of several thousand people. They have hurt the lives, the attitudes, of hundreds of millions of people. They have turned America from joy to fear. And that fear is being pushed around the world and multiplied into a paranoid frenzy.

As information about the hijackers is slowly released, Islam is dragged through the mud and it is open season on Muslims and the Qur'an, seemingly a deadly threat to civilisation.

Apparently, some of the hijackers were looking forward to the 72 virgins they will get in Paradise, for being martyrs for Islam. I am outraged, but unheard. This is all nonsense; it's not in the Qur'an, it's part of the body of Arab tribal culture and superstition that has been wrapped around Islam and it is degrading to our faith. But it's plausible that some of the gullible and brainwashed hijackers actually really believed this, and the non-Islamic world is led to think that this is authentic Islam.

The Christian fundamentalists are having a field day. Now they can attack Islam and the Qur'an as much as they want, and no one objects. There is much talk of horrible verses in the Qur'an, urging war on Christians and Jews. I feel like I've been through this before. It's the inability to distinguish between immediate tactical advice, and eternal spiritual guidance. The early Muslims were a vulnerable group, often struggling to survive against hostile clans, idol-worshippers, tribes nominally Jewish or Christian. Sometimes they were forced to be at war, and sometimes they were advised to make peace. The Qur'an directed them strategically in the most expedient way, just as books of the Bible directed the Jews in ways to ensure their own survival. Interpretation in context is required; not everything is to be taken as literally true and eternally binding.

But it's also true that many Muslims are unable to make this distinction, confused about what Islam is, and without access to a Qur'an that they can understand, so it's hardly surprising that non-Muslims think this really is Islam.

Whenever a fundamentalist Christian quotes these war-like verses on television, I am infuriated that no one answers back with verses from the Bible: directions to *slay every man, woman and child* in a particular town; instructions to stone your own children to death if they exhibit unruly drunkenness; *Psalm 137* extolling the joy of smashing your enemies' children against the rocks. No one mentions these at all – not even Muslims who are forced to defend and explain the Qur'an's selected horrible verses.

My personal experience of post 9/11 intolerance is limited, thankfully. I'm in my car one morning and have a slight disagreement with an on-coming van driver in a narrow road. I actually say through my open window, 'I'm not interested in having an argument', and his idea of abuse is to call me a 'typical Middle East person'.

Madrid
2000 Age: 37 Madrid

I make a trip to Madrid on business for GE. The Iberia aircraft lands and taxis to a position away from the gate; we will be transported to the terminal by shuttle buses. It is sunny and very hot when I step out of the aircraft, onto the top of the staircase. I'm sure that it must be 91 degrees. I descend the steps and stride to the nearest bus.

I'm standing in this bus, waiting for it to fill up and depart, and I'm looking casually at the other bus parked a few yards away. Sean Wheeler is on that bus! It's definitely him. I grab my cell phone and turn it on. It takes a few moments to come to life and a few more agonising moments to find a local network. I retrieve his cell phone number and dial it. He answers and the look on his face is priceless, as I ask him whether he is in Madrid, whether he is at the airport, and whether he is on a shuttle bus, waiting to get to the terminal. He looks all around and sees me waving from the other bus.

We meet after passport control and chat for a few minutes. We are not able to organise dinner on this trip (our itineraries will not allow it), but this is an amazing coincidence.

Puddle Jumper
2001 Age: 39 US

It's October and I'm on my first trip to America since 9/11. I fly Delta to Atlanta, spend one night in the airport Sheraton, and then head for Connecticut and check in at my favourite Sheraton there. I spend a week in Stamford, and then have a few days back in Atlanta, visiting GE Power Systems and staying in the nearby Sheraton Galleria.

American flags are everywhere, but people are still nice to me. I ask directions of a middle-aged woman driving a car draped with US flags and *Proud to be American* stickers, and she is as friendly as can be. She doesn't look at me as if I might be a terrorist. I don't feel as if I'm being singled out or treated with suspicion in any way, anywhere, apart from one incident on the trip from Connecticut back to Atlanta.

I'm taking the 6:00 a.m. flight out of White Plains airport. Because of 'enhanced security measures', everyone has been told countless times to check in at least two hours before the scheduled departure time of any domestic flight (and three hours for international ones). After leaving the Sheraton Stamford in pitch darkness and being driven through the charming Connecticut countryside to the small local airport that is White Plains, I am the first to get in line at 3:50 a.m. A few people arrive and queue behind me, but no one shows up to open the desk until 5:00 a.m., only an hour before the flight. This really doesn't prove to be a problem; since 9/11 many US airports have gone eerily quiet and this flight has only ten passengers.

The aircraft is relatively small, with about fifteen rows of seats. Despite the flight being at only about 15% of full capacity, I have been placed next to someone. I want some space to sleep, so I wait until all the passengers appear to have boarded, and then move forward to an empty pair of bulkhead seats. The youngish African-American flight attendant immediately challenges me, asking me what my seat number is. I tell her and make a show of settling down comfortably (and harmlessly) in the two empty seats, resting my head against the window in an obvious bid to sleep. She goes to the cockpit and I hear her telling the pilot that I have moved from my assigned seat. He nods, looks back at me, but doesn't do anything.

I'm spending the weekend in Atlanta, before my business meetings during the week. I rent a car and explore some of the backwaters of Georgia and South Carolina. I definitely feel like I would be somewhat out of place in some of the communities which I drive through, with their countless pick-up trucks and gun-racks. From what I've heard in some media reports, some of these people may shoot me on sight as a suspected terrorist. (Now, I'm becoming paranoid.) Minneapolis, where I lived for five years, was quite a cosmopolitan place.

This trip to the US goes well. I never feel any hostility towards me, except for that slight suspicion on the puddle jumper.

Lucid
2001 Age: 39 Milwaukee

For my meetings at GE Healthcare, I arrive in Milwaukee and drive a rental car to the Sheraton. As I walk down the corridor to my room, I pass a door from behind which I can hear a woman gently moaning in the act of making love. Hotels are such erotic places, and hearing the woman just reminds me of how miserable and barren my life is in this dimension.

I go to bed and fall asleep relatively easily, since I've just flown from London, which is six hours ahead …

… I wake up in the middle of the night. I am not in the Sheraton Milwaukee. I am in what looks like some old English country hotel, reminiscent of the ones I often stayed in when I was travelling on audits in England, years ago. Outside it is dark and the wind is howling. There are oak trees swaying severely in the wind, in what looks like an old market town. I am not asleep and I am not dreaming; I am wide awake. This is all real and lucid. I am worried, because I don't want my life disrupted in some supernatural way that I don't understand and can't control. I am not looking for an adventure in time travel or alternative universes.

There is only one way back that I can think of. I return to bed, can't sleep easily, but eventually drift off …

… I awake in the morning in the Sheraton Milwaukee. It is bright, but bitterly cold outside. I don't have any explanation for what happened and, of course, I never tell anyone.

I AM
2002 Age: 39 Gatwick

In March, I make a business trip to Atlanta and fly Northwest Airlines, in the hope of clinging to some frequent flyer status. On the return trip, I fly out of Minneapolis to Gatwick overnight and I have a bulkhead aisle seat in Business Class. When we arrive at the gate at Gatwick, I very expertly extract my attaché case from the overhead bin, weave around the other passengers struggling with their huge carry-on luggage, and quickly reach the area of the exit door.

The flight attendant here has her back to me; her attention is taken by some procedure at the door. I circle around behind her and I am standing next to her, with my back to Economy Class, when she turns around and sees me for the first time. As I move towards the door, she blocks my way and says, rather abruptly: 'You'll have to wait for Business Class to exit first.' (*'You'll have to wait for Michael Jackson to arrive.'*)

'**I *am*** from Business Class,' I retort, outraged. I wave my boarding card in front of her face and push angrily past her towards the door and onto the jet bridge.

As I stride away, I feel affronted, and yet I *know* that this is a silly little boy inside me, an *Ego* that has been offended by an honest mistake on the part of the flight attendant. She really *believed* that I was from Economy Class, because I appeared to her to have come from that direction.

Why did I have to take it so *personally*? I could see that it was an understandable error. Is my self-esteem so fragile that it hangs on the thread of my Business Class status? *What kind of person am I?* When did I become like this? I am ashamed.

Ganesh
2002 Age: 39 India

I begin to spend more time with the Indians at GE's software division, on behalf of Corporate. I've introduced them to GE Power in Atlanta and we need to demonstrate to that huge division that our new India-based service business can meet some of their global information technology needs.

In February, I travel to India again and stay a couple of weeks. As before, everyone is wonderfully warm, welcoming and human. The Indians in GE have some additional characteristics. GE prides itself on its core values: integrity, passion, energy and so on. The Indians I work with demonstrate these to the ultimate degree. They are so professional, so energised, so competent and they work so hard; they make me feel ashamed of my own laziness and occasional complacency. It is a privilege to work with them.

On Saturday morning, I fly from Hyderabad to Delhi, and check in to the Taj Palace hotel, which is hospitable and elegant beyond description. Agra, the site of the Taj Mahal, is a four-hour drive from Delhi. I have never been to the Taj Mahal, and this weekend will be my opportunity.

However, there are some terrible Hindu-Muslim riots taking place right now. There has just been a fire on a train, passing through a predominantly Muslim area, in which 60 Hindus were killed. These Hindus were returning home from a ceremony to prepare for the building of a Hindu temple on the site of the Babri mosque in Ayodhya. The Babri mosque was destroyed in 1992, by Hindu fundamentalists, who want to reclaim the site, believing that Ayodhya is the birthplace of Lord Ram. This mosque had been built in the 16th century, and some Hindus believe that a temple to Ram had originally stood on that site and had been destroyed to make way for the mosque. (India at that time had Muslim rulers, although they were in the minority.)

Now, as a result of the Hindu deaths on the train, there is rioting taking place in the state of Gujarat, and hundreds (eventually thousands) of Muslims are being killed; many are being burned to death. The police and authorities appear unable (or unwilling) to protect them. The Chief Minister of Gujarat, someone named Narendra Modi, appears indifferent (possibly complicit), ordering no discernible action to curtail the rioters.* We see in a newspaper a telephoto picture of a Muslim man on the roof of his house, his family cowering behind him, extending his hands in the prayer gesture, begging the Hindu mob below not to kill them. The caption notes that they were then burned to death. (Journalists have access to the violence, but police and army are nowhere to be seen.)

India is a huge and diverse country, so although this news is coming in and everyone is aware of what is happening, life in Delhi, as I observe it, is continuing as normal. It's as if the horrors are taking place in another world.

But I *am* affected, although in a selfish and mundane way. Because of the riots, GE issues a ban on employee non-essential travel to certain regions, and Agra is included. As this is a business trip that I am on currently, this applies

---

* Sanjiv Bhatt, a Hindu senior police officer, later alleged that he was present in a meeting at which Narendra Modi instructed that the Hindus should be allowed to 'vent out their anger' against the Muslims. Bhatt was persecuted and eventually fired when Modi became Prime Minister. Because of this apparent complicity in the riots, Narendra Modi's US visa was cancelled by the administration of George W Bush and he was denied entry to the US for ten years. Only when he became Prime Minister of India was this ban lifted, as a matter of expediency.

to me. But this opportunity to visit the Taj Mahal is too precious to waste. Without telling anyone at work, I arrange a car and driver at the hotel, and head for Agra on Sunday morning.

My driver is a well-groomed Hindu man in a smart uniform. He talks just enough to be polite, but not enough to impose on me, as I stare out of the window at the Agra Highway. This should not be confused with an American freeway – judging from the goats, bullocks and carts – but is nonetheless a good road by local standards. About halfway to Agra, we pull into a rest stop. This is a charming compound, with a number of low-level stone buildings. The 'tourist' restroom is clean, and manned by a very attentive employee, to whom I give the customary tip. This restroom has no other users when I am there; the driver has obviously gone elsewhere.

There is a peaceful, ornate walled garden, which leads to a restaurant. A central fountain provides tranquillity, and there are statues in niches all around the walls. I am alone in this garden. I stroll gently through it, and stop to consider a statue of Ganesh, the elephant-headed Hindu god who is the remover of obstacles, the god of harmony and success. He seems to be one of the most popular gods; I've seen him on many people's desks. One of my Indian colleagues gave me a ride last week and I noticed a small Ganesh stuck on top of his dashboard. This worried me a little at the time. Having an idol of a false god in your car is a sure way to anger God/Allah and to invite Him to punish you with an accident.

This is the dilemma that I am struggling with. Whatever induced these people long ago to imagine and create these non-existent gods, to give them form in statues, and then to start worshipping them, passing this reverence down the millennia? It seems utterly insane. Belief in many gods is wicked; that is a core belief of Islam, Christianity and Judaism. *There is only one God!* As a good Muslim, the morally righteous thing for me to do right now is to smash these false idols in this garden and to proclaim to all these non-Believers: 'There is no god, but the One God!' That is the rational course of action to be ultimately consistent with my system of belief. Even if the outraged non-Believers kill me, it won't matter; God will reward me in Paradise.

Even though I know that this is the logical thing to do, if I believe as I do, I know intuitively that it is *not* the right thing to do. Is this cowardice, or something else? Am I a coward, or do I not really believe? It troubles me.

And … how can someone's *belief* be evil? Actions are evil, but people believe what they think is true; how can that be evil? If Hindus believe in many gods, that is because they don't know any better. It's not wicked; it's just ignorance. It doesn't stop them being warm, kind, compassionate, generous human beings, as they always seem to me.

The One God obviously isn't happy that Hindus believe in many false gods, but does this mean that they live their entire lives without any divine assistance? That all of their prayers and devotions go nowhere, energy lost forever into an infinite void? But that's what Magnus – the Christian evangelist at university who was always trying to convert me – said about me: 'When *you* pray, there's no one listening.'

I contemplate Ganesh intently. He is expertly balanced on one leg, three of his hands are holding objects, the fourth is extended with its palm forward in a gesture of peace, and he looks good-humoured. He seems to regard me right back. *There, now I'm doing it!* That's the danger with idols and images. We lapse into revering them with consciousness, with life and with abilities. That's why God doesn't like them and warns us against idolatry.

But … Ganesh and I now have a relationship, for me an uneasy one, and it troubles me. He's still good-humoured about it. I can see it in his face.

We resume the trip and, just before we arrive at the Taj Mahal, the driver stops to pick-up a bearded Muslim man. He is to be my guide, it seems. This was never discussed with me in the arrangement, but apparently he will show me around the Taj Mahal and I will pay him afterwards, whatever amount I think appropriate. (I realise later that this is an arrangement between the guide and the driver, who will surely receive a percentage.)

It is very good to have a guide; I don't have to queue at all and he knows exactly what to show and to tell me. Many people in the West think that the Taj Mahal is a mosque, but it isn't; it's a mausoleum, a tomb. The Muslim Emperor Shah Jahan so much mourned the loss of his beloved wife, Queen Mumtaz, that he almost bankrupted his Treasury by building this Taj Mahal; the splendour and intricate detail in it is breathtaking, almost unbelievable. It truly is a magnificent structure. Where do we draw the line between love and obsession?

I express an interest in visiting a local market, perhaps to buy a few souvenirs and gifts for Sabrina and Aleena. As we are driving away from the Taj Mahal, the guide is again sitting in the front passenger seat; he and the driver are talking in Hindi.

The driver says: 'I don't work for him. My job is with the hotel. I have to get back to Delhi before it gets dark; otherwise it will be hard to drive, and the traffic will be terrible. Just tell him that the market is closed today. I will take him to a store in Delhi. I don't work for him. It's not worth my while to stay late.'

The guide glances back at me; his face conveys a flicker of concern that I may be able to understand Hindi – but I'm staring indifferently out of the window, enjoying the sights and sounds of Agra.

I don't worry about the market. If the driver thinks we should get back to Delhi, I trust his judgement. I pay the guide more than he expected and we drop him off, before heading back to Delhi. The driver was right; as it gets dark, the traffic also gets very heavy. He does take me to a very elaborate and comfortable store in Delhi, with tourist prices (no bargaining), where they accept Visa. When he finally returns me to the Taj Palace hotel, I thank him genuinely and give him a gratuity that was considerably more than he anticipated. It's been an amazing day.

London
2003 Age: 40 London

I'm in the City of London, walking from one meeting to another. In Stonecutter Street I pass the office of Deloitte, my former consulting firm, the one which originally sent me to America all those years ago. Funnily enough, my friend Sean Wheeler now works for Deloitte. I recall with a wry grin our adventures in Texas, where we first met. I haven't spoken with Sean in a while, so I give him a call on my cell phone. I go straight through to his cell phone's voicemail. I leave him a message about not having met in a while, and how we must catch up soon.

Sixty seconds later, as I'm crossing a main road, my cell phone rings. It is my voicemail system, delivering a message. It is Sean, calling to say that we haven't met in a while, *but* he is *not* calling in response to my message; this is a spontaneous call of his own. His message mentions that he is out-of-town at the moment, but that we must catch-up soon.

I check the two call times carefully. At the precise moment that I had called Sean, he had called me, which is why both of our cell phones had gone straight to voicemail.

I've learned enough to know that there are no coincidences. The significance of Sean in my life will surely play itself out in due course.

Catfight
2002 Age: 39 Atlanta

At GE Power Systems in Atlanta, I am taken to lunch by a Senior Manager from Ernst & Young's management consulting business (now acquired by Cap Gemini). He wants to sell me Oracle consulting services to use on the big GE programme I'm involved in. There *is* such a thing as a free lunch!

I ask him if he knows of Lucy Mingam. He sounds exasperated and embarrassed as he tells me that she was fired a while back … after getting into a very loud and very abusive catfight with another woman from E&Y … in a client's office premises … in front of the client!

What I find amazing is that she survived another two years in E&Y after the Dell fiasco and the previous project catastrophes. I had written and submitted a comprehensive report, with validating references, of Lucy Mingam's misdemeanours with clients and her threatening behaviour towards other E&Y staff. Nothing was done.

But this is reflective of these management consulting firms being environments where true knowledge and competence are overshadowed by insecurity and politics. The Partners weren't competent enough to understand how utterly incompetent (and dangerous) she actually was.

Buttons
2002 Age: 39 Atlanta

On my next trip to Atlanta, I have a date with Melanie, whom I met on the Internet. We are having dinner and I'm hoping that she will come up to my hotel room later. She talks enthusiastically about a writer named Wayne Dyer (although she's not so enthusiastic about me – nothing happens, and she doesn't see me again*).

Later, I look up Wayne Dyer on Google, and I read an extraordinary and succinct guidance on living a spiritual life. It is very compelling and attractive. Most importantly, it does not require the reader to embrace Christian theology. On the basis of this, I go to the nearby Barnes & Noble and buy a copy of every single Wayne Dyer book. The woman at the checkout looks slightly bemused.

Wayne Dyer's writing is amazingly uplifting and empowering. This material is not Islamic, although strictly speaking, it's *not un-Islamic* – so I suppose that's okay. Dyer manages to avoid theology altogether, whilst defining what are essentially religious (or spiritual) practices. I start putting some of these into effect, even waking up early to meditate, which I find very calming and uplifting. I find myself looking forward to doing this each time, with excitement and anticipation.

Dyer gives me a completely different perspective on my life and all the unfairness I've encountered and on my miserable arranged marriage to a completely unreasonable and intolerable person – all because I wanted to please my parents with their regressive cultural constraints. According to Dyer, there is no point in me getting angry

---

* A recurring pattern: the Universe uses a beautiful woman to catch my attention (*it works!*), she conveys a lesson, then she disappears – her assignment completed. We all learn *and* teach, as the opportunities arise.

with Sabrina for pushing my buttons – no matter how unreasonable and provocative she is. **It is actually *her job* to push my buttons, as one of my Teachers in Life.** The real issue is inside me, and how I react to this provocation. It's a learning opportunity for me – I am completely empowered in how I react to the apparent unreasonableness. If I overcome my negative reactions, if I cultivate true peace in my heart, then the provocation will stop. (That's what Wayne Dyer thinks – but he's never met Sabrina.)

Dyer presents many other uplifting lessons, again avoiding overt religion, but not far-removed from the positive and peaceful ethos of the teachings of Jesus – as presented to me by Mr Campbell, the Headmaster at my primary school. This form of intuitive, heartfelt, moral behaviour has always been more appealing to me than that presented by the carrot-and-stick, Heaven-or-Hell motivation of organised religion – but that doesn't mean that Heaven and Hell aren't real. It would be eternally catastrophic to get this wrong.

On a plane from Detroit to Atlanta this evening, I'm reading a Wayne Dyer book and, as we bump onto the runway, I commit to try living my life with my heart filled with compassion and tolerance – not impatience, judgement and hate.

I implement this immediately (at the rental car counter, hotel front desk etc, it's no longer about *me, me, me*). It seems to work – I feel a lot better. But there's still an all-powerful sky-God. (I can be compassionate about gay people, but I'm still uncomfortable about them, because I don't think that God likes them, even though it was *He* who made them gay, and I'm not going to argue with God about the unreasonableness of this or anything else.)

Alien
2002 Age: 40 US

My seventy-second trip to the United States, in November, begins just like every other one in recent times. I arise at 5:00 a.m., shave, shower and dress. The car comes for me at 6:00 a.m. I am at Gatwick by 6:45 a.m. and Mr Singh, the familiar security officer, asks me the usual questions about my computer and other items, before putting another of his initialled airport security stickers on the back of my passport and letting me approach the check-in desk. I am checked in by 7:00 a.m. and have secured my usual seat.

Today, I'm sitting next to a bearded man who looks like a Taliban (although he is white). He turns out to be an American, from Georgia, who is with the Department of Defense, and is just returning home from his seventh trip to Pakistan. He cannot stop describing how wonderful the people are in the North, so hospitable, so generous, no matter how poor they are. He loves to have *paratha* for breakfast, and he bemoans the British with whom he works there, who complain endlessly if they can't have a traditional fat-soaked English breakfast, with the stewed tomatoes mutilated just right. He says he works in Information Technology. (But there's an implication that this is just a cover.)

There was only one sinister incident that took place during his time in Pakistan. He was walking through a traditional marketplace, when a man who was facing him began reaching inside his tunic. My American friend, thinking that the stranger was about to pull out a knife or a gun, acted as anyone would in the circumstances. He lunged at the man, knocked him over backwards and sat on him. The 'weapon' turned out to be a tobacco pipe. He apologised, helped the stranger up, and the two of them went about their business.

The plane lands in Atlanta and taxies to the gate. Immediately when the seatbelt light goes out, I slide smoothly from my seat, deftly extract my slim leather attaché case from the overhead and am waiting at the exit door by the forward galley in seconds – the first one off the plane as usual with the arrogance of familiar routine. As we wait for the door to open, the American Taliban-like IT specialist is chatting with the flight attendant. He mentions that he'll be home in about two hours, '*insh'Allah*'. 'What does that mean?' she asks him.

Their voices fade behind me as I stride swiftly through the jet bridge and into the terminal.

Atlanta Airport is a huge facility, with voluminous corridors and a massive immigration hall. Timing is everything here; if two or three other flights arrived just before yours, it can be chaotic, with huge lines, even for the Americans.

I'm the first person from my aircraft to reach the hall, and it looks like they are just finishing the remains of another flight. The six booths at the far side are for Visitors; the two furthest ones have the shortest queues. I do reverse profiling of INS officers. They can vary a lot in terms of friendliness and suspicion, but the worst that any of them has ever done is to ask to see my return ticket, to ensure that I'm not going to overstay, so it's no big deal really.

These two have the same profile; they are both white, middle-aged men. The one at the furthest booth has the shortest line of all, so I go there, with about six people in front of me. From the outset, it is apparent that these two men are Mr Friendly and Mr Grumpy. Mr Friendly is welcoming visitors to his country with a vociferous good humour that can be heard all around this end of the hall.

Mr Grumpy is persistent in his questioning and exudes a cold, cynical suspicion. I am in Mr Grumpy's queue and my immediate instinct is to switch lines, but I think: *'Why, what difference will it make? So he'll ask me about my job title in General Electric and want to see my return ticket – big deal. Switching lines is not necessary for someone who has nothing to hide.'*

Mr Grumpy finishes hassling the scruffy young Frenchman in front of me and then it's my turn. I approach confidently, say 'Hello' cheerfully, and put down in front of him my completed forms and my burgundy double passport (new passport and older full passport taped together) with 68 US entry stamps in it, (as well as countless others). His first question takes me completely by surprise: 'Have you been to the United States before?'

I resist the very American behaviour of prefacing my response with, 'Duh…' which is used to indicate that this is a stupid question with an obvious answer. Instead I reply calmly, 'Yes, many times.'

From there it goes downhill fast. Noticing that I was born in Karachi, and the presence of a Pakistan multiple-entry visa, he becomes fixated on the possibility that I might be a dual national. He does not seem to notice the significance of the fact that I also have an Indian visa. How many people have *both* of those?

My seventy-second entry into the United States does not go well. The final question is the clincher. He is reading from a piece of paper taped-up inside his booth and he asks me if I am over 45. I reply that I am not. *Wham!* I've been profiled. I fit the three criteria of a potential terrorist: born in a listed country; male; aged between 18 and 45 years.

Mr Grumpy gathers my documents into a neat pile, places them inside a bright red folder and hands this bundle to me. For the first time *ever*, I am being sent for secondary questioning. The bright red folder that I am holding ensures that I cannot slip out of the immigration hall into the baggage claim area. Instead, a guard points me towards the secondary inspection room.

This is a sombre place. A few huddled masses sit on plastic chairs, waiting to be called for questioning by INS officers, who are behind a counter. Assimilating the process for the first time, I place my red folder into a rack on the counter, where it is in a proxy queue on my behalf, with other folders representing their human subjects.

I'm feeling hot, nervous, outraged, afraid; there's a sense of bureaucratic miscarriage. I don't belong here: I am *British.* I'm a Vice President in a respected American company. This is my seventy-second arrival into the United States. I lived here for five years. I travel the globe with impunity. Why am I sitting with suspicious foreigners in an interrogation room? Duh, it's because *I am* a suspicious foreigner.

The INS officer at the counter is questioning a South American girl about the fact that she now seems to be living in the US. *How is she supporting herself, when she is not authorised to work?* I answer the same question in my mind, visualising the Corporate American Express card in my slim leather wallet. (I don't think that she has one.)

An attractive blonde female INS officer emerges from a backroom and deliberately seeks and removes my folder from the rack (ahead of the queue). What is going on? They've been alerted to this mistake, obviously.

She stares at a computer screen and then speaks to the officer next to her. 'It says: *Appears to be innocent.* What does that mean?' He is not sure.

I am grateful to Mr Grumpy for at least entering that into his computer, before giving me a red folder.

She looks up and identifies me sitting in the front row and calls for me by name. What happens next is completely bizarre.

She and another INS officer (cheerful, friendly and chubby) take me outside the questioning room and lead me towards a special booth at the very far side of the hall. But, as we proceed, they are both discussing *why* I have been selected for 'Alien Special Registration'. They are not really sure, but figure that it must be because I *might* be a Pakistani-British dual national. Ms Attractive is cynical about whether it is really necessary for me to undergo Special Registration. 'But he comes here *all* the time,' she argues. (I like her – although it may be because of the uniform, the gun, and the handcuffs.)

Mr Cheerful is sympathetic, but cautious. They decide to leave me waiting at the Special Registration booth and go to ask their supervisor.

This is a strange experience. I am left standing by myself at a remote booth with some special equipment. Everyone from my flight has gone through Immigration already. An entire flight of French people is processed while I wait. I watch them disappearing into the baggage claim area.

The great hall is eerily silent when Ms Attractive and Mr Cheerful return. They are apologetic, sympathetic and wonderfully friendly, but regret that I must be subjected to Special Registration. Ms Attractive is supposed to do it, but has never done this before, so Mr Cheerful offers to help her, and then ends up doing it himself when she is called away.

He does not appear to have done it himself for real either. We both struggle through the questions emitted by the computer and he keys my answers in. The response time is terrible. He helps me calculate the approximate years of my parents' births (I know the days and months) and laughs when I confirm that I have a US bank account, but quip that I don't have much in it. *When was I last at University, where, and what was the course?* 1987, Stirling in

Scotland, Chemistry PhD. (I don't say that it was unfinished – well, he doesn't ask.) He asks me how tall I am and how much I weigh. I slightly overstate the former and significantly understate the latter.

Another passing INS officer (Mr Helpful) shows him how to use the digital camera and add my mugshot to the computer record, along with my scanned fingerprints.

Finally, the computer gives me my very own Alien Special Registration Number, which Mr Cheerful writes into my passport, alongside my 90-day visa waiver entry stamp. He also gives me a helpful information pack about Special Registration and all that it entails. The key point is that if I should stay more than 30 days, then I must report into an INS office between the 30th and 40th day, to tell them what I've been doing and with documentary proof such as my hotel bills (or, if I've been staying with a friend, one of his utility bills). Also, when I'm leaving the US, I must check in with INS on the way out, so that they can confirm my departure.

Nearly two hours later than expected, I enter the baggage hall. My suitcase is waiting by itself, all the others long gone. I've done this arrival routine so many times before, but now everything feels different. I don't feel like a sophisticated globe-trotting James Bond anymore; I am a Special Registration Alien, a potential terrorist suspect. I feel different; *will people know it and treat me differently?*

At the rental car counter, the woman recognises me and tries hard to be friendly, but I'm feeling very down. I decline the talking Navigation System, because I know my way around Atlanta now and the $8 per day soon adds up.

I should have taken the Navigation System. The softly spoken, but firm and insistent, American female computer voice might have prevented me taking the wrong freeway out of the airport, so engrossed am I in replaying the events at the airport and trying to analyse what this all means.

I arrive at the GE Power office really late. I might as well have gone straight to the hotel. I enter the office using one of my Corporate ID cards. I have several of these, for different offices around the world. I'm reasonably senior; a lot of people report to me and ask me what to do and to authorise things. My Atlanta colleagues are friendly and welcoming as always, but now I don't feel comfortable. I feel as if I have something to hide, because I'm a Special Registration Alien. My long love affair with America has hit a rocky patch.

I leave the office and head for the Sheraton. Henry and Tatiana are at the front desk and greet me warmly as always. This place is my home in Atlanta. They have held my usual suite and they arrange for my luggage to be taken up. But I am different now. Would they treat me differently if they knew my sinister new status?

I can't convey how hurt I feel, how emotionally this has affected me; America doesn't trust *me* anymore. Somehow, I can't blame America – not mainstream, regular, middle-of-the road, optimistic America. She was hit very hard and completely by surprise that sinister day, when her easy-going trust was betrayed by men twisted and brainwashed into hatred by events and policies and actions of which the collective mass of America, for the most part, does not have any idea or understanding. This is a situation so complex that few have any grasp of it, and yet many suffered for the actions and arrogance of a few.

I don't blame America, but I still feel hurt, and I still replay the whole process in my mind.

This trip is a couple of weeks long, so I get to spend the weekend in the US. Ironically, I have arranged to visit Faisal, a cousin of Sabrina's, who lives near Washington, works for the Department of Homeland Security and reports directly to the White House. I haven't seen him since he came to London for our wedding. Like me, he was born in Karachi – but he is an American citizen, whereas I am British. Despite all of my accumulated time in the US, I have never visited him or Washington before (apart from a job interview conducted in a Washington Dulles Airport terminal once). Faisal shows me around with relaxed ease and I am impressed as he tells me about his job within the Bush Administration (the non-Classified stuff, of course).

This is the remarkable, reassuring part about this whole sad, complex affair. I learn from him that this Special Registration is not personal; it is America struggling to cope with an ugly reality thrust upon her. Everyone he works with knows that he is a Muslim of Pakistani origin, but his loyalty and integrity are not questioned. Faisal relates how a few days earlier, he was fasting (this being Ramadan) and was in the White House in a very senior level security meeting as sunset approached. An Admiral looked at his watch and asked him, 'Don't you need to go and break your fast right now?' Faisal acknowledged this and excused himself from the meeting for a few minutes, and no one thought anything of it.

I find this amazing and comforting. Nothing is as black-and-white as those who would like to deal only with simple, unquestioning hatred would like it to be (on all sides). I don't have an easy answer on the situation with Iraq, because I realise the incredible complexity of this whole tangled web, and that most of my sorry species prefer not to deal with complexity.

Faisal takes me to see the White House. This weekend it is not possible to take me inside, as there are massive preparations underway for a Bill signing event on Monday. I stand outside and am struck at how much smaller it is than I imagined, and how close we are able to stand. I take pictures and the Secret Service sniper on the roof, dressed all in black, waves nonchalantly.

A couple of important-looking men come outside, through the Security gate, and recognise Faisal. They stop and chat and he introduces me. They are extremely cordial, and I don't mention that I'm a Special Registration Alien. It doesn't seem to matter now.

Faisal tells me something interesting – George Bush is a really nice guy. He's extremely personable and friendly, and never passes anyone without saying hello. The other day he was walking between the White House and another building, and he stopped to chat to a black gardener who was on his knees doing some weeding. The gardener couldn't believe what was happening.

But Dick Cheney and Donald Rumsfeld – they are cold and aloof. They know who you are, but they pass you in the hallway without acknowledging your presence and without making eye contact.

My flight back to Atlanta is on Sunday night. Sitting at the gate at Washington-Dulles airport, I notice an extremely smartly dressed thirty-something white man from one of the higher socio-economic groups, waiting for the same flight. He has a smart briefcase and a leather suit carrier, and he looks well-educated. I know that these are subjective judgements, based on personal prejudice, but I'm pretty sure that my superficial evaluation is accurate. He probably has a Harvard MBA or similar. Looking at the people waiting to board this small jet, the person most likely to be a terrorist, based on simplistic demographics, would be … me.

When the flight is called, the Harvard MBA gets up to board first, as he is in First Class, but he is pulled aside for a very thorough personal search, which takes several minutes. I take my Economy seat without any problem. I am grateful that I'm not being profiled everywhere I go, that even in the aftermath of dehumanising terror, America at a federal level is struggling to be fair and unbiased.

A few days later my US trip comes to an end and I am back at Atlanta Airport, having checked in and been through security. As a Special Registration Alien, I have to register with the INS before boarding my flight, so that they have an airtight record of my departure. I wait at the information desk in the terminal and they phone the INS to send someone.

Forty minutes later he walks up from the arrivals hall. They've just had some flights come in and they were all busy. I am the sole Special Registration Alien waiting to be recorded. The INS officer is Indian, definitely not born in the US – he still has that slight hint of an offshore accent.

He is friendly and fills out the form, commenting, 'This is such a pain for you guys.'

I return to London overnight and I'm the first one off the plane, moving swiftly through a seemingly deserted Gatwick in the early hours of Saturday morning. I am not an Alien here; I feel nothing less than elation.

I'm the sole person approaching the immigration officers, holding my burgundy double passport. There are two of them, both women – one on the left and one on the right. Inexplicably, I veer to a different side at the last moment and the scorned woman says, 'There goes a man with no taste' as the other woman gives my passport photo a cursory glance.

They are joking with me. How glad I am to see them – they have no idea. And they make me feel like James Bond again.

Neale
2002 Age: 40 Atlanta

On this trip to the US, I meet Neale Donald Walsch at a lecture and book signing at a Barnes & Noble in Atlanta. Eagerly, I sit in the front row. He is dressed quite conventionally in a dark blue suit.

He talks about the need for us to be willing to *transcend* our faiths, in order to accommodate each other in peaceful coexistence and global human spiritual progress. He reads some passages from the Bible, which are demonstrably intolerant and not indicative of a loving God; for example, that your children who become drunk and behave badly should be stoned to death. He mentions that he could just as easily have taken unpleasant quotes from the Qur'an.

I think this is very fair of him. In the post-9/11 hysteria, the Christian evangelists have been having a field day, pulling horrible verses from the Qur'an and thus demonstrating what an evil religion Islam must be. I have never seen anyone challenge them back (Muslim or Christian), with absolutely equivalent hateful and intolerant verses from the Bible. The evangelists either don't know about such verses (ignorance) or they are deliberately overlooking them (hypocrisy).

Afterwards, at the book-signing, I apologise to Neale Donald Walsch for hating his guts and wanting to kill him when I first looked at *Conversations with God* in 1997. He looks at me slightly uncertainly, as if I'm possibly unstable and dangerous.

Everything written in the *Conversations with God* series indicates a loving, helpful God, who wants us all to progress – not an angry, judging sky-God.

5 - 2
2005 Age: 42 London

In early June, another of those deliciously exciting plain white envelopes arrives. But this time the content is not exciting … it is inexplicable, unreasonable, unjust and like a slap in the face.

This the only communication we've had since MI5 told me I passed the test. Now it says that I have 'not demonstrated adequate management experience' to qualify for one of these middle management positions. That's complete bullshit! I was a Senior Manager in Ernst & Young in America (that's the level just below Partner), I've been a Vice-President and a Director in different GE businesses – that's way more than enough to have 'middle management' experience in a non-commercial civil service organisation (actually, they call it 'Crown Service'). They could easily check all of that.

This makes no sense at all. MI5 *needs* people like me – people of my ethnic and religious background. The prevalent threat to Britain isn't Irish Catholics anymore, it's Muslims!

MI5 had already seen my extensive and impressive corporate history on my application form *before* they called me to sit the test; I passed the test; they told me I passed and to await further communication.

How can they *now* say that I haven't demonstrated adequate middle management experience, when they already knew what my level of experience was *before* the test. And we've had no interaction since the test – there's been no further evaluation, no chance for me to prove myself. (I did have a lovely chat with a nice old lady who was looking at houses in my cul-de-sac and mentioned that she worked for MI5 – but that was nothing to do with my application.)

I don't think this is racism, because we are in a new, enlightened Britain that is so much different from the grey, hostile landscape of my childhood – but this doesn't make any sense. I keep playing the whole tape in my mind, again and again. It doesn't make any sense.

Atman
2003 Age: 40 London

The *Bhagavad Gita*, the ancient Hindu scripture, is a wonderful source of spiritual knowledge, peace and wisdom. It is a mesmerising and moving book. The eternity of the soul is described beautifully in the *Bhagavad Gita*[*]:

Worn-out garments
Are shed by the body;
Worn-out bodies
Are shed by the dweller
Within the body.
New bodies are donned
By the dweller, like garments.

Not wounded by weapons,
Not burned by fire,
Not dried by the wind,
Not wetted by water:
Such is the Atman,

Not dried, not wetted,
Not burned, not wounded,
Innermost element,
Everywhere, always,
Beings of beings,
Changeless, eternal,
For ever and ever.

---

[*] English translation of the *Bhagavad Gita* by Swami Prabhavananda (1893-1976) and Christopher Isherwood (1904-1986).

The Atman is the eternal soul, both the universal one and the individual one, which are really One.

The need to rise above judgement and the 'tribal trap' is similarly expressed:

He who regards,
With an eye that is equal,
Friends and comrades,
The foe and the kinsman,
The vile, the wicked,
The men who judge him,
And those who belong
To neither faction;
He is the greatest.

I used to hate Hindu scripture without even reading it! In this I was no different from those evangelical American Christians who oppose any teaching about Islam or the Qur'an, even in so-called liberal arts colleges, even in courses about Religion!

Hindus are not really idol worshippers who believe in many gods. They actually emphasise the oneness of God, and the oneness of everything *with* God. Hinduism is really a wonderful philosophy. I foolishly made assumptions about Hindu beliefs, and I *assumed* that God would want me to hate Hindus because of their beliefs. Even more misguided was the idea that God would want me to hate anyone; God is Love and is incapable of hate.

In my life I have been so judgemental, so prejudiced and always convinced that my position was aligned with God's (because I was afraid of God and wanted to make sure that I toed His line). This is the outcome of being too God-fearing.

Jeep
2003 Age: 40 Maui

We are having a wonderful time in Hawaii, staying in the Sheraton Maui (using Sheraton miles). Despite Sabrina and me being estranged, when Aleena is with us the three of us can still function well as a family. We flew here Business Class on Northwest miles, and my Platinum status with Sheraton even got us a suite.

Life is good with miles!

One day, we are on the road from Hana, heading back to Kahului in our rented convertible. The Hana Highway has only one lane in each direction, but there are places where slower vehicles can pull in to allow others to pass. There is a red rental jeep in front of us and he is not in any hurry. I assume that he will let me pass at one of the passing places, and I drive very close to him with my lights on, to demonstrate that I'm in a hurry. Instead, he slams on his brakes to express anger at me for driving so close. I brake and we don't have an impact. Okay, never mind. We continue.

An opportunity comes for me to pass him safely; I put on my left turn signal and pull out to pass him. He deliberately pulls in front of me and slams on his brakes; I react just in time to avoid a collision. *What an idiot!* Can't he understand that this is *not a personal contest.* I am in a hurry, he is not – so why won't he let me pass? Why does he take my need to pass as a personal challenge?

We continue uneasily like this, but it starts to rain, his roof is down, and he is forced eventually to turn off the Hana Highway so that he can put his roof back up. Sabrina and I both give him the finger, as we pass him. *What an ass! Why wouldn't he let me pass and why did he take it as a personal affront?*

It doesn't take me long to remember the white van in 1990 and my behaviour then. *Karma always balances things out.* He was *me*, as I used to be. How can I hate him, when he was doing as I did, before I knew better?

Later, we are in Borders in Kahului, and I find that many of the Wayne Dyer books on the shelves have been signed by the author. I learn from the staff that Wayne Dyer lives nearby and often comes into the store. I imagine running into him somewhere nearby and telling him about all the amazing things that have happened, since I started reading his books.

Presidential
2003 Age: 40 India

In May, I am in India again on a business trip, and I am spending one weekend all alone at the Taj Palace hotel in Delhi. I decide to pass the days by the pool, reading a book, which I must select in the gift shop. As I approach the book section, a mental note filed away deep in my mind becomes active again and I think: '*What about that story of the boy stuck on the lifeboat with a tiger? What was it called?*' I wonder if they have it. I look up at the shelf and immediately my eyes fall upon it: *Life of Pi* – staring right at me. There is one copy and, rather than being placed on a shelf with only its spine exposed, it is standing with the cover facing outwards towards me.

Life of Pi is a great read and a remarkable story. The principal character is a boy who, while in India, becomes equally Muslim, Christian and Hindu. On the way to Canada he is shipwrecked and survives on a lifeboat with a tiger – with whom he develops an uneasy relationship.

Inter alia, the book addresses the fundamental issue that I have been coming to grips with: that every religion has *a piece of the puzzle.*

I spend a few days in Hyderabad, and on the last morning Rohit – the completely clueless and obdurate new boss, who has been forcing me to pursue strategies with which I have concerns about integrity – wants to have breakfast with me, along with Saurabh, our chubby and cheerful Sikh head of HR. (Saurabh and the senior leadership team all agreed with me about the integrity issue but, in typical Indian fashion, no one challenged the boss – except me.)

We meet in the restaurant of the Taj Krishna hotel, where we are both staying. I expect that he wants to talk about our strategy in Europe.

The conversation does not go as expected.

He wants to eliminate my job. He needs me to move on and find another position within GE. The fact is that my very highly-paid, senior-level job, based in London, is a huge overhead to his relatively small and growing business unit. He has a major challenge to make his required profit number, and eliminating my position will make a significant impact. He believes that he can have other people cover my responsibilities effectively, and they don't need to be based expensively in London. It's nothing personal, *but you know how it is in GE; you must make the numbers.*

I am speechless. I almost babble some disagreement, but his mind is made up. *I know this is because I challenged him on that directive he gave me!* He wanted me to lie to a UK business about our current capabilities, win the deal, and then figure out *afterwards* how to deliver. *But that's not how we operate in GE!* Integrity is everything.

There is nothing I can do about this, because he has all the power in this situation. This is so unfair.

I feel as if the carpet has been pulled from under me. I lose my appetite for the delicious buffet breakfast.

When I return to Delhi this evening, in a very melancholy mood, the Taj Hotels people give me a gratuitous upgrade. It is the Presidential Suite. The term *presidential* is not good enough. It is a *palatial* suite, with a huge living room, twelve-seat dining room, enormous bedroom, never-ending bathroom (it goes around two corners), steam room, study, treadmill, television screens and music everywhere. And fruit … bowls of fruit in every room.

The bittersweet irony is this. I checked in at 10:00 p.m. and I have to check out at 6:00 a.m., to get my flight back to London. *How I long to stay!*

I have a room service dinner with a local colleague, instead of going down to the restaurant as we had planned. We have a cook and a butler in the suite for this, using the suite's own kitchen. But having two attentive hotel staff standing nearby, in an uncomfortably quiet suite, is a real conversation killer!

After Ashish leaves, instead of wasting my time sleeping through the night, I nap for just an hour on one of the sofas. Then I get up and work out on the treadmill, followed by a long session in the steam room. (Note for future reference: next time, turn on steam before commencing exercise, then steam room will be ready at maximum steam strength when exercise is complete.)

After a long, cold shower, I potter around, repack my stuff, and then sit in the leather armchair in the study and stare out of the window, watching the sun come up.

My mood is sombre – I feel vulnerable again, uncertain and a little afraid. I've just been through the best few years of my professional life – working for GE has been amazing. From London, my field of operations has spanned Europe, the US and, unexpectedly, India. Thanks to visiting India, my childhood prejudices and Islamic school misconceptions about Hindus were completely decimated. Thanks to visiting the US, I had a transformative experience that completely changed my beliefs and personal philosophy – but no one will ever believe me, if and when I ever get around to writing about it in a book (as I'm supposed to do, according to the woman on the plane).

The reason my mood is sombre is that I haven't yet fully mastered detachment, surrender and going with the flow. I know that whatever happens completely outside my control is almost certainly for the best (*'Every disappointment is a blessing'*), but I still feel fear and insecurity.

What if I can't find the right kind of job in GE? Rohit didn't specify a time limit, but he made it clear that he wanted me to move on as soon as possible.

At 6:00 a.m., I head downstairs to leave this wonderful hotel (and country), with very mixed emotions. The same warm and friendly people, who checked me in last night, are still on duty downstairs.

I love India!

Sean
2003 Age: 41 London

Sean Wheeler and I finally catch-up for dinner in London. He's a Director and I'm a Vice-President, so we're both doing okay. We talk about the old times in Texas of course, and of how incredibly beautiful and elegant Lucretia was. The issues and characters on that project never cease to cause us amazement and amusement. I usually hesitate to discuss my recent experiences and change of outlook (what I think of as my 'Transformation'), as I'm afraid that people will laugh at me – but it seems silly to keep this from my friend Sean, so I tell him all about everything that happened to cause the profound change. All of it – even the unbelievable stuff.

His response is incredible. 'We never discussed spirituality and reincarnation when we were in Texas, did we? – but I've always believed in it. My mother's believed in it for years. You should meet her; she lives in Connecticut. She took me to a very good psychic once and she confirmed that the reason I'm drawn to England is that I've lived several successful past lives here.'

My head is spinning with the implications of this. One is that I'm not crazy after all. Another is that there must be many people in business suits (like us), who believe as we do, but don't talk about it openly.

Star the Rabbit
2004 - 2011 Age: 41 - 48 London

Now Aleena, who is eleven years old, wants a rabbit. Her mother supports her in this foolishness. I counter with all the logical and rational arguments about who will look after it, what happens when we go on vacation, and so on. But Aleena is on a charm offensive and 'Please, Daddy' is virtually impossible for me to resist – because I am blessed that Aleena's requests are usually quite reasonable.

The pet shop has already been identified and is nearby. The selected rabbit is a baby with shiny black fur and is a Dutch rabbit, apparently. A luxurious two-storey rabbit hutch is also procured, and I wish that I had brought a big towel to protect the beautiful cream leather of my Honda Legend's back seat, as the rabbit mansion won't fit into the boot.

Aleena names her 'Star the Rabbit'.

I have little interaction with Star initially, as the rabbit hutch is placed in the back garden, and Aleena (reminded by her mother) is responsible for feeding her. But one day we notice foxes lurking around the hutch – Star is obviously hiding inside an inner chamber. That settles the matter. Star moves inside the house, with a cat litter tray provided for her business. She is given (nearly) full run of the house and becomes (cliché alert) a member of the family. She seems to recognise her name and seems to understand that being yelled at means she's doing something we don't like. A daily routine is developed: she expects breakfast in the morning when she hears the humans wake up; she relaxes in the afternoons; she sits with us while we're watching television in the evening; at night she has the whole house to explore, untroubled.

I never allow Star into my study. Somehow, she senses that this is the one room of the house she has never been in.

One day, inadvertently I leave the study door ajar. The moment Star becomes aware that this particular door is open, she mischievously lurches in there and dives under my desk.

I run after her, sternly shouting, 'STAR! GET OUT!'

I am able to goad, nudge and push her out of my domain – but I discover that in just the short time that she was in there, she managed to chew through *four* cables. Fortunately, none of them was a live mains electrical cable – she would have been electrocuted.

One afternoon, Star is lazing on the ottoman in front of the French windows facing the back lawn, when she spots a fox in the wilderness out beyond the wire fence. She leaps to the floor, sprints out of the room and up the two staircases to the remote safety of the attic. We laugh at her reaction, but also I am troubled to ponder how terrifying it must have been for her when she spent the nights in the rabbit hutch outside (before we moved her inside the house) ... and surely the foxes must have come and tormented her as they tried to get at her. No matter how futile it was for the foxes, it must have been terrifying for Star.

In the middle of the night, I am woken by Star thumping her back feet heavily and frantically on the floor. From the back garden, we can hear the shrieking of foxes, and Star seems to be reacting to this. Although she's safe inside the house, obviously, nonetheless she seems terrified of the foxes and is thumping her back feet as loudly as possible. I lift her up on to the bed and reassure her as best I can, gently stroking her fur and speaking to her softly. The foxes are loud, though, and they do sound frightening!

The next day I read on the Internet that rabbits thump their back feet to warn of danger. But how did she learn to do this? Apart from her first couple of weeks in the safety of the pet shop, Star has never spent time in the company of other rabbits. How is this behaviour acquired? It must be in her DNA!

One weekend, Star is clearly unwell. She is not eating, lethargic and severely weak. We call the vet and he agrees to meet us at his surgery opposite the local station.

The vet is holding Star in his arms very gently, and clearly she is shaking with fear. He gives her an injection of antibiotics and says he'll have to keep her here for now. They will monitor her, give her medicines, try to get her to eat and drink. But she may not survive the night.

Two days later, when I arrive at the station after work, it's actually a few minutes after closing time – but I persuade the vet's assistant to let me in to see Star the Rabbit. She is so much better! The assistant says it looks like she'll be okay.

I thank her excitedly and I walk home, leaping with joy almost. *Star the Rabbit is going to be okay!*

Over the years, I come to love Star the Rabbit. She responds to her first name very obviously. She recognises me and shows affection. When she is given her favourite foods, like broccoli and coriander, I can sense the gratitude. She rubs up against me when I'm writing in the solitude of the night, as if to remind me that I'm not alone.

All of this experience totally demolishes my long-held scientific assertion that animals have no self-awareness or consciousness, and my theological assertion that they have no souls (because surely they don't have to be *judged* for Heaven or Hell).

Now Star confirms what I read in Rumi and in the *Bhagavad Gita* – the most amazing Hindu text. Star has consciousness and a soul, and is a spark of the Divine on the same journey as me.

The night Star passes over is one of the most extraordinary events of my life. In July 2011, Star is now seven-and-a-half years of age – which is old for a Dutch rabbit, apparently. I'm on a two-week visit back to the UK; I've just returned from visiting Milton in Scotland; and I am spending *only one night* in this house before flying back to Malaysia tomorrow.

In the middle of the night, in the quiet of my bedroom, Star wakes me somehow, leaping about, knocking her water dish, and then lying down, stretching out and gasping loudly two times – then being absolutely still. In the silence there is beautiful music that cannot be heard with my ears; in the dimness there is a light that cannot be seen with my eyes; I can hear Star, but there's no sound; she is still here with me, but she's gone.

I begin to cry.

Debt
2007 Age: 44 London

Every morning when I wake up, it's the first thing I think about – the burden of Debt. All the balances on all the credit cards. It drains me. It sucks away my entire income every month and then grows a little more. It's always there – hanging over me.

How did it come to this? When I succeeded at getting into Unilever, I was a star. I was smart and responsible and disciplined. I was identified as a high potential corporate leader. At that time, I controlled every penny that I spent, and I knew every pound that I had – in my current account, in my savings account, in my pocket, and the balance on my credit card – which I *always* paid in full every month without fail. When I bought my first house, I lived on literally a few pounds every month. I had everything under control.

What changed?

I was conned into marrying the daughter of a *faux* millionaire who brought total chaos to every aspect of my life, and I allowed it to happen. I loosened financial control because I assumed that it would all be okay – that some part of those 'millions' would flow in my direction, so it didn't matter if I relaxed and let her spend whatever she wanted to. I bought a luxury house with a huge mortgage, because her father told me it was only a temporary measure — he would pay off the mortgage shortly. Setting up a joint bank account was one of the biggest mistakes of my life. If I could go back in time and give myself one piece of advice it would be: 'Never get into a joint bank account!' (Or maybe it should be: 'Marry *only* for Love.' But … the bank account advice would remain valid, no matter who I married.)

No matter how senior I became, what prestigious job I had, how much money I earned – it could never be enough.

She would never fill out cheque stubs (I had no idea how much she had spent and on what); she always bought more food than we could ever eat (and left it in bags to rot *outside* the fridge); she insisted on managing one of the credit cards and never made the payments on time; she always wanted to look at bigger houses … And whenever I tried to discuss spending, she would yell and make out that it was my fault … and also be abusive.

On top of all this, there was no sex or even intelligent, meaningful conversation.

Both of us … miserable.

This is the outcome of having a responsible and wisely arranged marriage, where my parents, family and community have *carefully* considered everything and worked diligently to ensure a positive match leading to a happy and stable future. It's complete BS!

You should *only* marry for love – it can't be worse than *this*, even if you don't have lots of money.

Spiral
2004 Age: 41 London

Karen Armstrong, in her excellent new book, *The Spiral Staircase,* talks extensively about the dangers of people who have *absolute certainty* in their hearts, and the extreme acts that *absolute certainty* can compel. This is similar to Neale Donald Walsch talking about the need for us to *transcend* our religious faiths, and not be hung up on the need to be exclusively *right.* I recognise Karen Armstrong's term *absolute certainty* extensively in my experience of people's religious convictions, including my own.

Karen also relates a very interesting event from her life. She had spent three years at Oxford, studying for a doctorate in English Literature. At her oral exam, one of the examiners was a visiting professor with a huge ego, whose own views were somewhat different from those presented in Karen's thesis. This individual exhibited extreme arrogance and attacked her every idea, totally demolishing her. The other professor was meek and intimidated by the fame and reputation of the visitor. There were procedural anomalies as well, and this whole process was totally unfair – but no one would stand-up for Karen and she was denied her doctorate.

Had she received her doctorate, English Literature is almost certainly the path that her career would have taken. Instead, she has followed her (unqualified) passion, and is now probably the world's most popular expert in theology. Like so many people, she had a major disappointment that turned out to be for the best.

'Every disappointment is a blessing,' Alex, the wise and gentle security guard in Nigeria, told me long ago. Which was the *key* disappointment in my life, the one that turned out to be for the best? I'm not sure – *I've had so many.*

Bombers
2005 Age: 42 London

The day of July 7th, I'm working from home and there's some news story in the morning about an explosion in the London Underground train network (the 'Tube'). I've worried for a long time that suicide bombing in London is inevitable and I am afraid. Then the apparent explosion is attributed to a 'power surge' and I am relieved. But then there are three 'power surges', which is impossibly optimistic, and I am afraid again – the inevitable reality emerges slowly but surely. It has finally happened. The story unfolds and it's 9/11 all over again, but this time it's here, at home in London – humble London, cheerful, polite, friendly, swinging London that has always managed, complaining and yet really *uncomplaining* about the weather and the traffic and the bloody trains. Always soldiering on and always there for me, London. Now the trains are bloody in the worst possible way; just as they were in the IRA years of the seventies and eighties.

Please God, it will be some North Africans who slipped in as asylum seekers, never intended to build a life for themselves, *bloody foreigners*. But it gets worse. Three of the suicide bombers are British-born young men of Pakistani origin, from somewhere up North, where there are lots of Pakistanis.

The contempt and anger which I feel are tinged with a helpless understanding. They were sold the lie of separation from the moment of their birth, from family who meant well and knew no better. Too many immigrants, especially 'up North', recoil in horror at the drunken, lecherous, shameless, drug-crazed, vomiting-on-the-pavement, wanton depravity that seems to have become the norm for young people in British society and, unable to find a comfortable middle ground, they veer forcefully to the other extreme – absolute, joyless, religious drudgery and partition.

They have discovered the easy familiarity and comfort of creating their own separated community-states (little-Pakistans, little-Bangladeshs) and hold these isolated bubbles of existence, frozen in time; not appreciating any of the potential of the indigenous society; labouring forever under the excuses of racism and decadence; harking back with false sentimentality to an idealised vision of the morally upright, decent, just and pious society *back home* – a vision that is a myth, a lie.

From within such a bubble, boys like these can see throughout their entire lives the sensual delights of the outer world – women, music, dancing, freedom, careers, convertibles – and yet are forbidden these for an enforced life of miserable Puritanism, bad theology and *assumed* second-class citizenship. Going to Qur'anic school for several hours a week drains from them any ability to achieve academic excellence in regular school, condemns them to tired mediocrity. They are instilled with an inferiority complex, a belief that they have no right to seek their own happiness and that Western society (because it struggles to accommodate *everyone* tolerantly and even-handedly) is somehow decadent and wicked. They have no freedom of choice and no expectation of ever having happiness in this life.

On top of all this is the intense sexual frustration that can be neither discussed nor fulfilled, but not to worry, a 'nice girl' from the village back home will be imported, so that the boy is not corrupted by a vivacious, feisty, challenging and independent white woman. I can imagine what was said to them. (*'She won't be the best, you are hard sell, you are not doctor, what can we say you are? … you don't even have proper job … but she'll be good girl … she won't be educated … no need of education … she will cook and clean, won't cause you any problem, won't ask for anything … the educated ones are trouble … but you are hard sell … what to say for job? … at least you have British passport … don't be too fussy.'*)

Faced with this misery, they were willing to believe the old lie – whether Protestant, Catholic, Sunni, Shia, it's all the same – that the purpose of your one chance at life is to secure your place in Heaven and to avoid Hell. Once you believe this, you look for short cuts and guaranteed routes. The truly Islamic way is to spend your life doing good deeds, with humility and self-discipline. But this seems quite arduous and takes too long, especially if life seems dull and unfulfilling, and is under the shadow of that miserable arranged marriage. So if someone authoritative – a silk-tongued confident leader with a powerful persona, hiding his own fear and cynical political agenda – presents a shortcut, based on the intense glorious passion of hatred and destruction, rather than of Love, it seems irresistible. No more dull, grey semi-existence – instead a thrilling top secret mission against the 'evil empire' and eternal glory thereafter. *Allahu Akbar! God is Great!*

They were willing to die because, in their own perception of reality, they had nothing to live for.

But what if the purpose of life is *not* to gain Heaven and to avoid Hell? What if the purpose of life is to *make the most of life* as an opportunity, a joy, a privilege to exist and live and love and make a difference … a good difference, not a bitter, twisted-metal-and-charred-flesh difference. What if every problem cannot be blown away, but has to be healed, and if you don't take the responsibility of dealing with it, you try to explode your way out of it, you are destined to come back and face it again … and again … until you get it right.

That would require a change of approach, wouldn't it?

5 - ?
2005 Age: 42 London

It's a beautiful late May evening when I arrive home from work and park my black Honda Legend outside our elegant house in this tranquil cul-de-sac. Ever since we moved back from America, it's been a bit of an adjustment to live in a house about one-third the size of our Minnesota house – but by UK standards this *is* a lovely house. Unfortunately, Sabrina and I now have less space to put between us, so tensions can run high very easily. It is very difficult for me to escape her enforced chaos throughout the house – but I do have my study, which is a place of dignified intellect and calm order (as long as Star the Rabbit doesn't get in there).

I pause to stand outside surveying the lawn and flower beds (the grass needs cutting again), but mainly to enjoy the evening sunshine and the civilised calmness of middle-class England in the spring.

A pleasant-looking, sprightly, sixty-something English woman with grey hair, whom I've never met before, comes up to me on her bicycle and engages me in conversation about this cul-de-sac and these houses. She is looking to move and wonders how old these houses are, and what the public transport is like around here. We have a friendly and polite conversation. I love this about Britain – most people have inherently good manners and are respectful to strangers, even foreign looking ones.

I tell her that the nearby station has an excellent service to London; it's only a twenty-minute walk, but there's also a bus you can catch from just outside the cul-de-sac which goes to the station every fifteen minutes. Sometimes I walk, sometimes I take the bus, sometimes I drive the car (although the station car park is really expensive). She asks me where my office is (it is assumed that I work in an office and not on a building site), and I tell her it's on the Strand – I walk there from Waterloo Station.

Out of polite interest, I ask her: 'Where do *you* work?'

Suddenly, almost imperceptibly, her mood changes, and she replies coyly, almost hesitantly: 'Thames House.'

'Thames House?!' I exclaim, surprised. 'But … that's MI5!'

Again coyly, she acknowledges this. I ask her about working for MI5 and we have quite an interesting conversation. Of course, she doesn't disclose anything confidential, but just gives me a general feel for the place. She says it's not as secret as it used to be, and the problem now is that terrorist-types can find out who you are and where you live. MI5 doesn't have unlimited resources, of course, but the nature of threats is broadening and increasing in severity. The working hours can be long and stressful (I'm used to that in Unilever, Ernst & Young, General Electric …).

On a practical note, she tells me that she drives there every day, instead of taking the train, as it's more flexible – you can't be sure what time you'll finish each day and you might miss the last train. They have a staff car park. I've never been a fan of driving into central London – to do so every day during rush hour would be quite stressful. But having the use of a private car park would certainly make things easier.

I can't resist. As she's getting back on her bicycle to be on her way, I say (with a confidential tone): 'I actually have an application in progress with MI5 at the moment. I passed the test and I'm just waiting to hear about the next steps.'

Cheerfully she wishes me luck and cycles off.

I'm feeling really exhilarated. MI5 employees are actually normal, friendly, cheerful, polite, good mannered, middle-class people – just like me.

Dad
2004 Age: 41 London

My probationary period at Xansa ends and they have no interest in retaining me. I have no desire to remain with Xansa either (there are some real idiots at the most senior level), but I was hoping to find another job before this happened. Now I am unemployed, with a mortgage and school fees to pay. I should be worried, but it is a relief to not be in Xansa; it did not make me proud to belong.

What I want most desperately is to return to GE, if only I can find a suitable London position that is a match for me. I see a job advertised on the GE website for one of the smaller business units, and I feel a sudden and inexplicable wave of emotion about it. I cannot explain this strange experience, but I do apply for the job. Christine, the American woman who used to work for me in London, now works for this business unit at its US headquarters in Richmond. I send her an e-mail and she replies that she would be delighted to recommend me. All I can do now is wait, and keep applying for every job that I can find which looks vaguely suitable.

I have a dream about my father. He is looking smart in his airline uniform, with the three gold stripes he eventually acquired (although he's retired now), and he's running around trying to help me out in some way, as he always does. I have a problem with my car and my airline ticket. I need to get my Honda Legend checked into the cargo hold of the aircraft, on this trip I'm going on.

My father looks young, cheerful and upbeat as always. He tells me not to worry about it; he will take care of it. He will get *both* the car and me on that airplane.

I wake up on Sunday morning and I think about my father. He is such a wonderful and warm man, and he has always been good to me, forgiving, patient and generous. Currently I have not seen him for a while, although he's been bugging me to fix his computer. (He never has been very good with the Internet.)

I decide to visit my parents, although I had not planned to do so today. At my parents' house I fix my father's computer and get his AOL e-mail working again. My brother Rehan has dropped in as well. I spend some time with my parents and give them both a hug and a kiss when I leave. They are getting ready to go to a wedding downtown, at the Hyatt Hotel near the American Embassy.

I go home, do some gardening, and I've just come out of the shower when my cell phone rings. I see it is my parents' cell phone calling, and I am concerned. When I hear the voice not of my father, but of a family friend, I know it cannot be good. He tells me that my father has had a heart attack and is on the way to hospital in an ambulance. My mother is in the ambulance with him, and has given the friend my father's cell phone. This is all the information that I receive.

I call my brother Rehan, pick him up at his house and drive downtown with him to the hospital. I am thinking thoughts like, *'Most heart attacks aren't fatal'* but, because of the dream, I know that this will be a significant event.

At the hospital, the receptionist shows us the way, without saying anything. My mother and a family friend are in a private room and my father is on a trolley. He has gone.

On seeing my father lying on the hospital trolley, I feel a deep, heavy weight in my chest at my loss – but there is also an unspeakable sense of joy, of something magnificent having happened. I can see from his faint smile and the look of absolute peace on his face that he has not died, but returned home, and this has been a wonderful, blissful event. I am so happy for him, that he escaped from the dream with such dignity.

He had gone suddenly, when he was sitting on a chair at the wedding. Being a Pakistani wedding, there were at least three doctors in the crowd who came to his aid immediately, but he was gone in an instant, of a massive heart attack caused by cholesterol. There had been no sign of life in the ambulance at all. He had gone immediately. My mother says that he was always in a hurry, which is true. He would have seen the Light and hurried towards it, not wanting to be late (in case it left without him).

My brother says later that he had also dreamed of our father during an afternoon nap, so it was definitely his time. He says that as he awoke, he felt a thought from our father: '*Always remember the happy memories of childhood, don't dwell on the bad ones.*' (It was shortly after this that I called my brother with the limited news that our Dad had had a heart attack and had been taken to hospital.)

They say that healthy people go suddenly; this was definitely the case with my Dad, who was seventy, fit, and swam most days. He was a kind, generous, forgiving and always cheerful soul. I loved him and I will miss him so much, but he had a good life and it was his time. The look on his face was very happy and gracious. I know that he is fine, and we just have to accept it.

I also know without a doubt that I will see him again, when he comes to get me (*no hurry, Dad*).

The next day, Monday, I have a job interview first thing in the morning. My father wakes me early. I go through the motions of shaving, knotting a tie, taking the train. I don't really want this particular one, but I have no choice; I need a job. It seems to go okay, as long as I keep my thoughts focused away from my father.

Later I drive to Heathrow to pick up our brother Rizwan, who has flown in from Tokyo, where he lives with his Japanese wife.

The funeral is to be on Thursday, and the call from the small GE business comes the day before. I see them a week later; they are upbeat, sharp and professional as always. They offer me the job just a week after that. I return to GE. *Thank you, God.*

And thanks, Dad, for everything.

Dalai Lama
2004 Age: 42 US

In November, I'm on a business trip to America again – my first since returning to GE. The INS computer at Newark Airport kicks out my name again, and I am sent to Secondary. The two INS officers sitting behind the desk – one a young white man, the other an attractive Hispanic woman – are implausibly friendly and great fun to chat with, while they enter me to the system as a Special Registration Alien.

I drive from Richmond, Virginia, to Raleigh, North Carolina, and back, listening to an audio book about the Dalai Lama, called *The Wisdom of Forgiveness.* Whatever doubts I have about the potential for forgiveness in the most extreme circumstances, this puts them to rest.

There are many examples. The 15-year-old Irish Catholic boy who forgave the British soldier whose rubber bullets cost the boy his sight. The black South African woman who forgave the white, apartheid-era policemen who pushed her breasts into a drawer and pummelled them to a near pulp. The Tibetan man who was daily tortured by Chinese soldiers and whose main concern was that he would stop having compassion for his captors. The list goes on.

Forgiveness is always possible and is *always* the wisest course.

Kingston Bridge
2011 Age: 49 London

For the Christmas and New Year holiday period, I fly back to London from Kuala Lumpur and stay at our house with Sabrina and Aleena, and Sabrina's boyfriend Chris. He's an American she met on e-Harmony. Chris is a really nice guy and we have many great conversations. Sabrina seems happy and is not being miserable and abusive all the time. She's really a lovely person — obviously it was her frustration and unhappiness in the enforced (for her) marriage which made her behave to me as she did. (It turned both of us into horrible people.) Sadly, the house seems a bit empty without Star the Rabbit.

My diet-and-exercise programme continues and every day I go on a long and vigorous walk that takes me over Kingston Bridge. My trousers are now loose, as the weight is literally falling off me!

[Unknown to me at this time, every day I am walking past an apartment building next to Kingston Bridge in which one unit has been rented for the holiday period by a woman from thousands of miles away — her name is Nina.]

Village People
2006 Age: 44 London

I don't go as often as I should, but I go to the mosque this Friday, because the main prayer is being followed by the funeral of my late father's best friend. Hounslow Jamia Masjid is a very impressive, elegant modern mosque, presenting an image of Muslim success and achievement in Britain.

The sermon is in Urdu: long and dull and completely lost on the non-Pakistanis present, who presumably also are Muslims. After the sermon (but before the prayer), another elderly man in a suit tries to discuss mosque business, in English. He is reading rather formally from some prepared notes. From his comments, I gather that there have been some 'irregularities' in the election of the mosque trustees, and for this reason there is going to be another election in September. This time, a private security firm has been engaged to validate the identities of those voting. He says that it is essential to bring a photo ID ('... a Pakistani passport, or an English passport...') and a utility bill, to provide proof of address. He says that no one will be allowed to vote without providing these.

He continues to read out some other points, but some people became impatient, calling out in Urdu: 'Start the prayer!' Others shout, 'Let him finish!' also in Urdu. For an agonising period of time, the hall seems to devolve into chaos, with all this shouting going on, back and forth. The Africans, Arabs, Bosnians and white Englishmen look on in bewilderment, at this heated Urdu/Punjabi exchange.

At this moment, I realise something. These people shouting and arguing are ignorant, self-obsessed savages. They want to bring the tribalism and selfish arrogance of their Pakistani villages to this mosque in London. They want it to be a Pakistani mosque, with all the baggage that comes with that. Why else are the sermons in Urdu, not English? Why else would there be 'irregularities', if not because the election was run along Pakistani lines, with a Pakistani mindset? (This means that cheating and vote-rigging are the norm.) Why is such a significant Muslim institution in London being run solely for the benefit of Pakistanis, rather than all British Muslims?

Observing the Pakistani behaviour in the mosque on Friday is profoundly shocking and makes me feel ashamed. I also realise something else. These people are too ignorant and too self-absorbed to have even registered the impact and implications of the July 7th bombings; they are too detached from the reality of mainstream life in Britain to worry about those events (and future terrorist events) and to consider what role their own attitudes and behaviour play in all of this. They have no concept of the current risk being posed to peaceful Muslim existence in British society.

They just can't grasp the enormity of what is happening. They are too inept to be terrorists, but also too clueless to identify and stamp out the seeds of terrorism and extremism.

Sejanus
2003 Age: 40 Budapest

Soon after New Year I have to attend some important meetings of GE in Budapest, Hungary – a place I've never been to before. I fly overnight from Atlanta to Gatwick, go home, have a shower, return to Gatwick and fly to Budapest.

I take a taxi to the Marriott, check in and go up to my room.

After unpacking, I return to the hotel reception area, searching for any sign of my colleagues. I look into the bar, where there are a few seductively dressed and overly made up women sitting by themselves; they look at me expectantly. I hurriedly retreat back into the lobby. Patrick Stewart walks past me, heading for the elevator. His wife, Wendy Neuss, is with him.

Not entirely sure what I'm going to do, I decide spontaneously to return to my room. They are waiting for the elevator; I join them. I don't say a word to them in the elevator, but when I head for my room on the 8th floor, they are walking right behind me (towards their unmarked suite). Outside my room, I apologise for intruding (they stop and listen), I state that I appreciate his work and, in a stroke of genius, I compliment him on his role in *I, Claudius* (from nearly 30 years ago).

Patrick Stewart shakes my hand and says, 'Thank you.' I apologise to his wife for the intrusion, and then I disappear into my room. (I learn later that he is in Budapest filming *The Lion in Winter*.) I imagine that not many of the gibbering idiots that he meets *all the time* compliment him for *I, Claudius* rather than *Star Trek*.

Heartless
2010 Age: 48 Kuala Lumpur

I'm living in Kuala Lumpur when our 74-year-old mother decides to make an *Umra* (lesser pilgrimage) to Mecca and Medina, and goes with a Muslim tour group from London. Afterwards, my brother Rehan in London tells me what happened.

Within the grounds of the Holy Mosque in Mecca, her money belt containing her passport, bank cards and cash was stolen. She went to the British Embassy, who treated her well, but advised that a local police report was required for them to issue a new passport (which she would need to get home, obviously). She went to the police station in Mecca and was completely ignored. She was invisible. No one would listen to her or pay any attention to her whatsoever. They were completely heartless. But without a police report she could not get a replacement passport, leaving her stranded in a foreign country. The tour group moved on and left her to deal with this.

Fortunately, her cousin was still working in Jeddah, and he had a client whose father was a retired police officer. The arrangements were made through this gentleman for her to go to a police station in Jeddah, where she lied (as directed) that her money belt had been stolen in Jeddah (not Mecca), and under the jurisdiction of *this* police station, her police report was issued. She was able to get a new passport and make it home.

What is worrying about this account is that, without a local connection, my mother would have been totally stranded – an elderly woman in a foreign country, with no money or bank cards, where no one 'in authority' had the slightest inclination to help her. She would have been left destitute, until some kind of intervention could be organised to rescue her. I have absolutely no trust in the Saudis, who behave with a complete disregard for truth and the welfare of others. They have totally failed in their responsibility as supposed guardians of Islam. They can finance medievalism and wars and terrorism around the world – but they can't be bothered to provide an old woman with a police report so that she can get home.

Darkness
1999 Age: 36 Devon

It's early August and I take a Northwest Airlines flight from Minneapolis to London on Saturday evening, eventually reaching my parents' house early on Sunday morning. I've brought my Whittman-Hart laptop computer and, by plugging it into a phone socket in the living room, I'm able to effectively 'work from home' on Monday.

But I have booked the next three days as leave, and on Tuesday morning I travel to central London and get on a delightfully slow and comfortable train to Torquay, Devon in the southwest of England – it takes over three hours. I stare out of the window at the familiar, beautiful countryside and remember what Kirk said in *Wrath Of Khan* when Spock asked him where he was going. '*Home*,' he replied, with deep emotion, almost choking on the word.

Where is home for me? There seem to be several answers: my parent's house; England in general; (strangely) wherever Milton is. (It's definitely not the big luxury house in Minneapolis with the huge mortgage and the abusive wife.)

Torquay is always a popular seaside town, but is particularly busy right now. Milton meets me at the station, and we stroll to the cottage he has rented for the week – along with his girlfriend, his brother and his mother. Fortunately, there are plenty of bedrooms and bathrooms. He marvels at how often I seem to be travelling between America and the UK. 'I need the miles to keep my Platinum status,' I explain. Of course, in the evening we have fish and chips.

The next day, we head out at mid-morning and take up positions facing out to sea. There are many people doing the same, but it is not as crowded as I expected it to be. Unfortunately, the sky is very overcast and there is no chance of this being as visually spectacular as we would like. The appointed time comes and there is a noticeable darkening of the sky, but disappointingly it doesn't become like night-time. I'm peering into the thick clouds through the cardboard spectacles we all have, and for just a moment I do glimpse part of a black circle.

'I see it!' I exclaim to Milton and the others.

But then it's gone.

Oh!
2013 Age: 50 Kuala Lumpur

The Executive Roundtable meeting is during afternoon tea at the J. W. Marriott hotel.

In the meeting room, one of the women CEOs catches my attention immediately. She is the Chief Executive of one of this region's most influential and powerful media empires, including Malaysia's cable television network, Astro. She has a beautiful face and exquisite figure; she is elegantly dressed; she carries herself with graceful poise and absolute confidence; she speaks perfect, sophisticated English. Despite being a Southeast Asian woman, she exhibits not one iota of meekness, subservience or dependence. She is the perfect combination of beauty and empowerment – exactly the specification of woman I gave to God over 25-years-ago, when I was looking for the perfect wife and asking Him to deliver her.

Her name is Rohana Rozhan.

5 - !
2018 Age: 56 Langkawi

I'm sitting in a hotel restaurant in Langkawi (a beautiful archipelago in Malaysia) with my occasional friend Frank Gardner, the Security Correspondent of the BBC, who in 2004 was shot six times by Islamist nut-jobs in Saudi Arabia, miraculously survived, and now uses a wheelchair; but he doesn't allow this to constrain him in any way from doing his job – reporting from faraway, inaccessible and dangerous places – as well as skiing, scuba-diving etc. He is also an amazing example of not allowing negative events to take away one's personal empowerment by being consumed with *bitterness and self-pity*. He *should* be seething with *anger and resentmen*t about what was so unjustly done to him – but he isn't. Also, most significantly, he holds no grudge against Muslims *in general*, because of what these *particular* so-called Muslims did to him. He is truly an extraordinary man.

Because it's been thirteen years, I think it's okay to tell Frank about my application to MI5 – I don't think the confidentiality requirement really matters anymore. He knows people in MI5 and MI6. I emphasise that I was applying for an office job, not an operational role as an agent 'in the field'. I explain that I passed the test, which was really difficult, and I don't think that most members of the public would be able to think logically enough and recognise their own assumptions enough to pass.

He says: 'You're too posh to be credible as a field agent. But a job in which you were evaluating data and writing reports and making recommendations – I think you'd be good at that.'

I explain that, after telling me that I'd passed the test and to await further communication, they then wrote to say that I had 'not demonstrated adequate middle management experience' for these particular jobs and that my application was unsuccessful. But that was complete BS. I had been a Senior Manager and a Vice President and a Director in really demanding commercial organisations. To say that I had not demonstrated 'middle management' experience was nonsense.

I then tell Frank about the delightful grey-haired lady on the bicycle who rode up to me and engaged me in conversation, who worked for MI5, and whom I could not resist telling that I had an application in progress. Frank bursts out laughing.

'There's the reason, right there. She was sent to determine if you could keep your mouth shut, and you couldn't.'

I am defensive. 'But literally no one knew that I had applied to MI5, except MI5 itself – so I figured if she was from MI5, it wouldn't matter if I mentioned it to her.'

'She may not have been an actual employee of MI5. She was probably one of the contractors they use for the recruitment evaluations and her job was to see if she could get you to mention that you had applied. Which you did.'

I sigh. She was such a nice old lady, we had such an enjoyable and engaging conversation, and it was *irresistible* for me not to mention it.

Damyanti
2010 Age: 47 Kuala Lumpur

After my speaking event, I am driven over to Sharon Bakar's house for her husband's birthday party. It's a vibrant gathering, with live music provided by Sharon's husband and his mates. The chairs and tables are laid out elegantly on the lawn, and there's a wonderful, joyful atmosphere that resonates comfortably with me. Many of Sharon's friends are writers, so I feel very energised. I am enjoying my experience of Malaysia.

That beautiful woman I met at the Festival in Bali last year is here – the one who was moderating some sessions. I try to connect with her, but she's politely disinterested. [I learn later that I am not her type, being a man.]

I start chatting with a beautiful, young Indian Hindu woman named Damyanti – she is also a writer. Damyanti tells me about her experience during the Gujarat riots of 2002.

At the height of the insanity, she and some Hindu friends were in a Muslim area, and had to take refuge in a hostel. An enraged Muslim crowd gathered outside: armed with swords and machetes; yelling that they knew of the presence of Hindu girls inside the hostel; pounding on the doors; demanding that the Hindus be given up. It was the most terrifying night of her life.

And it was a long time before Damyanti could return to a 'normal' view of her many Muslim friends.

She tells me that she knew the riots were provoked deliberately by politicians. Some of the Hindu rioters were found with computer printouts of names and addresses of Muslims to be killed. This could hardly be explained as the 'heat of the moment'. It was all orchestrated for political gain.

I tell Damyanti about my visit to India at the time of the riots. I was a Vice President in one of GE's Delhi-based companies and I loved working with India. By that time I had developed a respectful understanding of Hinduism – which was sadly lacking in my youth.

I remember reading about the Gujarat riots, while safe in the Taj Palace Hotel, and wondering if I might be affected …

Integrity
1984 Age: 22 Stoke-on-Trent

Janice and I are exchanging letters every week. She is back at our beloved Stirling University – having returned from her year at the University of California in San Diego on the Exchange Programme. I am at North Staffordshire Polytechnic in Stoke-on-Trent – doing the final year here because I failed the Honours Qualifying exam (partly because I was sullen that I did not go on the Exchange Programme, and mainly because I didn't do enough work to pass and God did not intervene as expected).

One day on my walk to college, I stop at the little post office on London Road to get stamps.

At the counter I ask the friendly middle-aged local woman for five First Class stamps. She passes the strip of 17-pence stamps across the counter towards me.

'That's 85 pence, duck,' she says cheerfully and with the casual familiarity that is endemic around here (not always the case back in London).

I notice something amiss. The strip of stamps on the counter in front of me has *seven* stamps, not five.

Hurriedly, I pick up the strip of stamps and slip it into my wallet, simultaneously handing over a pound coin to pay. I wait for the change, thank her, and hurry out of the post office with false nonchalance.

Safely outside, I'm feeling a sense of glee at my good luck just now – I only paid for five First Class stamps, but I received seven. I feel like I just won something.

A little later the same day, I begin to feel regret. *Why did I do that?* I should have pointed out to her that she had given me seven stamps. I should have returned the extra two … or paid for them. My first instinct had *not* been to remedy the situation, but to take advantage of the mistake. And yet, this is not how I see myself. I see myself as a 'good' person who would not have taken something given in error.

Now it's too late. I can't go back there and return them. It would be obvious that I had known and had taken advantage. There doesn't seem to be any way to fix this.

But I should stop worrying – it's only a minor matter. The Post Office is a multi-multi-million pound organisation that isn't going to worry about two stamps (even First Class ones).

35 Years Later

I learn something that I didn't know before. Individual postmasters are responsible for balancing their own books and are themselves financially liable for any cash discrepancies. In effect, I stole directly from that kind, friendly woman.

And why? Was I really so poor that I needed to grab 34 pence worth of stamps given in error? If I hadn't noticed, it wouldn't have mattered – it would have been an oversight by both of us. But I *did* notice! I saw it the moment she put the stamps on the counter. So that was my true nature in operation.

And now it really is too late to do anything about it.

What we *choose* to do is in principle what defines us – not the *magnitude* of our success in doing it. I stole 34 pence from an innocent, kind, good-natured, hardworking individual.

What does that say about me?

Transformation

1986 Age: 23

I have a mysterious dream. It is a long time ago, in a place that seems to be Atlantis. It is a peaceful, civilised time, advanced in philosophy and science.

I am in Atlantis with some old friends. We are wearing white robes, and there is architecture reminiscent of ancient Greece. There is at least one man and one woman, in addition to myself. We are very close, and there are *warm* feelings of friendship and love. This is the most poignant, lingering aspect of the dream – the *warmth* of the friendship (even though I cannot identify who my friends are).

But there is also a bittersweet aspect. We are saying goodbye, but it is understood that we will meet again for sure, in another, later life.

I awake and it is a bright Saturday morning. I am in my sparse student room, in the wooden bed that is so narrow, one wonders if it is really true that some students have sex sometimes.

I lie here, looking towards the window. Well, this dream doesn't make any sense at all. I have never given Atlantis a thought (outside of that crass television series *The Man From Atlantis*), and as for meeting again in a later life, what kind of nonsense is that? It sounds like Hindu reincarnation theology. We have only one life. Only Islam or Christianity can be the true religion, and I'm sure that it's Islam.

But the warmth of the feelings of friendship lingers on. I can still feel it. It is tangible.

I am still young and in my life I have not experienced the depth of friendship which the dream conveyed. Such friendships would take a very long time to grow, a lot of shared experience.

Later in the day, I see Julian Hamilton-Peach in his room. I tell him all about this strange dream with its alien concepts. Julian, in his characteristic way, does not perform any obvious analysis, but instead focuses on my use of the word 'warm', and what a good word that is for conveying certain emotional feelings. *Warm.* Yes, it's a good word; it does convey the feelings.

1993 Age: 31

Sleeping in the 'television room' – the upstairs bedroom where we keep the television, video, hi-fi (on which I never get to play anything, because Sabrina doesn't want to hear Joni Mitchell, Paul Simon, Janis Ian or Mozart) and a sofa bed – I have a strange and vivid dream.

All of us – a group of humanity, a group of friends – have assembled in the gym of Hampton Grammar School. We discuss how we each have performed in the life we have just led, what lessons we have learned, and what the game plan is for the future. There seems to be a Coach who is leading this discussion, using a blackboard to illustrate points. It reminds me of when Mr Foster was explaining the rules of rugby on the blackboard, before our first ever game. I couldn't see a thing, because my glasses were in the changing room – but I was too afraid to ask if I could go to get them. But this dream session is not as sombre as that one in my memory.

After the discussion, we all leave the gym and start another life. The details of the actual life are obscured. At the conclusion of this life, we each return to the gym, until the crowd of us has reassembled there again. Once again, the Coach goes over how we have performed, what lessons we have learned, and what the strategy is for the next 'game'. Then, we again disperse, live another life, die and reassemble in the gym.

This cycle continues indefinitely. Each time we live a life, die and reassemble. Death is not a traumatic event in this process; it is just a part of the 'game'. Reassembling and meeting everyone again is fun, and the gym reverberates with all of our chatter, until everyone is back, and we quieten down for the review to start formally. We learn from the lives just lived, plan to do better, and depart for the next round. And so it goes, on and on, *the swirling cycle of life and death and life.*

I awake from this dream, puzzled by the alien concepts. It doesn't make any sense. *Reincarnation.* This is nonsense. Reincarnation is Hindu nonsense. I hate Hinduism, because it makes God angry. The only potential candidates for the one true religion are Islam and Christianity, and there is *no* reincarnation in them. There is only one life, then Heaven or Hell, and God will decide.

Anyway, reincarnation is about punishment and reward – everyone knows that. If you're good, you come back as a wealthy, privileged person. If you're bad, you return as some lowly and humiliating animal. It's a stupid, primitive belief. But in this dream, reincarnation was not about punishment and reward – it was just a game to enable learning and development. It doesn't make any sense.

But it was a very vivid dream. It reminds me of the dream I had back in 1986, in which I lived in Atlantis with a group of very close friends, and we were going our separate ways, but we agreed that we would meet again, in another life.

Where did I get such strange ideas?

2002 Age: 39

My London-based position is being eliminated, as GE Capital Corporate has decided that the Oracle global programme office has run its course, and I need to find a new job within General Electric. Apparently, this is nothing to worry about. Jack Welch always said that you should destroy your job (i.e. create so much new efficiency that your job becomes unnecessary) and then carve yourself a new opportunity within GE. But I still feel a twinge of fear – our house, Aleena's schooling, my entire life – it's all built on a steady and generous income stream. GE has been the best job I've ever had – I feel proud to belong amongst so many sharp, intelligent and driven people. When I think of the ineptness and downright deceit I witnessed in my consulting firms, I feel ashamed. I don't want to have to go back there.

But HR is very supportive, and I'm to visit Stamford in Connecticut in June to have a series of meetings about various open positions. I particularly want a job at Corporate, as I think that gives me more exposure and is better for my career. It also keeps me close to America – which still pulls me.

So, I book a week off first and, using my huge reserves of airline and hotel miles, I take Sabrina and Aleena to New York City for one week. We stay in the Sheraton Manhattan, in a rather cramped room, but it doesn't matter – this trip is about the city, not the hotel. Because of the time change, we're always wide-awake by 5:00 a.m. We spend our days finding places to eat breakfast, lunch and dinner; we do all the usual tourist things like the Empire State Building; we always seem to end up in a Barnes & Noble somewhere.

At the end of the week, they fly back to London, and I head for Stamford, to the Sheraton hotel – a place which I associate with optimism and success. It's the only place that I've ever stayed in Stamford. I first came here for my interviews with GE, when my job in Whittman-Hart was falling apart – the huge stock options were a lie, and worthless anyway, and the company was nose-diving into non-existence. Norman Keith, the mysterious headhunter who had walked into my life once before and taken me to Ernst & Young, suddenly reappeared and led me to the perfect job with GE. It all worked out impeccably. GE moved us back to London just in time for Aleena to start at Lady Eleanor Holles School – the girls' school next to my old boys' school.

The job at GE has been very satisfying, and I have always enjoyed visiting Corporate in Stamford, of retaining that connection with America. Everything seems to have been divinely managed and I am very grateful. And the Sheraton in Stamford always provides the backdrop to this success.

Because of my membership status at the Sheraton, they very kindly upgrade me to a junior suite – which is a very large room with a generous sitting area. The meetings in the first week go well, and most of next week will be spent on a Green Belt six sigma quality training course.

I'm spending the weekend here in Connecticut, so on Saturday afternoon I have a leisurely drive to Westport and pull into Barnes & Noble. I buy a venti cappuccino, and wander around the store, eventually coming upon the big New Age section. *I can't believe how many bookcases it now has!* I am filled with utter contempt. It never fails to amaze me that people can believe this utter nonsense – it's superstitious, it endorses the Occult, and it's offensive to the One true God. But disturbingly, the movement seems to be growing, judging by the number of books.

I know what I can do! I will read a New Age book and deconstruct it with my superior Islamic knowledge and intellect, demonstrating logically why it's complete garbage. That will be a good use of my Saturday afternoon – constructive, fun and fulfilling. I step into the New Age section *(I shouldn't really be here),* randomly pull a book from the shelf and sit down with it. It is *The Power of Karma* by Mary T Browne, a supposed psychic. *Oh, this is going to be some of that pseudo-Hindu rubbish.* I'm not threatened by Hindu philosophy, which is patent nonsense. I will read it and be able to see the flaws in it easily, from my superior Islamic perspective.

It doesn't go quite as I expected.

I settle into the armchair, with the venti cappuccino perched on one arm, and I read the entire book in one sitting, as it is unexpectedly compelling. It has strange and alien concepts: spirit guides; Karma; reincarnation as a path to spiritual development, rather than as punishment and reward. I never heard about this before.

According to the book, Karma is a universal law that ensures balance and facilitates our spiritual growth. It is impartial and extends no favours and holds no grudges. Adverse events and circumstances are really an *opportunity* for spiritual progress, rather than a *punishment* for sins. However, every negative action performed by a soul does have a consequential impact on that same soul. Thus, Karma helps us to learn. It operates without judgement and favouritism, and no one is exempt – whatever their religious belief or special relationship with God.

This spiritual growth takes place over multiple lifetimes. The circumstances of each lifetime are determined by the soul's Karmic needs arising from previous lifetimes.

We are all souls who chose to incarnate into this physical world to undergo lessons and training in this vast simulation we think of as *Life*. A spirit guide is a more experienced soul, who is still in the real world keeping an eye on how we are doing in this game, and who is responsible for nudging us along the agreed path, ensuring that the right events occur to give us the best opportunity for growth.

A great many of us alive today have had past lives in Atlantis, which was a great civilisation that has passed away.

This is a completely different perspective on reincarnation from the one that I have been holding all these years, which is that reincarnation is a form of punishment or reward (contradictory to the Islamic-Christian Heaven and Hell, with only God as the angry judge).

Something extraordinary and unexpected happens inside me. This book resonates with those mysterious dreams I had in 1986 and 1993 – about living in Atlantis, and meeting in the school gymnasium between lives, to discuss spiritual progress and development needs. What this book is saying exactly matches the content of those vivid dreams. Suddenly, it all comes together. I feel like crying, so great is the emotional upheaval. I remember the love I felt for my old friends in the Atlantis dream. And this business of reincarnation for spiritual growth is *exactly* the story conveyed in my dream about the school gym.

I think about the evidence for Karma in my own life. What about that little shit who sabotaged my Renault 5? He got his comeuppance. *I mean*, what about that *fellow soul* who stole my oil cap, without considering what the consequences might be for me? He later suffered those very same consequences.

Oh ... what about that time I pushed Mansoor down the stairs? (No one knows about this – it's not something to brag about.) I tumbled down the stairs exactly the same way within about a year or so. *Oh boy.* I contemplate this sombrely. *But I was just a kid … but so was Mansoor.* And I *did know* that pushing him down the stairs was wrong. I can't hide behind childish innocence. It was kind of fair that I also experienced what I did to him.

This is turning my world upside down. *God will be so angry.* I'm not even supposed to go into the New Age section. It's all superstitious nonsense, that Satan has created to lead people away from the one true God. (*But it's making sense.*) I am completely shaken. If this is true, virtually everything I've always believed is wrong. If it's not true, then the very fact that I'm even entertaining these ideas in my mind is going to alert God (who can read my thoughts) and He is going to get very angry with me for wandering into this deceitful nonsense. *He's always been good to me, always helped me out, and this is how I show my gratitude?*

But Karma makes more sense. The idea of an omnipotent God who is going to punish people for what they did in circumstances that He imposed on them has always been somewhat problematic. I never saw a viable alternative before.

I leave Barnes & Noble, carrying the world's greatest dilemma on my shoulders and drive carefully, very carefully, back to Stamford.

This evening, in my suite in the Sheraton, I look in the phone book and find that Mary T Browne does indeed live in nearby New York City, in Greenwich Village. I feel like calling her, but I'm not sure what I would say. But I think of a way that I can test this new worldview in a rational, almost scientific manner. I articulate a challenge to my theoretical spirit guide, if I *really* have one, to contact Mary T Browne's spirit guide, and get her to call me in my suite. They (our two spirit guides) can give her the phone number of the hotel and the number of my suite. If she calls, I will believe. If she does not, I won't have to believe. (I hope that God does not get offended by my faith being so shaken up.) Nervous with anticipation, I leave it at that and go to bed. I can't quite drift off to sleep, wondering if the phone will ring – I'm terrified that it will and that everything I thought I knew with *absolute certainty* is actually wrong.

There is no call.

On Sunday morning, I'm talking to Milton in Scotland on the phone about all this. He listens with deep interest; he's my sounding board. I tell him the whole story: the Atlantis dream; the gymnasium dream; the information about Karma and reincarnation and spirit guides given in the book; how it all fits together; my challenge to the alleged spirit guides; my relief that the challenge was not answered.

I'm walking around the room, talking on the cordless phone, when I find a small white feather on the central coffee table of my otherwise cluttered suite. The only other thing on that table is a copy of *A Return to Love* by Marianne Williamson, which I left there. (I picked up this book in Barnes & Noble last week in New York City, but have not read it. It was the beautiful brunette woman on the cover that caught my eye.) I remember hearing that some people believe that feathers are left by angels, but that is clearly nonsensical. The idea that angels have feathery wings which they flap in order to fly to Heaven in the clouds is primitive, medieval Christian thinking – Heaven isn't in the clouds, it's in another dimension, and it's not somewhere that you can get to by flapping wings. I laugh about this with Milton. I can relax somewhat; my world is not being turned upside down. I tell Milton it was a wild thought for a time, but I'm not going to change my position.

But still, this has intrigued me, and I want more information – more data with which to make a rational, scientific evaluation. On Monday evening I go out looking for Mary T Browne's other book, *Life After Death.* The local Barnes & Noble doesn't have it, but Borders in Stamford tells me there is a copy in the branch in Danbury, 30 miles away.

I drive over there on Tuesday and eat dinner in Borders – spending the evening reading *Life After Death*, which talks about her spirit guide a lot more than in *The Power of Karma.* But there isn't really anything compelling or profound in this book to cause me to change my position.

On Wednesday evening, after leaving Corporate headquarters, I'm driving back to the Sheraton … when the penny drops, and I suddenly make the connection. Mary T Browne's spirit guide is called *White Feather.* It hits me like a slap in the face.

What did I do with that feather? I don't know. I drive hurriedly back to the Sheraton, park the car somewhat frantically, rush back up to the suite, open the door, step inside the room, and look across at the coffee table. The feather is not there. *Where could it be?* Strangely – instead of consciously turning my head left and right and scanning the room with my eyes as I would do naturally and instinctively – I find that my head tips forward *entirely of its own accord* (as if I'm a puppet on a string) and I see the feather on the carpet right in front of me, precisely in between my two feet. There is something entirely strange about this action – I had no control over it. I pick up the feather, examine it reverently, and keep it safe. Then I scour this hotel suite, looking for a source for this feather. I figure that if I can find another one, then this means nothing. I vigorously thump the sofas, the pillows, the comforter – hoping that another such feather will fall out from somewhere. Nothing. I can't find another feather like it.

(Who left this feather? Is this a satanic conspiracy? Am I rapidly going off the right path? Did I fail to keep my faith and avoid the forbidden knowledge?)

I'm excited and afraid.

On Thursday evening I return to Barnes & Noble in Westport, where all this craziness started. I have decided that I need more data to formulate an opinion, so I head for the New Age section to randomly select another book. I have the intention to read whatever book comes to me and assimilate the information – using it to further evaluate what must be true and what must be false. I walk into the forbidden place and randomly reach for a book. My hand and eye both fall on the selected volume at the same time, as I yank it from the shelf. I feel *utter shock* when I look at the title and especially the subtitle.

It is *Sacred Feathers* by Maril Crabtree. *The Power of One Feather to Change Your Life.*

I stop breathing; overwhelmed and giddy – I feel like I'm going to faint.

With trembling fingers, I examine the book. It's fifty stories about how feathers changed people's lives! I never knew feathers were a phenomenon. I can't believe it. No, that's the problem … *I do believe it!* My head is swimming; I feel weak. I'm delirious with excitement and joy. *This can't be a coincidence! That would be ridiculously unlikely.* We *do* live in a benevolent Universe and we *are* being helped. *It's all true!* Reincarnation, spirit guides, spiritual growth, psychics, passing over, near death experiences, *What Dreams May Come*, it's all true!

Where does this leave Islam and the Qur'an? I don't know – I'll have to figure it out later.

I pause for breath. I sit and read *Sacred Feathers* with utter exhilaration. As stated on the cover, it's a collection of accounts about how feathers appear in people's lives in miraculous and transformational ways, carrying some profound meaning or acting as a sign. According to the book, feathers are a common way for the Universe to provide a sign of some sort. (It is nothing to do with medieval angels flapping wings!) In my case, it was in answer to my challenge to Mary T Browne's spirit guide, *White Feather.*

And where the feather was left is also significant. It was on the coffee table, the most obvious place in the room, and next to a seminal work about spirituality, *A Return to Love.*

Okay, I'll buy all this, but Astrology, Numerology and Tarot, that's all bad. I'm *never* going there.

Hey, does this mean that I don't have to dislike gay people anymore? What a relief! *They are always so nice.*

There is a colleague at headquarters, Mike Cohen, who is a very interesting person. I have known him ever since I started at GE. I cautiously, *very cautiously*, discuss some of this experience with Mike. He comes out of the closet, as it were. He understands Karma, reincarnation, spirit guides and so on, and he believes in it all; there's nothing weird about it. Mike tells me about the feather. He says that it's not a *metaphysical* feather, it's a real feather, from this world. It wasn't created out of nothing. The important thing is that someone trying to help me out, to guide me, moved that feather into my hotel room and onto that table, making it significant to me at a certain moment in time. That's what spirit guides often do; they help out, they provide *signs*.

I'm amazed to find someone in GE who not only understands this, but also believes in it. It's a good thing that I chose Mike to discuss it with.

Let's not forget why I'm in Connecticut; it's about my next job in GE. I want one of the headquarters corporate jobs – but my boss, our software division in India and the people at GE Power all want me to take a position where I liaise between GE India and GE Power. It will be London-based, but I will be working with India, and visiting Atlanta a lot. This is the job which I take in the end.

My new title is Vice President, so I guess that means I've made it. *Who would have thought it? And in an Indian company, too!*

But all this spirit guides and reincarnation stuff, I can't talk about it; most people will think I'm crazy.

2002 Age: 40

I give up eating by myself in a restaurant most nights in Atlanta and instead eat a grilled sandwich and a slice of dessert in the Barnes & Noble next to my Sheraton hotel, and I try to read at least one book from the so-called New Age section each day.

What does amaze me is the level of consistency between all the books on all the topics. They combine in my mind to form a coherent model that makes very good sense. (Of course, I stay away from Astrology, Numerology and Tarot, as these are deceptions of Satan.)

There is one common and very strong theme. We are all on a path of spiritual growth, learning lessons over multiple lifetimes that help us to release our *fear* and fill our hearts with *love*. These are the two basic choices: *fear* or *love*. We can react to every situation and every person we encounter with either *fear* or *love*. We can react to 9/11 with *fear* or *love*. It seems too simple, but it really is true.

Even wholly within Islam, this choice is apparent. Sufis seek to lose themselves in the *love* of God. Wahhabis are driven by *fear* of God. We know that the 9/11 hijackers were not Sufis.

We have spirit guides, who are helping us along our paths – much of which we have mapped out before this incarnation. In retrospect, I'm now very suspicious about that kilt-wearing Scotsman I passed on the walk up the mountain in 1981. I was brand new to Scotland at that time, and I assumed that it was normal to see a man in a kilt. But after spending many years in Scotland, I realised that a man in a kilt, halfway up a mountain on a cold, windy day, was *not* normal. And the meeting that I had on top of that mountain, in which Dr Porter told me how to excel in exams – that was absolutely critical to my progress and success in life.

These life paths, which we have planned in advance, put us into situations that give us opportunities to choose between fear and love, and to act accordingly. We have agreements, *sacred contracts* (as described by Caroline Myss) with our guides and other souls with whom we relate in this life, about what will be achieved in this life and what roles will be played. Spirit guides operate at the level of looking after us individually, whilst Angels operate at a higher level, generally looking after the well-being of Humanity collectively.

There are myriad countless Angels, many with specialised areas of responsibility. I read that there's even an Angel responsible for helping us to find parking spaces. *Gimme a break!* Oh wait … what about that miraculous parking space I found in front of the exam hall when I was late, back in 1990. (*Thank you!*)

Our lives are nudged along *more or less* pre-determined paths that put us into certain necessary situations. When such nudges take place, they appear as coincidences, or synchronicities. This is our *SynchroDestiny*, as Deepak Chopra describes it. (*Oh yeah, Deepak's actually not a charlatan mumbo jumbo faker, after all.*)

In mapping out our intended journeys, we may also agree certain signs and signposts that will appear to us, to reassure us that we are on the right path. It's like leaving little reminder notes for ourselves along the way.

I wonder: *What are my sacred contracts? What is my life's purpose?*

Sometimes, we wander so far off our planned path that a major course correction is required. This can appear catastrophic at the time: a major accident, a serious illness, divorce, job-loss, a career failure. And yet, how many people have we all heard say, in reference to such an event: '*It was the best thing that ever happened to me.*'

However, this life is like a dream, an illusion. It's a simulation for the purpose of learning and spiritual growth. Our destination is a return to God, the source of Love. In so doing, we will extinguish our egos and realise that our separation from one another is an illusion; we are all *One* and we are all part of God.

We create our own realities, to a large extent. I learn about *creative visualisation*, which is a method of gently nudging reality to reflect your goals. God does not do things *to us*. It wasn't that I didn't go to medical school *because* God wouldn't let me. I didn't go because I couldn't be bothered to make it happen. Religions give us hints of this: '*God helps those who help themselves.*' Conversely, I got the first class degree because I *did* make it happen. I visualised getting a First, imagined the joy of it, figured out what was necessary, and focused on doing that. (We are not denied the fruits of our labours, unless it so contravenes one of our sacred contracts that it is not good for us, and is prevented by our guides for our own ultimate good.)

I had done the same with the Unilever selection process. I had looked at the brochure and imagined myself having one of those exciting corporate careers. I imagined the joy of receiving a job offer. That was nothing less than creative visualisation, even though I did not know there was such a thing at the time. I was more worried in case God decided I didn't deserve it.

Another example is Milton and his fear of flying. Milton was always terrified and apprehensive about flying – so much so that whenever he did fly, something frightening had to happen.

God does not make earthquakes, hurricanes and volcanic eruptions happen, to punish us. These are part of our situational reality, as is our own empowerment. We have separated from God for some reason; He just wants us to come home in due course. Sufism and Kabbalah are identical on this.

Our personal *empowerment* is the blasphemy that fundamentalist Judaism, Christianity and Islam all seek to keep from us. They intimidate us into surrendering our personal power to a frightening, punishing entity. And fear of God and Hell was always the main driver, the threat presented to me by Islam and Christianity.

'*The Kingdom of Heaven is inside you,*' said Jesus. And also: '*Ye are gods.*' What strange statements. Conventional Islamic theology cannot assimilate these words, and dismisses them as Christian fabrication in the scriptures. But they do not fit conventional Christian theology either. With these words, Jesus is telling us that we are responsible for our own destinies and we are *empowered*, if only we would wake up to this. He also said: 'Unless a man be *born again*, he cannot see the Kingdom of God.' He was talking about reincarnation! It's a miracle that these statements survived centuries of scriptural bleaching.

Organised religions are useful to give us some ritual and framework, especially when we are young, but they can also hinder our growth if we become afraid to transcend them. Perhaps the core truth is common and quite simple.

In one book, I read a Christian pastor's account of his extended visit to the *Other Side*, during a long near-death experience (NDE). He asked, *'Which religion is the true one?'* and was answered, *'Whichever makes you feel closest to God.'* What a wonderful answer, and so unexpected, given the background of the narrator.

I stay late in the Atlanta office one evening and I get into a very interesting conversation with a local colleague. It is about something that happened when Anna was in her twenties, with three young children. She was driving alone on a mountain road late one night, when she lost control of the car and it hit a tree. Anna was critically injured and taken into emergency surgery. She found herself detached from her body in the operating theatre, and became aware of a wonderful, bright, Love-filled light, that she wanted to throw herself into. She moved towards the Light, but her deceased grandmother and aunt appeared and blocked her way. They told Anna that this was not a good time, that her children needed her, and asked her to return – but she did have a free choice in the matter. Anna agreed to return; her surgery was successful and saved her life (although the doctor told her later that she had been clinically dead at one point). She went on to raise her three children and enjoy a successful business career.

This is the first time that I have heard such a story, directly from the source. Anna considers herself to be a Christian, and is perhaps unaware that *strict* Christian theology does not support this experience. Dead people are supposed to be asleep until the Day of Resurrection (in both Christian and Islamic belief). Also, in these theologies, people already dead could not possibly have any influence on whether someone *chooses* to live on in this world, or to return to the Light. That decision could only be with God. Of course, in my new way of thinking, I have no problems with this experience; it is a wonderful and uplifting story.

2002 Age: 40

Near Christmas, I'm in Atlanta, chatting on the phone with a woman I met online and who claims to be psychic. She tells me that it's time to start my life's work, and *what do I think this is*? I don't hesitate. I have thought about it a lot and *I know*. I say that I think it's to help make peace between India and Pakistan, and other parties locked in ongoing conflicts. I want to be a teacher of peace.

'Boy, you really picked an easy one,' she says.

The next evening, I'm in my favourite aisle seat on the overnight flight from Atlanta to London. An attractive middle-aged woman takes the window seat next to me. We start chatting. I have a strange feeling, so I jump straight to the point. The words come out of my mouth as if I have no control over them. I ask her if she is the sort of person one would find in the New Age section of Barnes & Noble. She looks pleasantly surprised and says 'Yes', that she is a psychic, and that she also does Astrology, Numerology and Tarot. She works in a metaphysical store in Arizona and she is writing a book about Tarot. Her name is Kaycie.

Astrology, Numerology and Tarot! Oh no! I always said adamantly that I would *never* go there, but the Universe seems to have other ideas. There are mysterious forces at work here, bigger than I ever imagined. I decide to go with the flow. I surrender.

I tell Kaycie that I have come a long way recently, I have opened up to a lot of possibilities, but I still have issues with Astrology, Numerology and Tarot. I'm afraid that these are deceptions of Satan, which is what both Islam and Christianity preach.

Kaycie's reply is quite disarming: 'Did *God* tell you this?'

She explains that Tarot is a form of self-analysis, not a bad contact with evil spirits. It helps to put us in touch with our higher spiritual selves, by bypassing the Ego and Intellect. Numerology and Astrology are signposts; they point towards how we have charted the directions of our lives in advance, but no outcome is absolutely fixed.

I tell her about my Hong Kong suits and the number *7051* in the labels. Before I say anything about this subsequently becoming my employee number at Ernst & Young, she tells me that *7051* is a number related to my work and career.

I tell her the story about the Scotsman in the kilt I passed on my walk up the mountain towards my 'random' meeting with Dr Porter. That meeting on Dumyat was *absolutely critical* to my life's journey – without that meeting, I would have been an academic failure and almost certainly would not be sitting here on this plane right now. She confirms my recent suspicion that the mysterious Scotsman wearing a kilt was probably my spirit guide making a humorous appearance – for me to figure out many years later.

She tells me that I have had an enjoyable and successful career, and that so far I have been living my life through my career but, now that I am forty, my true life's work *must* begin. She pauses, considers, and then says that I am to be a *teacher of peace.* These are her words. I never said *anything* to her about being a teacher. A shudder runs through me; not fear, but joy. She asks me if I am okay.

Kaycie warns me that if people resist doing their life's work for too long or wander too far off course, the Universe has a tendency to make 'course corrections' – and these can be quite traumatic when they occur.

I apologise to Kaycie that her original flight to London was cancelled and that she was rerouted through Atlanta to sit next to me and teach me what I needed to know.

She gives me her business card and we say goodbye at Gatwick, having talked all night. I have been profoundly transformed, pushed even further down a path unimagined.

I realise that I must begin my life's work and I know what this is. I have been given some gifts to help. I have an incredible memory for detail, which allows me to recall every significant event in my life, my thoughts and emotions at the time, and piece together my own personal development. I have the gift of writing, which allows me to convey events and thoughts in what I hope is an engaging way, without it feeling like 'work' – it just flows easily and naturally! I know that I've always been able to put myself in other people's shoes and see both sides of an argument, and to empathise with both parties. I remember how I saw the misunderstanding between Mr Hughes and that young girl, back in junior school, when he articulated the exam question rhetorically and the girl took him literally. I do seem to have certain skills.

I've been very judgemental of others and had *absolute certainty* – and I've now seen that totally obliterated.

The obvious way to me seems to be to write, but where do I start? And when will I find the time?

It's been an extraordinary year! My perspective on everything has changed completely, in a totally unimagined way. Most especially, the energy of my attitude to God has been transformed – from constant FEAR and deep insecurity to a peaceful and calm knowing that I'm not going to be sent to Hell for misdemeanours.

Best of all, I no longer have to hate people that *I think* God expects me to hate because He hates them – especially gay people. God isn't a Mafia Godfather!

And the journey continues …

Love

2010 Age: 47

This is a strange and painful state for me to be in, in January 2010. Unemployed, broke, in debt – the bottom of the barrel. What a contrast from my executive days of business travel, smart hotels and self-indulgent dinners on the corporate credit card. I was Platinum with Northwest Airlines and Platinum with Sheraton. I even miss the meetings and teleconferences – at least they gave me a sense of purpose, of self-worth even, shallow as they were for this. The Global Financial Crisis changed everything.

And yet life seems to go on as usual. Money keeps coming just as I need it: the tax refund; the renewal of the screen option on my book *Unimagined*; writing an article for the *Daily Mail*; Milton loaning me one thousand pounds (although he insists it is to be treated as a gift, not a loan). Aleena's school gave her 100% financial aid, so that issue – which is my true Achilles' Heel – is okay. For Aleena to be kicked out of her school because I couldn't pay the bill would have been a burden truly too painful to bear – it would have caused me such a sense of utter failure. But I have been spared that.

Although we are in a terrible recession, applying for jobs is relatively easy on the Internet. For each position, I just tailor my standard covering letter, load my CV and click 'Submit'. I spend some time each day searching and reviewing the new positions on various job sites and applying to any opening where there's a glimmer of compatibility.

I'm applying for jobs which match my career experience. Most of these seem to be in the financial services industry. But the truth is that my heart really isn't in this – I'm tired of that ugly corporate world and don't really want to go back there. But what choice do I have?

I make an application to Standard Chartered bank, and to Ernst & Young, which is once again growing its consulting business. It seems like a lifetime ago that I worked there in Minneapolis, or at least a different century. Putting on a suit and returning to the City of London on the train and tube is a sobering prospect – I had once dared to think that I was free of all that (by being a writer), but material needs and the responsibility of providing for Aleena have tugged me back to harsh reality.

The interviews seem to go well, and the recruiters who connected me are optimistic. It looks like I may even have a choice of jobs: Standard Chartered bank or Ernst & Young management consulting (again). I'm bound to get at least one of them. The probability of being rejected by both seems so low – but causes me a deep twinge of fear.

I have just parked my car outside Aleena's school, to drop her and a couple of her friends off in the morning. (Despite all the difficult circumstances, this is something I really enjoy and appreciate every day – taking Aleena to school and afterwards possibly stopping by to see my mother at the only house I have ever truly considered to be *home*.)

My cell phone rings and I take the call – it's the recruiter from Standard Chartered bank. My heart leaps with anticipation – it will be such a relief to be back in respectable employment again. The girls getting out of the car slip out of my awareness as I focus on the call.

It doesn't go as I expect.

The recruiter advises me that they will not be proceeding with my application. For some reason, I failed to make clear to the interviewers what activities and projects I had undertaken at General Electric which were relevant and applicable to this position. He expresses his regret. I thank him politely and hang up.

So, it will be Ernst & Young again. I'm completely comfortable with that. I still have all the polo shirts in different colours, with the Ernst & Young logo. And all sorts of other E&Y branded items, including a personal organiser, a sports bag, a leather pouch to hang on my belt, an alarm clock, a slim calculator with world time, and a compass (in case I'm lost in the wilderness or need to figure out the direction of Mecca). I will be returning to the familiar, reassuring world of management consulting: business travel and corporate meetings and endless (meaningless) deadlines.

I am in line at the post office, when my cell phone rings. It's the headhunter who introduced me to Ernst & Young.

It goes as I feared.

The headhunter advises me that something just didn't gel at the interview – even though I was well-qualified, and even though Ernst & Young is currently hiring everyone they can get their hands on. For some reason, I failed to convince them that I was right for the job, even though my résumé was a perfect fit.

I hang up with a deep sense of foreboding. Fear grips my body, as my mind runs through the ramifications of being unemployed and without a source of income any longer.

In February, a new position catches my eye on one of the employment websites. It's for a Business Process Outsourcing company in Kuala Lumpur in Malaysia. All the experience I have with outsourcing in GE, working with India, is absolutely entirely relevant. But it's in Kuala Lumpur. That just doesn't fit in my reality. I can't see myself moving to Malaysia.

But I don't have the luxury of choice. Very soon, the life I have precariously built on regular income and limitless credit will collapse totally. Sabrina will helpfully remind me what a complete failure I am in every dimension, and Aleena will be traumatised and so disappointed in her father.

I apply for the job in Kuala Lumpur with Symphony BPO – I give it my best shot. I really am very well qualified.

The recruiter calls me just a couple of days after my Internet application and conducts the preliminary screening. Then I have the initial call from Symphony's HR department, and then the telephone interview with the VP of HR. And during the call I persuade him that this job, which entails developing business with customers in Europe, can actually best be done from London, with occasional travel to Symphony headquarters in Kuala Lumpur. He agrees that this makes sense.

The face-to-face interview in a London hotel goes very well. The executive from Symphony is an amenable, middle-aged Irishman named Jack, who has been living in Malaysia for years. We seem to hit it off.

Three weeks later, I arrive in KL on a Sunday afternoon, for two days of meetings and interviews with Symphony's senior leadership team. Malaysia is a lush, tropical and humid environment – but with signs of high technology and wealth everywhere. The Saujana Hotel is a golf resort, with the attractive open architecture I first encountered in Bali when I was invited to the Ubud Writers and Readers Festival back in 2008. Everyone is gentle, friendly and speaks English – although it's sometimes hard to make out what they are saying.

After unpacking, I go for a walk. This is clearly a suburb of KL (named Petaling Jaya, or PJ), judging from the greenery and the residential construction. A giant billboard for an exclusive development of condominiums shows a white couple standing on their balcony – she is in an evening dress and he, a blond man, is wearing a tuxedo. Does it seem entirely plausible in this ninety-degree heat and near 100% humidity? (What I come to learn over time is that Malaysia is in its *nouveau riche* phase, in which western brands and images mean a great deal – they are aspirational.)

On Monday morning a hotel shuttle takes me to Symphony House – an elegant modern 12-storey building with impressive facilities, including a San Francisco Coffee House on the ground floor. The two days of meetings go well, they agree that it makes sense for the role to be based in London, but that it would begin with about six-to-eight weeks in Malaysia, to learn about the company and plan the role. By dinner on Tuesday, they are asking me when I can start.

'In about ten days.' (I don't want to sound too desperate.)

So I'm going to be away in Kuala Lumpur for six-to-eight weeks. But I finally have a job, and a good one at that – Vice President of Business Development. There is tangible relief in our family. I think that even Star the Rabbit can sense it. Aleena is heading into the critical final year of secondary school, in which her performance has to be absolutely impeccable if she is to get into medical school, which is her own genuine wish (not imposed by me). Sabrina is studying Neurolinguistic Programming (NLP) and counselling. Star the Rabbit is eating broccoli and coriander.

Sabrina and I – estranged by years of resentment, remoteness and occasional hostility – suddenly grow up. Sabrina suggests that we have an Islamic divorce, so that we can both be free. (The more troublesome and complex

English divorce can follow later.) Something is driving her to this, there is a new spark of life in her. It's funny – it never occurred to me that *she* might be the one who wanted the liberty to look elsewhere; it was always *me* who wanted to be free since forever (or at least since the so-called honeymoon … *honey-moon* … what a stupid word, it will always carry huge negative baggage for me).

We give ourselves an Islamic divorce without involving anyone else (my mother has no idea); I give Sabrina three *Talaqs* ('I divorce thee' three times) without the customary one-month intervals between them and without the accompanying counselling. She accepts and we both laugh with relief. Suddenly, a huge burden has been lifted from both of us. Finally.

All the financial stuff and the stuffy English divorce can be deferred. She is the mother of my child, and obviously I am not going to leave her in a sorry state financially – Aleena would expect me to take care of her mother. But being truly free, for the first time in my life – it's an amazing feeling.

The only person I know in Kuala Lumpur is Sharon Bakar, a middle-aged Englishwoman I met at the Festival in Bali, who is a creative writing teacher and seems to be well-connected to the local literary scene. She is married to a Malay man. I get in touch and we meet for tea in the Saujana Hotel, where I am staying during this couple of months. I ask Sharon about doing a speaking event in Kuala Lumpur, and she says that's a great idea and she will definitely work something out.

True to her word, Sharon fixes up for me to do a speaking event one Saturday afternoon at the Instant Café House of Art and Ideas (CHAI), a bungalow in PJ which is the headquarters of an innovative and progressive theatre company. I take a taxi from the Saujana and we eventually find the bungalow.

There is quite a sizeable audience, perhaps fifty people, and the atmosphere is quite relaxed. I deliver my usual narrative performance about my publishing journey, and they are very receptive and laugh a lot. I seem to be quite good at this. I tell the audience I'm only visiting KL for a few weeks, and I thought I'd drop into CHAI. They demonstrate their appreciation with generous applause.

Afterwards, I have dinner at Sharon's house – it's her husband's birthday and it's quite a party. The neat lawn is laid out with tables and chairs, and there's a delicious buffet of spicy foods. Sharon kindly introduces me to many people, telling them I'm a writer who has written a wonderful book. Sharon's guests are cultured, articulate people, and they seem quite interested in me. And I am free to explore and be myself – whatever, whoever that is. I seem to be discovering this for the first time.

18 Months Later

It's the last week of September and the Khazanah Megatrends Forum 2011 has just ended and it seems to be a great success. It's a two-day private conference of the business elite from Kuala Lumpur, held in the exclusive Mandarin Oriental hotel, and involves a series of panel discussions and keynote addresses delivered by 'thought leaders' from around the world. As Director of Knowledge Management at Khazanah – the Malaysian government's strategic investment company, dedicated to the economic, educational, business and cultural development of the nation – KMF is under my remit, and so I can feel proud that it's gone so well. I am particularly happy that certain important people from my past were able to participate as speakers – Ronald Stones, of the Green School in Bali, and Tom Berquist, a colleague from my consulting days in Minneapolis. And now the final event is the Open House dinner, held in the Mandarin Oriental's biggest hall, and to which about one thousand people are invited.

I am walking around the busy banquet hall, feeling very pleased with myself, in my smartest blue suit and sharpest tie. Life has turned out so well, in such an unimagined way. I feel truly on top of the world. There is only one missing component – I am still alone, but surely not for much longer. I know that I am ready, and I know the Universe will deliver.

An attractive Malay woman with intensely dark eyes suddenly approaches me, and says in perfect English, 'I know you! I was at your event at CHAI – that was over a year ago.'

She introduces herself as Salwah, a lawyer who does some corporate work for Khazanah. Her memory is very good. 'What are you still doing here? I thought you were only visiting KL for a few weeks.'

'At that time, I was. But I ended up working for Khazanah at the beginning of this year and moving to Kuala Lumpur. They were looking for someone with a solid business background who could write in an engaging way. They read my CV and my book, and they hired me. If someone had told me a year ago that I would be living in Malaysia with an office in the Petronas Towers and an apartment with an amazing view towards downtown, I never would have believed them.'

Salwah mentions how much she enjoyed my talk and how she wanted to read my book, but she couldn't find a copy in KL. I just happen to have a hardback copy on me (I was giving them away to our guest speakers), so I inscribe and sign it for her.

'Please would you consider giving your talk at my law firm? Everyone would love it.'

'I think of it as a narrative performance, rather than a talk, and sure – I'd be delighted to do that. I always say 'yes' to a speaking invitation, as long as you can promise me an audience. I hate it when I'm performing and there's no one there – I need the audience to give me energy.'

Salwah assures me that it won't be a problem – that she will have the entire firm, partners and staff, there to hear me.

We say goodbye and shake hands rather affectionately.

A few days later I meet up with Shireen Muhiudeen – a Scottish-Malay woman who is the CEO of an asset management company and was one of my guest speakers at KMF. This incredible combination of Malaysia and Scotland – coupled with her intelligence, education, independence and general vivaciousness – give me a strong sense of my 'ideal woman'. It's a pity she is married.

We have tea at the Vienna Café in the mall below the Petronas Towers, and Shireen buys three copies of my book, which she wants made out to friends of hers – she is sure that they will enjoy it. I inscribe the books somewhat mechanically – the usual wish that I hope the recipient enjoys the journey – and I don't pay any attention to the names that Shireen is spelling out to me.

The next day I get a most unexpected e-mail from Salwah.

'I have just returned to my desk from a meeting, to find *another* signed copy of your book inscribed to me – this one from my friend and client Shireen. This is a sign – you *must* give a talk at my law firm.'

We have the Khazanah year-end management retreat at Langkawi, a beautiful tropical archipelago a few hundred miles from KL. Langkawi is a favourite destination for off-site meetings, events and conferences. As usual, I travel there on FireFly – a budget airline which operates propeller planes out of the delightfully un-frantic Subang airport, just twenty minutes from my place. Even the most obstructive taxi driver can't claim he doesn't know where it is. Subang airport only has four gates, which are actually French windows facing out from the waiting area, and we walk out to our plane when called. This experience is always such a joyful contrast from the urgency and crowds of Kuala Lumpur International Airport. As we approach Langkawi about an hour later, from my window I observe the string of lush islands and the alluring blue-green waters of the archipelago.

As always in Malaysia, each of our meetings in the hotel is framed by food: breakfast, morning snack, lunch, afternoon snack, early evening snack, dinner. The food is always delicate and exotic and delicious – a far cry from the bland and unimaginative food that characterised my business meetings in America (but I still used to eat it, to try to fill that aching void inside me).

After lunch one day, I return to my comfortable, modern hotel room to freshen up. There is an electronic scale in the room, and I step on it. The figure which glares up at me leaves me reeling with shock. Even allowing a generous deduction for my clothes, I now weigh over 200 pounds! This is an appalling state of affairs – it completely undermines my self-image and destroys any credibility in my longstanding assertion that I look like how James Bond is supposed to look like.

Mentally, I draw a line in the sand – *this far and no further!* I *am* going to lose weight, I *am* going to be slim. I *am* going to be the attractive man I'm supposed to be. How else will I ever attract that beautiful, intelligent, vivacious woman I am so longing for.

After the next meeting, I emerge from the conference room to find a buffet of afternoon snacks has been laid out. I don't touch it.

It's a rainy December afternoon when I travel to Salwah's office. She arrives in a black 7-series BMW, complete with driver, and collects me from outside the Petronas Towers. Salwah delivers on her promise – the conference room is completely packed for my narrative performance. Even some of the retired partners come in especially for this event. Being Malaysia there is, of course, a generous buffet of delicious spicy and sweet food laid out for everyone. I sample just a little of the food; give the talk; enjoy just a tiny little bit more food; sign and sell all the books I brought with me; get my photo taken with various people; and have a generally affirmative afternoon – being very careful to keep my ego in check. (But it's nice to be appreciated.)

January is an exciting time. I am making a trip to America to meet with my US publisher, to do some marketing preparation for the April launch, and to attend a couple of industry conventions (one for booksellers and one for librarians). The journey from Kuala Lumpur to New York is an odyssey: seven hours to Dubai and then over thirteen hours to JFK. Miraculously, in a throwback to my Platinum days, I am mysteriously upgraded from Business to First on the shiny new Airbus A380. I do something I never imagined – I have a shower in a luxurious bathroom (which is bigger than my bathroom at home) just an hour before landing at JFK.

The INS officer is friendly and welcoming, and takes a good look at the copy of my book which I show him. (It's become apparent to me that, if you are a terrorist or someone else with evil intent, all you have to do to get past Homeland Security is publish a book and place it on the counter – especially if it has a cute childhood picture of you on the cover.)

New York is brilliantly sunny, but bitterly cold, especially compared to the unrelenting warmth of Malaysia. The icy wind cuts deep into my skin – I now seem to have less body fat to provide insulation.

After some time spent with my publisher in Park Avenue, I fly to New Orleans for the American Booksellers Association winter convention. Our publisher arranges for four writers, including myself, to meet a large number of booksellers over dinner in a private room in a restaurant. There are four circular tables, occupied by booksellers, but each with one 'writer's chair'. We writers take turns occupying the 'writer's chair' on each table, rotating around to the next table after each course.

I don't even spend 24 hours in New Orleans, before I'm heading to Dallas for the American Librarians Association convention. In Dallas, the weather is perfect – sunny and warm, but not too hot. These days are perfect as well – I'm manning a booth at a convention, not to sell software or consulting services or Business Process Outsourcing to hardnosed cynical corporate people, but to promote my book to wonderful, friendly warmhearted librarians. Life could not be better.

On our last evening, the marketing people have arranged for four writers to have dinner with about ten librarians in a private room in a Mexican restaurant. I've had many such dinners in my corporate career, but not with writers, librarians and publishers – I never even dreamed of this. Librarians, in particular, seem to be very intelligent and compassionate people – probably because they are largely free of the almighty Profit goal.

As the conversation becomes warmer and the participants more relaxed, Kaite from Kansas City mentions that she does Tarot. She takes a Tarot pack from her handbag and starts to do readings for people at the table. Although I don't have the same enraged hostility to Tarot which I did before my transformative experience, I've never actually participated – perhaps being a little afraid still. But now I feel that the time is right – for some reason I feel compelled. I ask Kaite to give me a reading.

She spreads the cards facedown, and I run my hands over them, trying to be as relaxed, as intuitive as possible, as I select my cards. Kaite says that her analysis refers to something occurring anytime over the next two months: 'It could be tomorrow, it could be weeks from now.'

She studies my cards and declares that what's coming is 'partnership and emotional connection'.

'Could that be a woman?' I ask, excitedly.

'Yes … [*pause*] … if you are open.'

I knew it! I am ready. I've moved to Kuala Lumpur, where I am free to discover and define myself; I've sorted out my marital status (finally); I've got a wonderful apartment with stunning views (and a daybed for relaxing on to enjoy the stunning views with my arm around someone special); I've lost thirty pounds in weight; I exercise rigorously and vigorously; I don't eat junk food (much); I have a job I really enjoy; money is flowing through my life in a positive way; I've learned a lot about Life and personal empowerment; I have all my hair – it's all there and it's all mine and it's still black.

I am truly ready. And the Universe will deliver now – I can feel it.

What does she mean: '… *if you are open*'? Well, of course I'm open. As long as it's an American or European woman who is mid-thirties with medium-sized breasts and who is definitely *not* Muslim, because I'm going to show the world, and especially my mother, that I am *free* of all those constraints which were imposed upon me in my childhood. I am a free and independent man. Of course I'm open.

Back in Kuala Lumpur, Salwah gets in touch by e-mail. She would like me to do another speaking event for her. This one will be at the office of a friend of hers. It will be a midday event on the first day of February, and they will take me to lunch. Of course, I agree to do it. I have a policy of always saying 'Yes' to speaking events, and Salwah has been very supportive.

I ask Salwah about the audience.

'Just some friends of mine.'

With a slightly suspicious feeling, I ask how many people will be there.

'About seven or eight.'

This is really annoying. The one thing I insist on for a speaking event is an audience. I don't like to get out of bed for less than twenty people. 'Seven or eight' people is hardly worth my while.

But since it's a lunchtime event on a Wednesday, it doesn't really matter. If it's like the event at the law firm, they will send a car to collect me from the office, give me lunch, and then deliver me back.

Then I discover that February 1st is actually a public holiday. I won't be at the office that day. I wouldn't have needed to go out at all and I wouldn't even have had to shave. Now I will have to make an effort for just 'seven or eight' people. It seems hardly worth the trouble. But I've already said 'Yes' to Salwah, so I let it be.

It is a beautiful day – one of those relatively rare blue sky days in Kuala Lumpur. I shave grudgingly and choose a blue silk casual shirt with tan cotton Hagar trousers. The trousers are quite loose now, of course. It's wonderful to be slim. I put about ten *Unimagined* hardbacks in a cloth bag and head out. The taxi I take from outside Amcorp Mall has trouble finding the place, as usual, but with Salwah's help on the phone we locate the office building in a quiet business park. Of course it's quiet – it's a public holiday. I could have slept late and lounged about all day, maybe had a swim and relaxed by the pool. But never mind – as a matter of policy I always say 'yes' to a speaking engagement, even if it's only a handful of people.

There's an almost festive air in the office, as no one is here to work. It's just a group of Salwah's friends loitering and chatting, with an excited air of anticipation. Clearly, she has set their expectations rather high. My talk will be in a conference room, and I take my position at one end of the traditional long table. Salwah and her friends sit at the other end – four women and three men, all Malaysians.

I launch into my usual warm up jokes and then into the main narrative. The audience is receptive and smart. They get all the jokes – even the ones requiring verbal reasoning skills. This is a positive experience for me, despite the small audience.

From the very beginning, I notice a beautiful Malay woman in the group. She is perhaps early forties, but has a young, slim figure. She is elegantly dressed, in a western-style skirt suit and just the right amount of jewellery. She laughs at every joke, and her smile and radiance light up the room. Her eyes are delicious. Most of all, she has class and dignity and an aura which touches me tangibly, profoundly and deeply. I can barely take my gaze off her – but of course I have to distribute my attention evenly across the audience.

As a group, they laugh heartily at my incredible publishing journey, and the completely implausible experiences I have had. Their applause at the end more than makes up for their low number.

Afterwards, when I'm signing and selling books, the beautiful, enigmatic woman asks to buy three. I sign the first two, for someone called John and someone called David, and then she says, 'Can you make this one to Nina, please.'

'Nina. Is that you?'

Almost hesitantly, 'Yes.' It's a shyness completely at odds with her elegance and class. But there is an energy about her which reaches deep inside me and triggers off profound emotion. How can I rationally feel that I love this woman, when I have just met her? That makes no sense at all. I try to engage her in conversation, but it seems awkward – her apparent shyness persists.

I'm looking forward to having lunch with this group, and especially Nina, of course. Salwah comes up to me and tells me that Darhim, whose office this is, will be taking me to lunch. I follow him outside and, when he asks me, 'Where would you like to go?' I suddenly realise that this isn't going to be a group lunch at all. It's just Darhim taking *only me* to lunch, as my reward for giving the talk. This doesn't appeal to me at all. I think back to that IKEA store I saw on the way here, and of how I would like to get an armchair for my apartment, to lounge in more comfortably as I watch the entire series of *Battlestar Galactica* on DVD. I tell Darhim politely that lunch doesn't really matter, I'd rather go to IKEA. I turn back towards the office, wondering if I can get a ride.

Nina, Salwah and another woman come out of the office together, walking towards a bronze Porsche Cayenne which is waiting for them, complete with driver. Nina is leading the way, so I assume it's her vehicle. It's a stunning car, so beautiful and elegant.

I ask Nina directly, 'Are you going anywhere near IKEA?'

She is very friendly in her reply: 'I can certainly drop you there.'

Nina instructs me to sit in the front, and the three women sit in the back, Nina in the middle. As we set off, she explains that the driver will drop off the three women first, as they are going to a school reunion lunch, and then he will take me to IKEA. My mind is already machinating how best to take advantage of this kindness.

'This is extremely cheeky of me. I hope you don't mind. I know exactly what I'm going to get in IKEA – it's an armchair. My apartment is over at Amcorp Mall. Could your driver possibly take me back to my apartment with the armchair? I won't take long.'

Nina is extremely gracious. 'Oh, that's fine … But you'll owe me lunch for this.'

I leap at this without hesitation, and blurt out, 'Dinner! I'll take you to dinner at the Malaysian Petroleum Club.' My enthusiasm is absolutely obvious and unrestrained. 'You just tell me what evening you're free.'

(Some weeks later, as I hold her in my arms, Nina tells me that, at this moment, both the other women discreetly nudged her to encourage her to go for it.)

Back at my apartment, now with several large flat pack boxes, I scrutinise Nina's business card, holding it carefully, affectionately and reverently. She is a Director in a small, private company. Her cell phone number is on the card. Intently, I compose my carefully crafted text message to her – perfectly written, of course, without vulgar abbreviations.

> Dear Nina, Thank you so much for the use of your car and driver. It was a huge help. I really appreciate it. What evening can I take you to dinner? Best regards, Imran

Strangely, bizarrely, I can see a whole future with this woman I've just met. An irrational excitement courses through me. But this doesn't make any sense. She is so *not* what I have specified. I am expecting the Universe to send a mid-thirties American or European woman with medium-sized breasts, who is spiritual but not religious, and *definitely not* Muslim, so I don't have to deal with all the baggage that entails and so that I can demonstrate to the world, and *especially my mother*, that I am completely free of all the constraints which were placed upon me in my younger years, and that I can choose to have that which was previously *forbidden* to me … But this is a spindly Malay Muslim woman in her forties. My mother would absolutely love her. This so doesn't make sense.

Her response comes quickly.

> My pleasure. I'm glad it was helpful. I was only joking about dinner. Best, Nina

I feel completely deflated. My Heart aches suddenly and my energy drains away and I feel a disappointment to the core of my being. But then my Mind kicks in and brings me back to reality.

'Are you crazy? You can have a beautiful American or European woman in her mid-thirties with a perfect figure, who's not Muslim and doesn't come with all that baggage. Why would you give up your life to an older Malay Muslim woman with a tiny figure? What were you thinking?'

He's right. What was I thinking? I breathe a sigh of relief. It was crazy. What was I thinking? The perfect woman is out there somewhere, on a collision course with me.

I'm about to leave the apartment the next morning, when my BlackBerry beeps unexpectedly with a text message.

> I am holding you personally responsible for how I look this morning. I was up until the early hours reading your book and I didn't get much sleep and I haven't had time to do my make-up properly. I must look such a mess and you owe me dinner for this. Nina.

She meets me on Friday evening in the lobby of the Petronas Towers, looking more stunning and more elegant than ever. We shake hands and converse politely, as I take her up to the Malaysian Petroleum Club on the 42nd floor, and into the Temana Brasserie. I have reserved my usual corner table by the windows; the view is spectacular, of course. (Just a short time ago, when I was unemployed and completely broke in London, it would have been unimaginable to me that I would have a favourite table in the Malaysian Petroleum Club in the Petronas Towers in Kuala Lumpur.)

Our conversation is formal at first, but we soon relax and are able to talk quite intimately. She did her A-levels in the UK, almost accepted an offer to study at Stirling University at exactly the same time that I was there, but went to a university in the north of England instead. Her father married her off to a Malay man also studying in England, even while she was doing her undergraduate degree. She had no choice in the matter. Her marriage was long and difficult, and she only recently got divorced. She is finally free for the first time in 30 years – or it's more like 50 years really if you consider her whole life. (Amazingly, she is 50 years old.)

She mentions that she spent the Christmas and New Year holiday period that's just passed in a rented apartment by Kingston Bridge. 'I walked past that building every day!' I gasp.

At the end of dinner, she asks if I would like to see her again, and of course I reply, 'Oh, yes.'

Nina gives me a ride back to Amcorp Mall in her beautiful Porsche Cayenne (no driver this time). Parked outside the apartment entrance, we talk a little while longer. We seem to have connected very well – both passionate people who had long, passionless arranged marriages. I sit holding her hand – it seems the most natural thing to do.

I'm not sure what the protocols are in Malaysia. She makes it easy for me: 'It's okay, you can kiss me.'

It's quick, but gentle and intense and delicious and charged.

The first of many.

We have lunches and dinners, but sometimes Nina comes over to my place for the evening. She relaxes on the daybed, perhaps looking at her work papers, preparing for her next board meeting. I have Mozart playing and I give her Earl Grey tea and massage her feet – sitting cross-legged on the daybed, rubbing lotion into her skin. She closes her eyes, tilts her head back on the pillows and moans softly, 'That's sooo nice …' with her delightful Malaysian twang. The sound of her voice, and the joy in it, with her delicious accent – it makes my heart leap.

Occasionally she says, 'You're too good to be true' or 'What have I done to deserve you?' The best is: 'I was thanking God in my prayers last night – for you.'

These words bring me such joy, and the act of massaging her feet makes me feel so unburdened by selfishness or ego. Afterwards, as I lie on the daybed with my arms wrapped around her – enjoying the caress and the scent of her – it seems like my heart is going to burst. I'm 49 years old, and this is the *first time* in my life I have felt this way. Everything else seems to fade into irrelevance: my job at Khazanah; the launch of my book in the US; the 50-city US speaking tour I'm supposed to be intently planning. Nothing else matters. *This* is what I've wanted, my whole life.

All too frequently, I tell her that I love her, and occasionally, just occasionally, she lets it slip out. On one occasion she says, 'Just remember – I loved you *before* your book made you famous.'

I reflect that if I hadn't been unemployed, broke and in debt, I *never* would have applied for that job in Malaysia. (*Thank God* I wasn't offered any of those jobs in London.) I would have kept to my old, established, familiar patterns – no matter how miserable they made me feel. And then I wouldn't be lying here right now, in the arms of this amazing woman – surely my soul mate.

It doesn't go quite as I expected.

To be continued …

Imran Ahmad will return in
The Gentle Man

Teacher

2018 Age: 56 Kuala Lumpur

Jasmina and I meet for dinner at least once a month, usually at the buffet restaurant of the Mandarin Oriental Kuala Lumpur. It's the most relaxed and informal venue in the MO (sometimes, with all the kids running around, it's more like a fast food restaurant in some tasteless crowded theme park), and the buffet allows me to eat self-indulgently whilst avoiding the dreaded carbs (which would otherwise put the pounds onto my aging belly).

Since we met at work, about four years ago, there's always been this comfortable ease between us. She is beautiful and slim and elegant, and there is possibly some sexual tension – but the essence of our relationship is a deep friendship of absolute trust and respect. Perhaps because we're both European foreigners in KL, it's easy for us to have some commonality, some shared perspective on life in Malaysia, with its quirky ups and downs.

We discuss the fact that Kuala Lumpur has been undergoing tremendous infrastructure improvement, which occasionally causes disruption to water and power, as well as traffic chaos. Jasmina says she's used to this. She recounts that, when she was in her twenties, there was a war going on during which her home city was attacked for a couple of months and she got used to running out to get supplies in between the periods when devastating bombs were falling from the sky. I listen intently and feel sad, although she seems at ease talking about it. She sounds quite matter-of-fact, not holding onto the experience with any bitterness.

Jasmina has been a bit down recently, because of personal matters which she confides to me. I try to cheer her up as best I can, and I'm not the only one. She shows me a personal video she received from someone back home – he's a Muslim imam. He is one of her closest friends from years back – although Jasmina's own background is Orthodox Christian. On her iPhone, I see a neatly-bearded man who looks not-quite-Arab, not-quite-European – something in-between. I can just about hear the soundtrack, against the noisy background of the restaurant. He addresses her kindly and familiarly in a language which is completely alien to me – I recognise only her name 'Jasmina' repeated several times. He then starts singing in a gently passionate and deeply affectionate manner, without musical accompaniment. It is extraordinary to watch and to listen to – it strikes me as the most moving and unselfconscious display of 'friendship love' I have ever witnessed.

I am convinced that Jasmina is one of my core group of soul friends who all incarnate together into successive shared lifetimes, to help each other with our spiritual development and resolution of acquired Karma. I have learned so much from her and deeply appreciate her insight, support and 'friendship love'. Just like Milton, who is definitely a soul from my core group. And Sean. And, of course, Nina.

We finish dinner and I pay with my debit card (I *never* use credit cards anymore). Jasmina hands me cash to cover her share.

I'm always slightly self-conscious as I walk out of the restaurant and through the elegant hotel lobby with her, as she is very tall and eye-catching, and I don't want people to get the wrong idea. Although it is somewhat exhilarating if they do get the wrong idea – my Ego still enjoys some gratification, not being completely conquered.

Outside the hotel entrance, our apartments are in opposite directions. We exchange appreciative pleasantries and agree to meet again soon. Before we head off, I give her a hug and three kisses on the cheeks alternately – as is the custom in her home country. Serbia.

AFTERWORD

2020 Age: 57

Dear Readers,

(I'm assuming optimistically that at least two people will read this book.)

I hope that you enjoyed this unimagined journey.

Again, I assure you that everything narrated here is absolutely true. You may draw different conclusions from me, based on the events described, or have a different theory to explain them – but we can have a mutual understanding that we are working from the same facts.

I have felt nervous about this sequel for years. Not only do I show myself to be far from 'the perfect gentleman', but the events of 'Transformation' may cause some to conclude that I have 'lost my marbles'. But there would be nothing to be gained by whitewashing myself or changing the events.

Here's one thing I know for sure: arranged marriage is very unlikely to find you the right person ... unless you let the Universe do the arranging. Don't let anyone hassle you into a marriage – if you have any intuitive doubts, *don't do it!* Your parents *do not* own you, and they *do not* know better than you what's right for *your* happiness.

So much more has happened – I have so much more to write about! And still more explaining to do. Let's see where this goes. The journey never ends – as long as we are living, we are learning.

The third book is titled: *The Gentle Man.* It's still unfolding (I'm still living it), but I promise I'm on it and it's not too far off.

Peace and best wishes,

Imran Ahmad

www.unimagined.co.uk
www.unimagined.org
Twitter: @unimagined

Note to Publisher: Trilogy would look great as a gift pack of three books in their own box. *I'm just sayin'.*

ADDENDUM

Just as this book was going to print, I learned that Mark Hemstedt passed away suddenly, a short time ago.

Mark was truly one of my great teachers. From him I learned that all the negativity, judgement and resentment I projected towards others had their foundations in my own insecurities and deficiencies.

Mark had a solid sense of self-empowerment, which I lacked in our Unilever days. I believed that being a (reasonably good) Muslim surely must give me some divinely sponsored advantage. It did not really work that way, but unfortunately it also made me judgemental of others. Mark steered his life on an amazing course — doing what he was passionate about and positively impacting the lives of countless people.

Mark: Thank you for everything. Cheers mate, see you later.

Made in the USA
Las Vegas, NV
23 October 2021